Modern Germany

Germany occupies a crucial political position in the European context. It also faces many new challenges which have come with reunification such as coming to terms with its history of Nazism. *Modern Germany* examines aspects of contemporary political, economic, social and cultural life in the new Germany.

Using a clearly structured approach, this book explains the electoral and political systems and underlines the significance of the federal system in Germany. The legendary German economy, industry, education system and training are analysed in the light of recent problems. *Modern Germany* also describes the media landscape of the nation and the recent reforms to the German language and cultural scene.

Modern Germany presents some of the key features of life in modern Germany. It provides an accessible introduction for students of German and European studies or the German language at all levels.

Peter James is Principal Lecturer in German Language and Politics and Head of German, Department of Modern Languages, University of Northumbria at Newcastle.

Modern Germany

Politics, society and culture

Edited by Peter James

London and New York

First published 1998 by Routledge
2 Park Square, Milton Park, Abingdon, Oxon, OX14 4RN

Simultaneously published in the USA and Canada
by Routledge
270 Madison Ave, New York NY 10016

Reprinted 2002

Transferred to Digital Printing 2005

Routledge is an imprint of the Taylor & Francis Group

Typeset in Times by
J&L Composition Ltd, Filey, N. Yorkshire

British Library Cataloguing in Publication Data
A catalogue record for this book is available from the
British Library

Library of Congress Cataloguing in Publication Data
James, Peter, 1946–
    Modern Germany: politics, society and culture/Peter James.
    p. cm.
    Includes bibliographical references and index.
    ISBN 0–415–15033–7. – ISBN 0–415–15034–5 (pbk.)
    1. Germany–Politics and government–1990–.
    2. Germany–Cultural policy. 3. Political parties–Germany.
    4. Germany–Economic policy. 5. National socialism–
    Psychological aspects. 6. Germany–Relations–Europe.
    7. Europe–Relations–Germany. I. Title.
    DD290.29.J36   1998
    943.087'–dc21   97–37584
                 CIP

ISBN 0–415–15033–7 (hbk)
ISBN 0–415–15034–5 (pbk)

Contents

List of contributors

Steffi Boothroyd is Lecturer in German at the University of Northumbria at Newcastle. Her research interests are in the area of German Cultural Studies. She has published on the politics of multiculturism in Germany and is currently conducting research on contemporary popular women's fiction.

Peter James is Principal Lecturer and Head of German at the University of Northumbria at Newcastle, where he teaches German language and a special-option course for final-year studentts on the Government and Institutions of Germnay. He is the author of *The Politics of Bavaria – An Exception To The Rule* and has published widely on the party and political systems of Bavaria and Germany.

David Kaufman is Senior Lecturer in German at the University of Northumbria at Newcastle, where he teaches German language, specialising in translation and remedial grammar. He has written several grammar manuals, including *Xenophobowski's Guide to Grammar* and *Xenophobowski's Guide to Declensional Decorum*. His research interests are neo-Nazi networks and the language of the Third Reich.

Sue Lawson is Senior Lecturer in German at the University of Northumbria at Newcastle. Her research interest is the GDR. She has written on the East German Church, GDR marriage guidance and women's roles in the GDR. She is a member of WIgS (Women in German Studies).

Hanna Ostermann is Senior Lecturer in German at the University of Northumbria at Newcastle, where she teaches German language and area studies concentrating on the economic and business environment of Germany. A graduate of Hamburg University, she has experience of working in the German education system and has a special interest in higher education. She is currently conducting research on the problems and challenges which face the present-day higher education system in Germany.

Ute E. Schmidt is Senior Lecturer in German at the University of Northumbria at Newcastle, where she teaches German language and German area studies, specialising in the economic environment of Germany. A German national, she received her qualifications at the Eberhard-Karls-Universität, Tübingen and the Staatliches Seminar für Schulpädagogik in Stuttgart thus gaining a practical insight into the country's education system. She entered the British Higher Education sector as a *DAAD-Lektorin*. Her current interest is the stereotypical perception of German culture in Great Britain.

Nigel Thomas is Senior Lecturer in German and French at the University of Northumbria at Newcastle. He is in charge of the Modern Languages Centre, heads the Business langauge Unit and is courseleader for the University's Langauge Elective Programme. He has written a series of books on twentieth-century military history and is completing a PhD on Germany and the eastern enlargement of NATO at the Institue for German Studies, University of Birmingham.

Preface

This book is aimed at all those who have an interest in life and society in modern Germany. It examines areas which are often required reading for students on courses which include German 'nation studies' (*Landeskunde*) from an interdisciplinary perspective. A knowledge of Germany and German culture is essential across a wide range of German, European Studies and similar courses in higher education today.

The focus of the book is on political, economic, social and cultural aspects of life in contemporary Germany. Clearly the text is not intended to be exhaustive. The authors have set out to highlight certain key areas of life in Germany today and address specific issues within these topic areas, which are outlined in the Introduction. The individual chapters may of course be read in isolation, although there are obvious links too. The chapter on the federal framework, for example, not only explains the nature of German federalism but also emphasises the fundamental effect of federalism on several aspects of life in the Federal Republic. It is important to understand how the federal structure works in order to appreciate fully its influence on some of the other aspects dealt with in later chapters – for example the political and education systems.

The approach has been to provide up-to-date, informative and analytical material. The current situation is placed in a historical context only in so far as this is necessary for a fuller appreciation of the contemporary scene. This book is for all those who need readily accessible information and explanation concerning life and society in the new German state, which emerged in the autumn of 1990; the new Germany is a key power both politically and economically in a changing Europe.

Introduction

Modern Germany sets out to examine and explain certain key aspects of German life and society today. One of these is the federal, or decentralised, nature of the Federal Republic of Germany (FRG). This is a fundamental feature and is addressed in Chapter 3. Federalism is a vital thread running through several facets of life in contemporary Germany. It affects people's daily lives in various ways. The German education and political systems, to give just two examples, are influenced by the federal structure.

The new Germany's changing European and global role, and the importance of its foreign policy initiatives are crucial to current and future developments. The final chapter looks at the developing relationship between Germany and its neighbours and the historic dilemma, usually referred to as the German Question. Chapter 5 reviews Germany's legendary position as a leading economic power, which now needs to be revisited in the light of the current debate on Germany as a location for industry.

For years the FRG was described as an economic giant but a political dwarf; the picture is very different today. Germany is nowadays a key player in the political arena, and the political and party systems are explained in Chapter 4. Chapter 7 takes a critical look at the need for reform of the German education system, focusing particularly on higher education, vocational training and the world of work.

Another central theme running through life and society in Germany is coming to terms with the past (*Vergangenheitsbewältigung*). This topic, and the more recent outbreaks of attacks on foreigners, are dealt with in Chapter 8. An area where the FRG has often been envied is that of social provision for its citizens (Chapter 6). Balancing the budget since Unification has meant that a number of hard decisions have been taken on financial grounds. These have, predictably, caused considerable resentment and controversy. Another controversial issue was the decision to return to Berlin as the capital of the new Germany, as well as its designation as the future seat of government. Berlin, in some ways a symbol of the new Germany, is the subject of Chapter 2.

The German media landscape (Chapter 9) has undergone a dramatic expansion process over the last decade or so. There has been a broadcasting revolution, accompanied by fresh challenges concerning the freedom and regulation of broadcasting. Culture and society, against a leisure-orientated background, with its prolific arts scene, are examined in Chapter 10. Finance, in this case in the form of funding and subsidies for the arts, again plays a vital role here. An unusual feature of this book is to be found in Chapter 11, which has a dual aim in taking a closer look at the German language. It draws the reader's attention to the relationship between the German and English languages, and examines the controversial German spelling reform, which is introducing changes that are going to be vitally important to all students of German.

Acknowledgements

The authors would like to acknowledge the support of the University of Northumbria at Newcastle, and in particular the Modern Languages departmental research committee, in allocating resources which supported the authors of this book. We also wish to acknowledge the support for the project and invaluable advice given by our Head of Department, Professor David Head. The authors are grateful to the modern languages technicians, David Crook, Seph Nesbit and Dave Marshall, for their patient and humorous assistance in the preparation of the manuscript. Any omissions and errors are of course the responsibility of the authors.

1 The new Germany eight years on

Peter James

'Bonn ist nicht Weimar.' This oft-quoted remark from the mid-1950s[1] was meant to indicate that the political system in West Germany, with Bonn as its (provisional) capital after 1949, was different from that of the ill-fated Weimar Republic (1919–33), Germany's first attempt at democracy. Experts in German politics[2] point out that the Berlin Republic, by which they mean the new Federal Republic of Germany, which has existed since the day of German Unity on 3 October 1990, is also different from the Bonn Republic. It has also been emphasised that Bonn was not built in a day. Neither was Berlin. The new Germany, with Berlin as its capital, was able to make good progress in a relatively short time – although not all its citizens might agree – but it will take many more years yet before the 'merger' of the two Germanys is complete.

Following the 1994 federal elections, the eminent Franco-German political scientist Alfred Grosser commented: 'das Ergebnis zeigt, daß die deutsche Einheit noch nicht vollendet ist' (the result shows that German Unity is not yet complete) (*Focus Wahlspezial* 1994: 19). That was a reference to, amongst other things, the very different voting patterns and political cultures between East and West (see Chapter 4). So, despite the numerous changes of the last seven or eight years, which many Germans and outside observers would, on balance, probably view as predominantly positive achievements, two things are quite clear: first, the unification process is still by no means over and, second, Unification brought not only pluses – there were minuses too.

When the former German Democratic Republic, the GDR[3] (die Deutsche Demokratische Republik, die DDR) – often referred to simply as East Germany – joined the former Federal Republic of Germany, the FGR, (die Bundesrepublik Deutschland, die BRD) – often referred to simply as West Germany – in the autumn of 1990,

Figure 1.1 The *Länder*

Federal Republic of Germany	
Capital:	Berlin
Area:	356,854 sq km
Population:	81.3 million

Schleswig-Holstein	
Capital:	Kiel
Area:	15,731 sq km
Population:	2.7 million

Bremen	
Capital:	Bremen
Area:	404 sq km
Population:	0.68 million

Lower Saxony	
Capital:	Hanover
Area:	47,351 sq km
Population:	7.6 million

North Rhine-Westphalia	
Capital:	Düsseldorf
Area:	34,070 sq km
Population:	17.7 million

Hesse	
Capital:	Wiesbaden
Area:	21,114 sq km
Population:	5.9 million

Rhineland-Palatinate	
Capital:	Mainz
Area:	19,849 sq km
Population:	3.9 million

Saarland	
Capital:	Saarbrücken
Area:	2,570 sq km
Population:	1.1 million

Baden-Württemberg	
Capital:	Stuttgart
Area:	35,751 sq km
Population:	10.2 million

Mecklenburg-Western Pomerania	
Capital:	Schwerin
Area:	23,559 sq km
Population:	1.9 million

Hamburg	
Capital:	Hamburg
Area:	755 sq km
Population:	1.7 million

Brandenburg	
Capital:	Potsdam
Area:	29,056 sq km
Population:	2.6 million

Berlin	
Capital:	Berlin
Area:	889 sq km
Population:	3.4 million

Saxony-Anhalt	
Capital:	Magdeburg
Area:	20,607 sq km
Population:	2.9 million

Saxony	
Capital:	Dresden
Area:	18,341 sq km
Population:	4.6 million

Thuringia	
Capital:	Erfurt
Area:	16,251 sq km
Population:	2.6 million

Bavaria	
Capital:	Munich
Area:	70,554 sq km
Population:	11.8 million

the new Germany, retaining the name FRG, was born. It consists of sixteen federal states or *Länder*: the ten so-called 'old' western states, the five 'new' eastern states, plus the new capital, a reunited Berlin (see Figure 1.1). Berlin is both a city and, with its surrounding area, a federal state known in German as a *Stadtstaat*, a city-state.

The new Germany ought to have been in an ideal position to understand the problems of both Western democracies and the countries of a changing Eastern Europe, following the breakdown of a number of socialist/communist systems. However, in the heady and euphoric days following the fall of the Berlin Wall and the opening of the East Berlin and East German borders, German politicians seemed to be obsessed with the political and economic problems, as they saw them, ignoring almost completely the social, cultural and psychological ones which have since reared their heads in no uncertain terms.

Nevertheless it must be acknowledged that the truly astonishing events of 1989/90, which even at the beginning of 1989 could not have been predicted, brought about the most exciting and far-reaching changes in life and society in Germany since 1945. This book sets out to highlight and explain several key aspects of political, economic, social and cultural life in contemporary Germany.

GERMANY'S NEW ROLE BRINGS NEW PROBLEMS

The first five-year census for the whole of the new Germany, the results of which were published in September 1996, revealed that between 1990 and 1995 the population increased by 1.7 million to a total of 81.6 million. That made Germany, after Russia, the country with the largest population in Europe, even though France and Spain are larger in terms of territory. Germany has borders with nine countries, including the Czech Republic and Poland in the East. It occupies a strategically important geopolitical position in the very heart of Europe; as such, the new, united Germany is ideally situated to influence policy decisions and play a vital role on the ever-changing European stage, as well as to act as an essential link between East and West in both a European and a global context.

In the intervening years since the historic events of 1989 and 1990 many Germans (51 per cent in one survey) spoke, and still speak, of the wall in people's heads (*die Mauer in den Köpfen*). This expression implies that, after living for more than forty years in two diametrically opposed systems, many Germans from the East ('*Ossis*') and from the West ('*Wessis*') – according to various surveys reported by the German news magazine *Der Spiegel* – still feel separated from one other in the new Germany: unified but not united.

In the mid-1990s a report by the respected public opinion researcher Elisabeth Noelle-Neumann, of the Allensbach Institute, asked Germans in the West and the East to compare their economic situation in 1995 with that before Unification. Only 6 per cent of those in the West said they were better off, whilst 32 per cent said they were worse off. In the East, however, 58 per cent reported that they were better off, whilst only 15 per cent thought they were worse off.[4] So a stark difference in perception of the effects of German unity in the old and new federal states is evident, and not just from the results of such polls.

In 1990, 47 per cent of East Germans (in the new states) had said in a survey that freedom (*Freiheit*) was more important than equality (*Gleichheit*). By 1996 only 35 per cent wanted freedom, whilst 47 per cent maintained that equality was more important (Allensbach survey, reported on in *Der Spiegel* in November 1996). This demand for equality applied to wages too. Although prices and rents were always much lower in the former GDR, so too were wages. In the initial years after Unification people used to ask why, for example, bus drivers in east Berlin earned considerably less than those in the western half of the city. Towards the end of 1996 a new minimum hourly wage on German building sites was introduced. Although the rates of pay for the old and the new *Länder* are now much closer, even in 1996 the rate was DM 17 in the West, but only DM 15.64 in the East (*Report* from the Federal Embassy of the FRG).

Over three-quarters of Germans in the East supported the call for more equality and fewer social differences (*Mehr Gleichheit, weniger soziale Unterschiede*). Obviously far more changed in the East than in the West, where some cynically claimed that originally only the post codes had changed – another reference to the fact that many citizens in the eastern states felt they had been taken over by the western states. In the survey someone from Halle (in the East) was quoted as saying that the citizens of the new states were 'the conquered new underclass' (*die besiegten neuen Untertanen*).

Clearly, the momentous events beginning on 9 November 1989 with the collapse of the Berlin Wall (built on 13 August 1961) and the fall of the regime in the GDR, accompanied by the collapse of communism in Eastern Europe, had tremendous implications for Germany's new role, both as a European and a world power. For the first time since Germany was originally unified in 1871, the current borders have been accepted. At most other times in Germany's eventful history its borders have been the subject of dispute and lively debate. In this sense it can be said that the new Germany is the 'first non-revisionist state since 1871' (Smith *et al.* 1996: 10). It could be argued that over the past century Great Britain, France and Germany have been the most powerful states in Europe. Yet Britain and France developed as nation-states much earlier than Germany, whose political history has been one of fragmentation and discontinuity (Paterson and Southern 1991: 1).

Amongst the many changes brought by Unification, one highly significant shift of emphasis was achieved simply by taking the decision to return to Berlin as the capital of a united Germany, and later deciding, albeit again by a narrow margin, to adopt the city as the seat of government for both houses of parliament, starting early in the twenty-first century. The geographical and psychological importance of moving from Bonn, situated only 60 kilometres (40 miles) from the Belgian border, to Berlin, about the same distance from the Polish border, was clear for all to see. The strategic significance of the geopolitical position of a united Germany at the centre of Europe, linking East and West, is equally clear.

THE ROAD TO UNITY

The so-called 'peaceful revolution' began on 2 May 1989, when the Hungarian authorities started to dismantle the barbed wire on their border fences. Five days later there were widespread protests in the GDR at the manipulation of local election results. In Leipzig over one hundred demonstrators were arrested by the feared and resented East German state security police – the Stasi (der Staatssicherheitsdienst – die Stasi). On 5 June the main newspaper of the ruling party in the GDR, the *Neues Deutschland*, justified the bloody treatment of the demonstrators in Beijing as 'the reply to the counter-revolutionary rebellion of an extremist minority'.

In August 1989 hundreds of East Germans fled to the West German embassies in East Berlin, Budapest and Prague. The number wishing to leave the GDR was estimated at around 1 million. A crucial turning-point came when Hungary fully opened its borders with Austria on 11 September, allowing East Germans already in Hungary to travel to the West, via Austria (at that time East Germans were of course allowed to travel only to countries in the Eastern bloc). On 25 September at a peaceful demonstration after Monday prayers for peace in Leipzig – the phrase 'Monday demonstrations' (*die Montagsdemonstrationen*) was coined when these gatherings became a regular weekly event – some 6,000 people demanded freedom of expression, assembly and travel.

On 7 October, Mikhail Gorbachev, attending the GDR's fortieth-anniversary celebrations, warned that anyone who 'missed the boat' would pay the price (his words were translated into German as 'wer zu spät kommt, den bestraft das Leben'). On 9 October the first mass demonstration of some 70,000 people took to the streets of Leipzig chanting the slogan that soon entered the history books: 'Wir sind das Volk' (we are the people). Nine days later the GDR state and party leader Erich Honecker was forced to resign. Egon Krenz took over as the new leader of what was the main political party in East Germany, the Socialist Unity Party, the SED (die Sozialistische Einheitspartei Deutschlands).

After more than 1 million people had joined a demonstration on the streets of East Berlin on 4 November demanding reforms, similar protests against SED policies in all the major East German cities followed. Thousands continued to leave the GDR every day, heading for Hungary via Poland or Czechoslovakia. A key date which has now entered the history books was 9 November 1989, when cabinet member Günter Schabowski announced, amidst some confusion, immediate freedom of travel for East German citizens. The Berlin Wall was opened amongst amazing scenes of euphoria and mass hysteria, as a multitude of East Germans poured into the West. Three days later the queues of mainly tiny East German *Trabis* (Trabant cars) stretched back 65 kilometres (over 40 miles) from Helmstedt, one of the border crossing points.

On 22 November, at one of the regular Leipzig Monday demonstrations, the crowd chanted the adapted slogan 'Wir sind *ein* Volk' (we are *one* people). Rather cynically, some Germans from the West were later heard to reply, 'Yes, so are we' (we are also one people, and we want to stay that way – 'wir sind auch ein Volk'), although it would be incorrect to assume that was the majority view. Helmut Kohl put forward a ten-point plan with the aim of, but no specific timetable for, unification of the two Germanys. In early December the Round Table (der Runde Tisch), based on the Hungarian and Polish models, brought together for the first time representatives from the SED, the churches, opposition groups, new democratic movements and the old *bloc* parties and mass organisations.

Kohl visited Dresden on 19 December, where demonstrators were demanding German unification; three days after that the Brandenburg Gate in Berlin was opened. On Christmas Eve 1989, West Germans were permitted to enter the GDR without a visa or the usual compulsory exchange of currency – *Zwangsumtausch (von Devisen)*. The latter had been a source of great annoyance to West Germans for many years, since they, and other visitors to the GDR, had always been forced to change set amounts of foreign currency per day in return for the virtually worthless East German *Ostmark*. Pre-1990 the East German authorities were especially keen to get West marks (DM) or US dollars, and even the ailing UK pound!

In January 1990 people power was again on the march in various East German cities as something approaching 200,000 demonstrators called for the reunification of the two German states (*die Wiedervereinigung beider deutschen Staaten*) and the exclusion of the SED. Demonstrators also occupied the Stasi headquarters in Berlin. The Round Table agreed on free elections in the GDR for 18 March 1990 (earlier than originally envisaged). At the beginning of February, Chancellor Kohl presented proposals for German Economic and Monetary Union (GEMU) to his cabinet in Bonn; on 12 February the so-called 'two-plus-four' talks between the two German states and the four victorious allies were agreed upon. Strange though it may seem, the original four powers which occupied Germany after the Second World War – the USA, Great Britain, France and the USSR – were also consulted, since Germany never had a peace treaty.

The first free elections in the GDR were then held on 18 March 1990. The Alliance for Germany, i.e. the CDU, the right-of-centre Conservatives, plus two smaller partners, gained 48.1 per cent of the vote. The SPD, the left-of-centre Social Democrats, who were then, and still are, the main opposition party in Bonn, polled 21.8 per cent; and the Party of Democratic Socialism, the PDS (Partei der demokratischen Sozialismus), the successor to the East German SED, gained 16.3 per cent. By mid-February 1990 the membership of the PDS was about 700,000. Its predecessor in the GDR, the SED, the ruling Socialist Unity Party, had boasted 2.3 million members only one year earlier. On 12 April the first freely elected government in the GDR was sworn in. The new minister president, Lothar de Maiziere, headed a Grand Coalition consisting of the two major parties, the CDU and the SPD, together with the Liberals, plus two smaller parties from the East.

Although the SPD in the West, and their leader Oskar Lafontaine, were in favour of all-German elections first and Unification second, in the event the view of Helmut Kohl and his party, the CDU, prevailed. German Unification took place on 3 October 1990, and the first all-German elections for fifty-eight years were held on 2 December 1990.

THE GERMAN PEOPLE: THE SEARCH FOR IDENTITY

One of the key points to emphasise about the German people is the tremendous variety and disparate nature of the characteristics displayed by the many different traditions and regions they represent. It has taken well over a thousand years for the German people to develop from various ethnic groupings and tribes, e.g. Swabians, Bavarians, Franks, Saxons, Celts and a range of Germanic groups. The Germans have always had difficulty with concepts such as *Nation* and *Volk*. Nationhood and the German identity have never been as clearly defined as in some other countries. Germany was a late developer as a nation-state. August Heinrich Hoffmann – he added *von* and the town where he was born, calling himself Hoffmann von Fallersleben – wrote a poem in 1841 which was set to music by Joseph Haydn. In 1922 it was adopted as the German national anthem. The opening lines of the first stanza were intended at the time to convey that the idea of creating a country called Germany was, above all, the key concept ('Deutschland, Deutschland über alles, Über alles in der Welt'). In the middle of the nineteenth century many Germans desperately wanted to establish a nation-state as their top priority.

The poem was written at a time when there were thirty-nine sovereign German states, thirty years before Germany existed. When it first appeared, the *Deutschlandlied*, as it is now known, was simply a call for a German nation and had none of the negative connotations later associated with Hitler and the National Socialists, who used only the first verse as Germany's national anthem. Ever since 1952, when it was adopted as the Federal Republic's national anthem, only the third verse, praising unity, justice and freedom ('Einigkeit und Recht und Freiheit'), has been used. That remains the case today.

Although the Holy Roman Empire (das Heilige Römische Reich deutscher Nation) from 768 onwards brought a certain amount of national feeling (*Nationalgefühl*), the concepts of nationalism and patriotism have always been difficult ones for the Germans. It has proved to be almost impossible to define precisely what constitutes the German identity. The vagaries of German history and Germany's changing geography have meant that it constitutes a special case in terms of nationhood and citizenship. Whereas in the United States or Great Britain nationality is determined by the place of birth (*ius soli*), the German nationality law of 1913, still valid, stipulates that nationality is determined by descent (*ius sanguinis*).

Germany's external borders have changed frequently, and there are very strong regional ties amongst its people. Even today some Germans feel they are first and foremost from a particular region or locality, be it Hesse, the Rhineland, Brandenburg or wherever. Just to take one example as an illustration of the point, many North American or British visitors have heard that the Bavarians are different from other Germans, but without realising that there are in fact seven different districts, each with its own traditions, within present-day Bavaria. The districts cover three distinct regions and dialects – Bavarian, Franconian and Swabian – plus a strong contingent of Sudeten Germans from the former Czechoslovakia, and Silesians too. Since Bavaria has existed since the sixth century (long before Germany), the Bavarians are extremely proud of their unique history, special customs and enduring traditions. Indeed, parts of present-day Bavaria are two thousand years old. So, given that there are substantial differences even within one federal state, and that you cannot generalise about 'the Bavarians', then the same must apply to 'the Germans'.

It would therefore be dangerous to try to describe in too much detail 'the German people', given that it is not only the Bavarians who are different. There are fifteen other federal states, not to mention the districts within those states. The local traditions, customs and regional idiosyncrasies in other areas of Germany, such as Hamburg, the Palatinate, Friesland, Saxony or Swabia, are just as colourful and fascinating, and the local dialects are certainly just as hard for the outsider to understand!

Partly as a result of the decentralised federal system operating in Germany today, which means that power is not all concentrated in one capital, as happens in London or Paris, the German regions and *Land* capitals have taken on considerable importance. This again strengthens the role of the federal states in the German way of life, since the *Land* has autonomy in four key areas: education, broadcasting/culture, health and police. This, in turn, means that many Germans feel a strong attachment to their particular *Land*, especially if they live in a rural setting, where regional differences tend to be more pronounced than in big cities.

The majority of Germany's population live in small towns and villages, with around one-third living in one of the eighty-four cities with more than 100,000 inhabitants, defined in German as *Großstädte* (*Facts About Germany* 1995: 66). Berlin (3.5 million), Hamburg (1.7 million) and Munich (1.3 million) are the largest cities, followed by Cologne, Frankfurt, Essen, Dortmund, Stuttgart, Düsseldorf and Bremen. Leipzig and Dresden, in the east, come just behind

Nuremberg, with just under half a million inhabitants each. Although it is not the norm, it is still possible today to find Germans living in rural communities who speak only dialect, hardly using High German (*Hochdeutsch*) at all and who feel far more attached to their particular local region than to Germany as a whole.

Until recently, when an influx of refugees came from Eastern Europe, Germany had one of the lowest birth rates in the world. Amongst a population of approximately 82 million, there are now around 7 million foreigners. The Turks are by far the largest group, with nearly 2 million, followed, in order of size, by those from the former Yugoslavia (this was always a large group, now swelled by the many war refugees), Italians, Greeks, Poles, Austrians, Romanians, Spaniards, Iranians, Portuguese, Americans, Dutch and many more (ibid.: 71). It is worth remembering two facts about Germany's foreign population. Nearly half of them have been living in Germany for at least ten years, and more than two-thirds of the children born to foreign parents were born in Germany, although being born in Germany does not give them German nationality (see p. 9).

NOTES

1 This quote, so often referred to in the context of West German politics, was first used by F. R. Allemann (1956) *Bonn ist nicht Weimar*, Cologne: Kiepenheuer und Witsch.
2 See for example Pulzer (1995).
3 For a concise summary of the economic and political systems of the former GDR (1949–90), see Parkes (1997: Chapter 1).
4 Figures taken from 'Die Einheit im Spiegel der Demoskopie', an article in the magazine *Deutschland*, no. 4 (August 1995).

RECOMMENDED READING

Facts About Germany (also published in German as *Tatsachen über Deutschland*) (1995), highly recommended to all students of German Studies, available free from the Embassy for the FRG in London.
Smith *et al.* (1996), especially the Introduction and final chapter.
Watson (1995), especially the Preface and Introduction.

BIBLIOGRAPHY

Facts about Germany (1995), Frankfurt: Societätsverlag.
Lewis, D. and McKenzie, J. R. P. (eds) (1995) *The New Germany*, Exeter: University of Exeter Press.
Parkes, S. (1997) *Understanding Contemporary Germany*, London and New York: Routledge.

Paterson, W. E. and Southern, D. (1991) *Governing Germany*, Oxford: Blackwell, especially Chapters 1 and 2.

Pulzer, P. (1995) *German Politics 1945–1995*, Oxford: Oxford University Press.

Smith, G., Paterson, W. E. and Padgett, S. (1996) *Developments in German Politics 2*, Basingstoke: Macmillan.

Watson, A. (1995) *The Germans: Who Are They Now?*, London: Mandarin.

2 Berlin

The new capital

Sue Lawson

Berlin is fascinating. Like no other German city, it symbolises German history. In 1871 it became the capital of the newly founded Germany, and it was a major site of the 1918 revolution. Berlin was the cultural centre of the 1920s and the 1930s, and in 1933 it became the capital of Hitler's National Socialist Reich. From 1949 to 1989 it was famous throughout the world as a divided city, until it was reunited in a blaze of television publicity. It is now once more the capital of the whole of Germany, and early in the twenty-first century it will become the seat of the German government. One short chapter cannot do justice to the exciting complexity which is Berlin, and this chapter does not attempt that. It merely attempts to give some indication of the atmosphere of Berlin, with particular reference to the building programme, the speed and extent of which is unique in present-day Europe and which profoundly affects this atmosphere. Of the many issues which could be discussed, two in particular have been highlighted: the choice of Berlin as capital and the unsuccessful attempt to merge the *Länder* of Berlin and Brandenburg.

BEGINNINGS AND DEVELOPMENT TILL THE SECOND WORLD WAR

In order to understand what Berlin is now, it is necessary to know something about what it was. Berlin's development as a city, both in size and in importance, has not been one of steady progress, more a series of leaps and setbacks. Although today it may seem the 'natural' capital of Germany, it was the united capital of a united Germany for a relatively short time.

Berlin began as two towns, Berlin and Cölln, which grew up as trading settlements halfway between the fortresses of Spandau and Köpenick. Berlin was on the north-east bank of the River Spree;

Cölln opposite it on an island in the Spree. This part of Berlin is still known as the Spreeinsel. The first documentary evidence of Cölln comes from 1237; Berlin, the older settlement, was first mentioned in 1244, though not as a town. Both places probably became towns around 1230. They remained separate until 1307, when they agreed a common defence policy.[1] The local rulers, the Margraves of the Province of Brandenburg, diverted the trade route between Spandau and Köpenick so that it ran through Berlin-Cölln, and the double town grew rapidly. In the fourteenth century, to defend themselves against spreading lawlessness outside the towns, Berlin and Cölln strengthened their co-operation with each other, and joined the Hanseatic League of Baltic towns. In 1448 the Electors of Brandenburg chose Berlin-Cölln as their official residence, and the town was to remain the home of the ruler – whether Elector (Kurfürst) of Brandenburg, King of Prussia, Emperor of Germany or Führer of the Reich – for the next five centuries, until the collapse of Nazi Germany in 1945.

The Thirty Years War (1618–48) reduced the population of Berlin by half. Thus the town was happy to welcome the Protestant Huguenots fleeing from persecution in France. About 6,000 of them found their way there. As the royal capital of Prussia, Berlin became an important economic, political and cultural centre. This was one of its first big leaps both in size and in area. Between 1700 and 1850 its population grew proportionately more than at any other time, from under 30,000 to nearly 430,000. New residential suburbs grew up, and in January 1710 Berlin, Cölln and the new suburbs were formally constituted into one town – Berlin. Since the old town walls made communications with the new, more spaciously built suburbs difficult, they were gradually demolished from 1734 onwards. The new city walls, finished in 1736, had fourteen gates, of which only one, the Brandenburger Tor, has survived. However, you can still trace the line of these walls by the streets linking the Underground stations which bear the names of the old gates. If driving from Hallesches Tor to Schlesisches Tor via Kottbusser Tor, or taking the train from Frankfurter Tor to Schönhauser Allee, you are travelling more or less along the line of the 1736 walls. The area thus surrounded was sufficient for Berlin's building needs until the late nineteenth century.

Berlin became the capital of Imperial Germany in 1871. This, combined with industrialisation, meant that between 1880 and 1905 the population grew from 1.1 million to over 2 million, and land and financial speculation was rife. In 1872 alone, 174 new companies were founded in Berlin, most of them short-lived. The mass housing built for the poorer sections of the population began to establish Berlin's reputation for having the largest concentration of tenement housing in the world. Many firms moved out to the suburbs, where new industrial estates[2] were being built. In 1902 its first Underground railway was opened. By 1903 this railway was transporting 30 million passengers a year. Berlin became a magnet for artists and scientists, but also attracted large numbers of unemployed.

This upswing came to an abrupt halt at the outbreak of the First World War (1914–18). After the war the Weimar Republic was established; in Berlin the Republic was actually proclaimed twice: by the Communist Karl Liebknecht at the Stadtschloß and by the Social Democrat Philipp Schneidemann at the Reichstag, the German parliament (Behrend 1992).

Berlin's next big leap in size was a purely administrative one. In 1920 eight towns, fifty-nine rural areas and twenty-seven landed estates were incorporated into Greater Berlin (*Gebietsreform*), giving it a population of 4 million. It was now the largest industrial town on the continent, the newspaper centre of Germany with 149 daily papers published here, and also an intellectual and cultural centre where cabaret and variety flourished. However, this golden age (1920–33) lasted only thirteen years, until Hitler came to power in 1933. This was to change the make-up of the city drastically, if only because virtually all the Jews disappeared.[3] The Nazi period and the resulting Second World War (1939–45) had a similar effect on Berlin to the Thirty Years War three centuries previously. By 1945, 600,000 dwellings had been destroyed and the population almost halved to 2.8 million.

BERLIN DIVIDED

After the Second World War, Berlin became a four-power city: that is, sovereignty over it belonged to all four Allied powers equally. However, the Western Allies (the UK, the USA and France) did not see eye to eye with their Soviet colleagues. The introduction of the Deutschmark into the British, French and American zones, but not into the Russian zone (*Währungsreform*), precipitated the division of Germany in 1949.[4] Even so, for a few months the many Berliners who lived in one sector of the as yet undivided city, and worked in another, found themselves being paid in money their local shops did not use.

Over the next forty years the Russian sector grew away from the others as the German Democratic Republic was gradually transformed into a Socialist state.[5] West Berlin, formed from the other three zones, came under Western influence, and acquired many of the characteristics of a West German *Land*. Both Berlins were in some measure untypical of life in the rest of the part-states they belonged to. West Berlin was the eleventh *Bundesland*, but its character was in part determined by the Western Allies. It could not be governed directly by the Federal Republic, and a number of Federal laws did not apply. Living or studying in West Berlin exempted you from military service. There were twenty-two members in the Bundestag, who were not directly elected but delegated by the Berlin parliament (Abgeordnetenhaus). These delegates had no vote in plenary sessions, nor could they participate in the election of the Chancellor.[6] On the other hand, Berlin was generously subsidised by the Bonn government.[7] As a part-city and an ex-capital, cut off from its natural hinterland, it would not otherwise have attracted investment. It was, however, politically important both that the standard of living in West Berlin should appear demonstrably higher than that of the East, and that the West Berliners should not feel abandoned by Bonn.

As citizens of a Socialist state, East Berliners might well have countered that your standard of living is not only a function of how much money you have to spend. 'Invisibles' like accessible child care and guaranteed employment also matter.[8] However, East Berlin was also subsidised. As the capital, for all practical purposes, of a command economy, it could ensure that the best of what was available got there. Moreover, in East Berlin the West lay next door, and most inhabitants knew someone[9] who after 1972 had access to the West of the city and could bring goods back.

THE BERLIN WALL

Physically Berlin remained one city until 1961. The Wall was erected during the night of 12/13 August 1961. It surrounded the Western sector and carved a jagged path across the city. Its declared – and in economic terms (though not in human ones) quite understandable – function was to stop East Germans from pouring to the West and thus depriving the GDR of much-needed manpower, brain power and dynamism. Its effect on families living on both sides was devastating. In Bernauer Strasse, for example, between Prenzlauer Berg in the East and Wedding in the West, the Wall split the street in two. When guards and a brigade of masons arrived to wall up tenement windows on the GDR side, people began jumping out of windows and into firemen's sheets below. This was documented on archive film at the time (Hadrow and Kirby 1994).

Over the years the GDR strengthened and realigned its defences until a tight network of 3m (10ft) wall, fencing, barbed wire, open death strips, watchtowers, searchlights, and dog and human patrols extended for 100 miles round West Berlin. Houses close to the border were pulled down to improve firing lines. Guards had orders to shoot to kill, and most obeyed them, having little choice. In all there were 258 killed while escaping, eighteen drowned, and twenty-five border guards killed.[10]

Despite the human costs of the Wall, the economic stability it brought to the GDR meant that the two German states could organise their relationship on a more permanent basis. By the 1980s it seemed that Berlin could well remain a divided city indefinitely. Plans were even put forward to incorporate the Wall into buildings (*zumauern*) on the Western side. And then the Wall fell, almost as suddenly and unexpectedly as it had risen. Its building, like Bismarck's 1871 Empire, had been imposed from above. To bring it down, the people took the law into their own hands.

In autumn 1989, Hungary opened its border with Austria. Thousands of GDR citizens could now leave for the West via Hungary,[11] as they could via Berlin before the Wall was built. The resulting mass exodus and the storming by East Germans of the West German embassies in Prague, Budapest and Warsaw prompted those who intended staying to demand reforms. Huge street demonstrations began in Leipzig and quickly spread to other East German cities, including Berlin. On 4 November 1989 around half a million people gathered on the Alexanderplatz to voice their protests. On 9 November the rumour spread that the Berlin Wall had been opened. Opinions differ as to whether this was formally true, but the people of Berlin made it true that very night. Thousands of East Berliners walked or drove to the crossing points of the Wall and demanded to be let through. Finally the numbers were too great for the crossing-point guards, who in any case had received no definite instructions, and the barriers were simply lifted. East and West Berliners walked through, on to and over the Wall. The mood was one of mass hysteria and euphoria; what happened that night in Berlin was broadcast live around the world on radio and television (Aust 1989). Hundreds of thousands celebrated throughout the city, and the frenzy of enthusiasm lasted for weeks.

The destruction of the infamous Wall began that same night. Pieces were chipped out almost immediately as souvenirs by the so-called 'woodpeckers of the Wall', the *Mauerspechte*. Over the next few days huge slices were carved out to make new crossing points. Six months after the opening of the Wall its systematic destruction began. Selected painted pieces were sold throughout the world, and the rest ground down to build roads. A year later 1 million tons of concrete had been disposed of. Roads that had been severed have been reconnected, and new buildings, grass and trees are covering the scars left by the Wall's removal. On the ground, its cross-city route is almost impossible to follow. Perhaps predictably, the pendulum eventually swung back once more. The one single watchtower left of the original 215 has been declared a national monument. In 1995 it was decided that the line of the Wall through the city should be marked. Test patches of coloured concrete, a copper and an aluminium strip, and double lines of paving stones have already been laid. This is a mainly Western interest; the East Berliners had other, more pressing problems. When the Wall was there, East Berliners avoided it as much as possible, leaving that area of Berlin to the tourists and the police (*Der Spiegel* 45/1995: 80–85).

BERLIN REUNITED?

Ironically, those who had said that in a sense there had 'always' been two Berlins were not entirely wrong. Even though there is no longer a physical barrier between East and West, there is still a psychological one (*die Mauer in den Köpfen*).[12] The Wall itself may be gone, but for most Berliners there is still an East and a West Berlin. According to a survey carried out by the *Berliner Zeitung* in 1991, only 7 per cent of West Berliners went regularly (more than once a week) to East Berlin, but 30 per cent of East Berliners went regularly to West Berlin; 64 per cent of these went shopping: the selection was better in West Berlin, and sometimes the prices were lower. Sixty per cent went for a look round. Only 4 per cent of West Berliners went to East Berlin to go shopping, and 49 per cent to look at the sights. Forty-five per cent of East Berliners wanted, now that it was possible, to see *all* of Berlin; only 30 per cent of West Berliners wanted to do so.

This is perhaps understandable. One could say that between 1961 and 1989 the East Berliners had been unable to travel anywhere very much, whereas West Berliners had had the run of the world. One could also say that, because Berlin had expanded so quickly during the nineteenth century and the early part of the twentieth, it had essentially remained a federation of only loosely connected and relatively independent small towns, each with its own centre. Thus the inhabitants of what was still basically Köpenick, though officially part of Greater Berlin, felt no particular need to go to other parts of Greater Berlin such as Reinickendorf or Weissensee. The post-Wall Berliner, therefore, still sticks to his or her own area.

It can also be argued that Unification had a more serious effect on employment prospects, and thus on the ability to travel, for the East Berliners than for the West Berliners, and particularly for the less well educated young. For some in the East, the world expanded with Unification. They could now travel, spend time learning abroad, and no longer had to fulfil the Marxist criteria of social acceptability to continue their education. But for others in the East the world narrowed. Every student and apprentice in the GDR including East Berlin knew that they would be allocated a job after training, and even the simplest and least demanding job had the status of a profession. These people were simply not used to applying for jobs in competition with others. Their parents did not necessarily know how to either, nor had they the connections and networks to help their offspring. Schools began providing courses in how to apply for jobs in a market economy, but because the special subsidies for Berlin had gone with the Wall the city was less interesting for investors. Many of the companies with training places in the East were closed down. The need for these young people to find jobs in an alien environment thus coincided with a reduction in the jobs available.

BERLIN AS CAPITAL: THE *HAUPTSTADTDEBATTE*

While Germany remained divided, Berlin was not supposed to be the capital of either part. East Berlin was none the less gradually incorporated into the GDR, and by the 1980s postcards of East Berlin, and motorway signs to it, bore the words 'Hauptstadt der DDR' (capital of the GDR). After Unification the prohibition of course lapsed, and in 1991 the Federal Parliament decided, after long debate and by a majority of only eighteen votes, that the capital and seat of government of the newly united Germany would be Berlin, not Bonn. Government departments have already begun moving, and by 2002 the whole administration (if the schedule is kept to) will have transferred to Berlin.

There were practical and economic arguments on each side. Moving to Berlin is proving enormously expensive, and the people of Bonn understandably feared that losing the German government would adversely affect the economy of their region. On the other hand, Bonn's loss might be Brandenburg's gain: making Berlin the capital might reinvigorate the economy of its surrounding areas. But this sort of decision is rarely made purely on practical grounds. Behind it lay the issue of how the unified Federal Republic saw itself, and how it was regarded in the rest of Europe. In a sense Berlin meant both change and continuity: a change from the immediate past, and continuity with an earlier past, not all aspects of which were acceptable. Going for Berlin as capital meant confronting Germany's imperial and Nazi past, and raising worries in the neighbouring countries about Germany's future role. The rest of Europe had felt relatively comfortable with Bonn as capital of West Germany. Chosen in the 1950s as a temporary capital partly because it clearly could not and would not rival Berlin, it had come to symbolise a Germany that had accepted democratic values, while Berlin recalled the non-democratic and imperialist past of Prussia. However, the feelings of the rest of Europe had to be balanced against the feelings of the East Germans. Had Bonn, which lay so far to the West, been confirmed as capital, the East Germans would have felt even more strongly that they had simply been taken over (Parkes 1997: 54). Perhaps Berlin did lie a trifle too far to the East; but unlike Bonn it was experiencing the effects of Unification at first hand. On another level, Bonn in all its forty years of capitalhood had never acquired the ambience and atmosphere of a lively metropolis, whereas united Berlin was rapidly rediscovering it (Watson 1995: 96–102). Despite the fact that Berlin was the united capital of a united Germany for a relatively short time,[13] one reason for the decision was undoubtedly the feeling that Berlin was somehow the 'natural' capital of Germany. Another was Helmut Kohl's emotional attachment to the idea of Berlin. He confessed on the day the vote was taken in Bonn that ever since that unforgettable night of 9 November 1989 he had been for Berlin (*Der Spiegel* 43/1995: 76–86).

REBUILDING BERLIN

Once the decision had been made to transfer the capital to Berlin, civic and federal authorities agreed that the old centre of Berlin should be revived. Private investors were quicker off (or on to!) the mark, and a veritable flood of planning applications came in. The political and administrative guidelines for future development were therefore formulated under great pressure of time. The historical street network was to remain or be reconstructed. The maximum building height was to be 22 metres to the eaves and 30 metres to the roof. At least 20 per cent of each building was to be residential.

The basic principle was to be the town house on one site; and the largest admissible site was the block (Kapitzki 1996: 16–17). Berlin had a lot of building to catch up on. In East Berlin the Socialist government could spend very little on repairing and maintaining the housing stock. It preferred – partly because it was cheaper – to give the people huge paved areas such as the Marx Engels Platz in which to foregather, and blocks of flats built of prefabricated concrete squares in which to live. The virtually complete destruction of the Wall, of the fortifications and of the 'death strip' presented the capital-in-waiting with a huge strip of derelict land right in its centre – a splendid opportunity for some visionary construction projects.

Few cities are given in peacetime such an opportunity to rebuild their centre. And what has happened in Berlin is that rebuilding after the destruction of the 1939–45 war was delayed by the division and the Wall. What we are now seeing there is effectively a speeded-up version of what in other European capitals has taken nearly fifty years. Clearly, such an enormous undertaking was never going to be uncontroversial. Equally clearly, Berlin could not afford to pass up such an opportunity for reconstruction and restoration. To give you some idea of the scale of the operation, think of a town of 100,000 inhabitants. The four largest building sites in central Berlin – Potsdamer Platz, Friedrichstraße, Leipziger Straße and Lehrter Bahnhof – were equal in area to a town that size. That is not counting the repair and rebuilding which is going on outside the centre. The noise, dust and inconvenience, for those who have to live there, are immense! Berlin has, however, made the best of things by successfully converting its huge building programme into a tourist attraction (*Die Welt*, 14 May 1996). The huge red 'Info-Box' on stilts in the centre of Potsdamer Platz showed up to 5,000 visitors a day an interactive electronic view of twenty-first-century Berlin. So successful has the 'Info-Box' proved that it will be used on other huge building sites elsewhere.

In the original town centre between Alexanderplatz and Potsdamer Platz the scars of the 1939–45 war, of unimaginative post-war rebuilding and of the building of the Wall will be finally removed. What in the eighteenth century were the suburbs (remember Berlin was much smaller then) of Dorotheenstadt and Friedrichstadt with their once splendid baroque squares, of which only fragments remain, will dictate the layout of Pariser Platz, Leipziger Platz, Mehringplatz and Spittelmarkt, but the buildings will be new. A huge shopping precinct has been built in Friedrichstraße; some very prestigious shops have already moved in, and others are awaited. The areas of

Spreeinsel and Wilhelmstrasse will contain ministries and embassies – the new federal government buildings proper will be west and south of the Brandenburg Gate, and will include the rebuilt Reichstag. New offices, shops and hotels will mingle with the existing opera house, theatre and university. The U-Bahn and S-Bahn lines severed by the building of the Wall have been rebuilt or reconnected already. As a reunited capital city Berlin will receive many more travellers per day than before, so its transport system needs not simply reconstructing, but extending and modernising. To connect it to the high-speed German railway network three large new intercity stations are planned – Lehrter Bahnhof (240,000 passengers per day), Papestraβe (79,000 ppd) and Spandau. Even so, the area around the Lehrter Bahnhof will be 30 per cent residential.

While this huge project takes place in the city centre, an extensive housing project is planned for the suburbs. The same principle obtains as for the town centre: use the traditional Berlin grid-system ground plan, and provide living accommodation, schools, kindergartens, shops, workplaces and greenery all within the same area, and preferably within walking distance. In the last five years 72,000 such homes have been planned or built for areas such as Biesdorf, Alt-Glieneke and Rudow.

In many ways the basic model for the rebuilding, particularly of the centre, is reminiscent of that other era of hectic building through which Berlin has gone, the end of the nineteenth century. At that time huge numbers of industrial workers came to Berlin, especially from the poorer, more easterly parts of Germany, as migrant workers in the 1950s came especially from the poorer, more easterly parts of Europe. They needed accommodation, and to provide it the town drew up in 1862 a blueprint for building until the end of the century. The plan envisaged a grid system of wide intersecting streets, generous rectangular sites interspersed with parks and greenery, decorated patrician houses on the outside of the blocks, facing on to the streets (*Vorderhäuser*), and humbler, plainer houses hidden behind these (*Hinterhäuser*), so that rich and poor could live, work and play happily in decent and appropriate accommodation side by side in the same areas. At least that was, and is, the idea.

This nineteenth-century plan both overestimated the town's interest in the common good, and underestimated the power of capital. In the long term it fostered land speculation. Thus, instead of the intended three- or four-storey dwellings, housing on the expensive sites was packed as densely as possible, with up to seven five-storey tenement *Hinterhäuser* behind each splendid *Vorderhaus*, and tiny boxed-in inner courtyards – the minimum area was that required for access and turning by the horsedrawn carriages of the fire brigade – into which no sun could penetrate. One way of dealing with this has been to demolish every alternate block in the system (to let in more light), and renovate what is left.

In the eyes of the civic authorities, Berlin today, newly united under a market system, clearly once again has to attract those with money. Concrete spaces are cheap to produce, but they bring no capital return.[14] If no one wanted to invest in the biggest building site in Europe, then the ambitious plans for Berlin would never be realised. This is partly why Berlin is targeting the well-off with this particular scheme, to persuade them not only to come and shop in Friedrichstraße but to live in the area as well, so that the property will be well maintained. The perceived alternative is the continued depopulation of the city centre and spreading of the city edges as the rich do their best to move out.[15]

In the centre of Europe, therefore, a fascinating experiment has begun (*Der Spiegel* 8/1995: 42–56). Developments which in other European cities took forty or fifty years are being accelerated. By 2002, if all goes according to plan, the long wound through the city left by the Wall will have been closed completely. But that is not all. From north to south, the following will have been built: a new central railway station on four levels, the government buildings with office space for 1,400, up to ten new foreign embassies and twelve *Land* offices, the huge business and residential area for Daimler Benz, Sony, ABB and Hertie in Potsdamer Platz, 750,000sqkm of office and shopping space in Leipziger Platz, and the five blocks of the business centre at the former Wall crossing point Checkpoint Charlie. Underneath all this, four tunnels will have been bored, for intercity and regional railways, for Underground and urban railway, and for a road under the Tiergarten. And that is still not all, for much of East Berlin is sadly in need of long-overdue repair and maintenance, and there is nearly as much building going on in the suburbs and outskirts as in the centre. In total around twenty housing projects are planned, for over 200,000 people. The plans are bold and worthy of a capital city. After sixty years Berlin is returning to the pace and vigour, the legendary 'Tempo' of the 'golden Twenties'.

ECONOMIC PROBLEMS

There is of course a downside to this growth. To finance the ambitious building programme, the *Land* Berlin will have to increase its debt by one-third, to DM 18,000 for every Berliner. The vast housing programme, needed in part because many repairs in East Berlin were neglected for forty years, will cost another DM 560m in debts. By 1998 one-third of Berlin's tax bill will go towards paying off interest on building subsidies.

Clearly, not everything can be afforded. In the East Berlin district of Hohenschönhausen in 1996, for example, DM 250m was needed for repairs: toilet facilities in almost all the schools were out of order; five gyms were unusable. The budget was DM 5m. Over 100,000 turn-of-the-century tenement buildings in Friedrichshain and Prenz-lauer Berg need attention if they are not to decline into slums. Demolishing every other *Hinterhaus* in each block to provide more space and let in more light, as the former GDR did when it could afford it, is least expensive in money terms. However, it means a loss of housing space, and the houses left standing still have to be modernised.

If the town cannot afford the repairs, can private funds be found? One problem here is that, if private individuals or companies buy the property, the rent can then rise out of reach.[16] This is happening in parts of West Berlin: in Kreuzberg, Schöneberg and Charlottenburg the poorer inhabitants are moving out because they can no longer afford the rents. Turkish shops and small businesses are giving way to bars and computer shops. The consequent loss of simple jobs has driven the unemployment rate in Kreuzberg up to 20 per cent. One solution may have been found in the privatisation programme encouraging tenants to buy. This may, however, lead to ghettoisation, the layering of society according to where people live: the antithesis of the specifically Berlin atmosphere created by different sections of society living and working in the same place, with shops and leisure facilities just round the corner – precisely what the town planners say they wish to preserve or re-create.

The restructuring of the old GDR economy was also reflected in Berlin. Since Unification nearly 300,000 jobs in Berlin have disap-peared. As in Germany as a whole, the overwhelming majority of them (about 250,000) were in the East but also about 50,000 in the West. Now unemployment is sinking in the East and rising in the West. The service sector is expanding, but in the old centre of Berlin, rather than in the West. By 1988 subsidies to West Berlin[17] had reached around DM 54 million annually. When they stopped, many investors, tem-porarily at least, left Berlin and moved into the cheaper environs. From 1994 to 1996 economic growth was greatest in the East German *Länder*. Although geographically in the East, the *Land* of Berlin's economy did not keep pace – in 1994 it even shrank a little (*Globus Kartendienst* Bb-2212), and in 1995 it grew more slowly than Dresden's or Leipzig's (*Globus Kartendienst* Bb-2924). In 1996 it merely maintained its position overall (*Globus Kartendienst* Bb-3245), but the economy of West Berlin sank by 1.5 per cent, while that of East Berlin grew by more than 5 per cent. Such growth as there was during these two years was attributed to the prospect of the Federal Government moving there and to the building programme. The latter appears the more important at present. Making Berlin the capital will actually only create about 16,000 new jobs, whereas 125,000 people are employed by the building programme.

BERLIN-BRANDENBURG: TWO INTO ONE DIDN'T GO[18]

Berlin will be the centre of the German building industry for only about the next ten years, and the frenetic pace will certainly slow down before then. One long-term way forward might have been to combine *Land* Berlin with its surrounding *Land* Brandenburg. Provision for this had been made in the Unification Treaty of 1990, perhaps as a first step towards the restructuring of the whole Federal Republic. The Berlin and Brandenburg parliaments voted in 1995 to accept the merger, subject to a referendum in both *Länder*, which took place on 6 May 1996. A narrow majority of Berliners voted in favour and a much larger majority of Brandenburgers voted against. The merger therefore failed, but the debate and the outcome are worth a closer look. The narrow majority in Berlin overall conceals the fact that a majority of West Berliners voted in favour and a majority of East Berliners against (see Table 2.1).

As with the Hauptstadtdebatte, there were economic and practical arguments on both sides. The merger was supported by the two *Land* governments, labour and employers' organisations in both *Länder*, and had the approval of Kohl and the Bundestag. The official pro-merger campaign was therefore immense, with a copy of the merger

Table 2.1 Voting in the Berlin–Brandenburg Referendum 1996 (per cent)

West Berlin			*East Berlin*			*Brandenburg*		
Pro	Anti	Turnout	Pro	Anti	Turnout	Pro	Anti	Turnout
58.7	40.3	59.8	44.5	54.7	54.7	24.3	62.7	66.6

Source: Statistisches Landesamt Berlin; figures from Mackay 1996

treaty for every household and an 'Info-Bus' touring the entire region.[19] The campaign stressed the economic advantages of the proposed merger. A unified Berlin-Brandenburg would form an extremely attractive region for investors. In many ways the area already operated as an economic unit;[20] unification would create optimum conditions for further growth, facilitate a coherent transport and communications policy, and end the costly duplication of administering two *Länder*.[21] The plan also had implications for the future structure of the Federal Republic as a whole, since the successful creation of a larger, financially viable *Land* could demonstrate one way of reducing the growing expense to the *Bund* of the federal system itself.

Its proponents were careful not to call the merger a *Vereinigung*, a union. Enough East Germans had in the event felt 'annexed' after Unification to make it inadvisable to invite any comparison – and Brandenburg lies in the territory of the former GDR. It was to be a 'fusion' or 'marriage' (*Länderfusion* or *Länderehe*) of equals, to form a new *Land* with a new name. None the less, two issues dominated the anti-merger campaign: Berlin's debts[22] and the balance of power. Neither *Land* really expected to gain financially from the merger, but the Brandenburgers feared they might be landed with Berlin's debts as well. The financial relationship envisaged between the city of Berlin and Brandenburg appeared complex, and very dependent on the hope of an economic upturn (Mackay 1996: 488). Another important issue was how the power in a united Berlin-Brandenburg would be divided. The Brandenburgers understandably felt that in a united *Landtag* Berlin would dominate.

The result of the referendum was no real surprise; opinion polls had consistently predicted the outcome accurately. In both areas of Berlin older people tended to vote in favour, and younger against. In the former East Berlin young people voted overwhelmingly against. Support for the PDS is highest in East Berlin, but more than just PDS members voted no. Mackay suggests that both West and East Berliners had been used to living in a city with special status. If the merger went ahead, the former West Berliners would be outnumbered two to one by former East Germans, whereas East Berliners' experiences since Unification might have made them sceptical of any promised benefits. In Brandenburg, as in Berlin, the merger was least popular with the young. Overall, however, the Brandenburg vote was essentially a vote against Berlin. Their fear of becoming a milch cow to service Berlin's debts reinforced their suspicions that as the capital

Berlin would once again enjoy a special status, this time at their expense.

CONCLUSION

This chapter has only skimmed the surface of the exhilarating city that is Berlin. Some there will see the present situation as a leap forward, others as a setback. In a city of that size (3.5 million inhabitants) and complexity it is not possible for everywhere to be doing well. In the future, as in the past, some areas will do better than others. But Berlin will survive somehow, and so will the Berliners, whose 'abiding spirit . . . has been to look forward, to move on from the past without . . . nostalgia or self-pity' (Watson 1995: 102). The best thing to do is to visit Berlin, perhaps even live there for a while, and appreciate the many things Berlin has to offer.

NOTES

1 Early European towns functioned in many ways as nation-states do nowadays. The walls, for instance, were for defence, and demarcation, and within them, though not necessarily outside, the writ of the town council kept the peace.
2 For example, Borsigwalde and Siemensstadt. Siemens now has its headquarters in Munich, but was originally established in Berlin.
3 In 1933 there were 173,000 Jews in Berlin; in 1946 there were 5,000. Now there are about 10,000 (*Der Spiegel* 40/1995: 142).
4 The Federal Republic was created in May, the GDR in October.
5 The GDR lies outside the scope of this chapter, but was a relatively successful socialist state.
6 The four representatives from West Berlin in the *Bundesrat* did not have full voting rights either. They were however allowed to vote for the Federal President.
7 Detailed information on precise subsidies lie outside the scope of this chapter.
8 See Chapter 6.
9 Men over 65, and women over 60, could visit the West for a maximum of thirty days a year.
10 Statistic from a memorial near the Reichstag. See also 'Third Reich and the Wall' in: Leitch (1993: 51–62).
11 See Chapter 1.
12 See Chapter 1, and p. 4.
13 Seventy-four years, from 1871 to 1945, and only fifteen of those years under democratic government.
14 Christian Villiers, *Senatsverwaltung für Bau und Wohnungswesen*, author's interview on 7 May 1996.
15 Ibid.

16 *Der Spiegel* 8/1995: 52.
17 See p. 16, this chapter.
18 I am greatly indebted to Joanna Mackay's 1996 article for this section.
19 The main opposition groups were the PDS, the Brandenburg Bündnis 90/ Die Grünen, various political parties not in the *Landtag* and the pressure group Bündnis für Brandenburg.
20 Around 200,000 workers commuted daily to Berlin from Brandenburg, and 50,000 the other way.
21 For a more detailed analysis of the referendum, see Mackay (1996: 485–502).
22 In 1996 these were DM 13.36 per inhabitant (Harenberg 1996: 528).

RECOMMENDED READING/WATCHING

Aust, S. (1989) *Fünf Wochen im Herbst*, Spiegel TV video on events leading up to the fall of the Berlin Wall.
Behrend, J. (1992) *Berlin*. Useful if you are visiting Berlin.
'Berlin: Baustelle der Nation', *Der Spiegel* 49/1996, pp. 22–34 on the pros and cons of the building programme.
Hadrow, J. and Kirby, T. (1994) *Walking the Wall*, BBC TV video. A retrospective look at events five years after the Wall fell. Personal memories in German (subtitled) and English.
Merian Extra (1994) *Hauptstadt Berlin*. Articles on various aspects of Berlin, with photographs.
Parkes, S. (1997) *Understanding Contemporary Germany* gives a short and clear statement of the arguments in the Hauptstadtdebatte (see especially pp. 52–54).
Watson (1995) pp. 96–102.

BIBLIOGRAPHY

Anon., 'Berlin ist die grösste Baustelle Europas – und stolz darauf', *Die Welt*, 14 May 1996.
Anon., 'Ihr müsst Berlin lieben', *Der Spiegel* 43/1995: 76–86.
Anon., 'Lied'l fum goldenen Land', *Der Spiegel* 40/1995: 134–142.
Anon., 'Schwer emotional besetzt', *Der Spiegel* 45/1995: 80–85.
Anon., 'Von New York lernen', *Der Spiegel* 8/1995: 42–56.
Aust, S. (1989) *Fünf Wochen im Herbst*, Spiegel TV video.
Behrend, J. (1992) *Berlin*, Insight Pocket Guide, APA Publications.
Globus Kartendienst (1994) Bb-2212.
——— (1995) Bb-2924.
——— (1996) Bb-3245.
Hadrow, J. and Kirby, T. (1994) *Walking the Wall*, BBC TV video.
Holland, J. and Gawthrop, J. (1995) *Berlin: the Rough Guide*, Rough Guides Ltd. (More detailed than Behrend.)
Kapitzki, C. (1996) *Berlin – Visionen werden Realität*, Jovis.
Leitch, M. (1993) *Slow Walks in Berlin*, Hodder and Stoughton, pp. 51–62.
Mackay, J. (1996) 'Berlin-Brandenburg? Nein danke! The Referendum on

the proposed *Länderfusion*', *German Politics*, vol. 5 no. 3 (December), pp. 485–502.

Parkes, S. (1997) *Understanding Contemporary Germany*, London and New York: Routledge.

Watson, A. (1995) 'Berlin', in Watson, A., *The Germans: Who Are They Now?*, London: Mandarin, especially pp. 96–102.

3 The federal framework

Peter James

INTRODUCTION

Even the name of the country – the Federal Republic of Germany (die Bundesrepublik Deutschland) – underlines the importance of the federal structure in Germany. The German term *Föderalismus*, derived from the Latin *foedus*, meaning federation or alliance, suggests a form of state organisation in which there is devolution of power from the centre to the constituent parts or regions; the concept of federalism, therefore, implies a **decentralised** system, in which there is real power-sharing, divided between a central government and several regional ones.

Gordon Smith (1979: 48) refers to the German federal system as being often underrated as a political institution. This chapter should be read in conjunction with the following one on the political system, since federalism is an integral part of the German polity, which is by no means the only aspect of German life and society influenced by the federal framework. It also affects, for example, schooling, the legal system, cultural matters, the organisation of the media, health and social provision.

Two points are of fundamental importance in understanding the concept of (German) federalism. First, there are both large and small countries which have federal systems. It is clearly effective to apply a federal, decentralised system to huge political units such as the USA, Canada or India because of their sheer size. However, small countries such as Switzerland and Austria – and indeed Germany itself is not large in comparative global terms – also have a federal system. In fact, the USA and the Swiss Confederation were key influences on the original decision to adopt a kind of confederate federalism for the German Confederation (der Deutsche Bund 1815–66).[1]

Second, the establishment of a federal system for the FRG in 1949 was not an innovation. It was a legacy from the past, building on a long federal tradition. When Germany was first unified as a nation-state in 1871, a federal component was introduced, despite Prussian hegemony, in the German Empire. The upper house of parliament at the time, the Bundesrat, had fifty-eight seats (Prussia had seventeen); it functioned as a sort of federalist/monarchist organ of state.[2] The Weimar Republic (1919–33) also had a second chamber, the Reichsrat, in a federal system.

The federal component was abolished between 1933 and 1945 by Hitler and the National Socialists, who ran a centralised, unitary state (*Einheitsstaat*), since federalism and dictatorship are incompatible. The Eastern (Soviet) zone of occupation, when it became the GDR in October 1949, originally contained a federal component too. This was, however, soon changed as fourteen administrative districts (*Bezirke*) took over from the five *Länder* and the East German *Landeskammer*, thus centralising power under a socialist system. In the three Western zones (US, British, French) the authors of the Basic Law, the West German constitution, were particularly keen to re-introduce a decentralised, democratic, federal structure in May 1949, as were the Western Allies themselves.

In this way West Germany adopted a federal system similar, though not identical, to that of the United States. The United Kingdom does *not* have a federal structure; in fact its political system is often criticised for concentrating too much power in London, at the expense of the regions. Calls for Scottish devolution and a Welsh parliament were evident yet again during the 1997 British general election campaign. Indeed, the view was often expressed in the UK between 1990 and 1997 that the British Prime Minister of the day, as well as some members of the cabinet, did not fully understand the term 'federalism', especially when speaking of a 'federal Europe'.

THE CONSTITUTIONAL DIMENSION

David Southern has pointed out that an essential feature of federalism is that the constituent states have a constitutionally entrenched position, as bearers of a limited form of sovereignty (Paterson and Southern 1991: 141). Germany's current federal system is characterised by a horizontal separation of powers between the legislature, the executive and the judiciary (see Chapter 4); there is also a vertical separation of powers between the Federation (*Bund*), the *Länder* and the local communes or municipalities (*Gemeinden*). In this vertical three-tier system (*Bund/Land/Gemeinde*), an additional district level (*Kreis*) sometimes occurs between the *Land* and *Gemeinde* tiers, though this is not the case in all states. Legislative matters are shared between the federation and the individual states, administration is fundamentally the responsibility of the federal states, and the two tiers work closely together in questions of jurisdiction.

A whole section (section two) of the German constitution, the Basic Law (*Grundgesetz* – GG) (see Chapter 4, pp. 45–46), is devoted to the question of the federation and the federal states. Each *Land* has its own constitution (which must conform to the federal constitution), its own state parliament and chief executive (Ministerpräsident). Article 30 (Art. 30 GG) states that exercising government power is the concern of the federal states (*Sache der Länder*), unless otherwise stated. Art. 31 GG makes it clear that federal law overrides *Land* law. Art. 28 (2) GG guarantees the independence and individual responsibility of local self-government for the lowest tier, the *Gemeinden*. Since the Basic Law was first introduced as a provisional constitution in 1949, there have been over forty amendments to it.

Perhaps the most crucial part of the constitution regarding federalism is Art. 79 (3) GG. This expressly excludes any alteration to the *Grundgesetz* that affects the division of the FRG into federal states, or the fundamental involvement of the *Länder* in the legislative process, or the basic rights and democratic principles laid down in Arts 1 and 20 GG.

Art. 29 GG covers in considerable detail the question of reorganisation of the federal territory, involving a referendum (direct democracy), as happened for example in Baden-Württemberg in 1952 and as was proposed but rejected with Brandenburg and Berlin in 1996 (see Chapter 2). The constitution gives the federal states the right to legislate, except where such powers are conferred on the federation (Art. 70.1 GG). In practice, however, there has been a shift in favour of the *Bund* in recent years.

There are basically three sets of areas of legislative competence: those where the federation has exclusive responsibility (defined by Arts 71 and 73 GG), those where the federal states have exclusive responsibility (Art. 70 GG) and those where it is shared, i.e. concurrent responsibility (Art. 72 GG). Article 106 covers the details of tax distribution (see p. 34). There are also certain areas where the federation is responsible for the provision of a general framework for more specific legislation (*Rahmengesetzgebung*) (see Table 3.1).

Table 3.1 The division of legislative responsibility in the FRG's federal system

Federation (Bund)	*Federal States* (Länder)
Foreign affairs	Culture/broadcasting
Defence	Education
Citizenship	Police
Passport, immigration/emigration	Health
Currency and monetary matters	
Customs and foreign trade	
Federal rail and air transport	
Post and telecommunications	
Framework legislation	
Higher education	
Hunting, nature conservation	
Land distribution, regional planning	
Residence registration, identity cards	
Press, film industry	
Concurrent legislative responsibility	
Civil law, criminal law and sentencing	
Registration of births, marriages and deaths	
Law of association and assembly	
Residence of aliens	
Production and utilisation of nuclear energy	

Land responsibilities

The four broad areas for which each of the sixteen *Länder* has exclusive responsibility (culture/broadcasting, education, police, health – see Table 3.1) exert a considerable influence on the everyday lives of German citizens.

For example, the school system varies, sometimes quite considerably, in terms of curriculum, types of school, the age at which you change schools, etc., according to which federal state you live in. A child whose family moves from Hamburg to Munich, for instance, or from Cologne to Stuttgart, usually has to adapt rapidly to a different system. Although the federal government has an education minister and the *Bund* has an influence as far as university education is concerned (via the framework legislation (Rahmengesetzgebung)), each *Land* has its own education ministry, which retains powers for its own state over both school and higher education. A Standing Committee of the Education Ministers (Kultusministerkonferenz) meets regularly, in order to maintain a degree of uniformity. For more detail on education and training, see Chapter 7.

The great cultural diversity (see Chapter 10) in German life affects theatres, museums, libraries, public monuments, etc. Such variety is a direct result of the federal system, as is the considerable regional variation which enriches the German broadcasting network. The latter concerns both radio and television, adding a regional flavour. The distribution of political power between the federal capital and the sixteen regional capitals has contributed to a wide variety and choice in the German media landscape (see Chapter 9). In countries with no federal system, such as France or Great Britain, greater press concentration in the capital (Paris, London) is evident.

Every state has its own police service, although expediency has meant that, in practice, a system of overall co-ordination across the *Länder* has proved necessary in the fight against serious crimes such as terrorist attacks or kidnapping. Health provision, addressed in Chapter 6, also comes under the auspices of the federal states, where austerity measures (*Sparpaket*) are proving necessary, with a view to making savings in Germany's massive health budget.

THE FISCAL DIMENSION

When it came to ordering financial and fiscal matters, two earlier German systems were taken into consideration. Under Bismarck in the German Empire (1871–1918) the central state, the *Reich*, was financially dependent on the *Länder*. During the Weimar Republic (1919–33) the reverse was true; in fact the financial position of the *Länder* was so catastrophic from 1930 to 1933 that they were not able to offer any real resistance to the rise of Hitler and the National Socialists, whose centralist state was anathema to the German federalist tradition.

The fiscal/financial dimension of federalism was, therefore, and still is, of paramount importance. A certain degree of financial autonomy is essential. There are around forty different taxes in Germany today, which go directly to one of three sources: into the coffers of the federation (*Bundeskasse*), the federal states (*Länderkasse*) or the local communes/municipalities (*Gemeindekasse*) (for examples, see Table 3.2).

However, some of the tax revenue collected is split either two or three ways. This applies to the biggest share of the tax bill paid in Germany (over 70 per cent), the so-called community taxes (*Gemeinschaftssteuern*), which cover four taxes: income tax (*Lohn-*

Table 3.2 Examples (%) of tax revenue distribution in Germany

Tax	Federation	States	Local
Income	42.5	42.5	15
Corporation	50	50	
Capital	50	50	
VAT	55	45*	
Business	20	20	60
Customs, excise	100		
Coffee, tea	100		
Brandy	100		
Beer		100	
Inheritance		100	
Vehicle tax		100	
Entertainment			100
Dog licences			100
Property			100

Source: Adapted from various sources, including Paterson and Southern (1991).
Note: *Until 1995 the ratio was 65/35 (see below).

und Einkommensteuer), value added tax (*Umsatz/Mehrwertsteuer*), corporation tax (*Körperschaftsteuer*) and tax on capital income (*Kapitalertragsteuer*). Income tax is the largest amount, 42.5 per cent going to the federation, 42.5 per cent to the states and the remaining 15 per cent to the communes (*Gemeinden*).

The second-largest source of tax revenue is value added tax (VAT). Originally 65 per cent of VAT flowed into the federation's coffers, with 35 per cent going to the federal states. In 1995 that was amended to a 55:45 ratio, as a result of changes needed after Unification. Corporation tax in Germany is split equally between the *Bund* and the *Länder*, as is the tax levied on capital income. Art. 106 of the constitution deals in detail with how tax revenue is apportioned.

There is a long list of taxes that accrue directly to the federation. These include customs and excise duties, tax on capital transfer, insurance, road freight, oil, tobacco, coffee, sugar, salt, brandy and sparkling wine, plus charges imposed by the European Community. Property transfer tax, wealth tax, inheritance and gift tax, motor vehicle tax and lottery/gambling taxes all go straight to the federal states. Any American or British student reading this who visits Germany and partakes in the popular German pastime of beer-drinking will also be contributing to the tax revenue of the *Länder*! Those who prefer sparkling wine or brandy will be paying a tax directly to the federation.

Taxes which go initially to the communes include a business tax (*Gewerbesteuer*). The communes give around 15 or 20 per cent of this income to the federation, and the same amount to the states, in return for their share of income tax. The precise percentage can vary from one local authority to another. Property tax, the income from hunting, fishing and dog licences, and entertainment taxes also benefit the local communities.

THE CO-OPERATIVE DIMENSION

Owing to the different powers exercised by the federation and its constituent parts, co-operation and co-ordination are essential features. The distribution of powers in Germany's political system, with its federalist component, is referred to in German as *Politikverflechtung*, literally an 'entanglement'. This term indicates that the two levels of government, the *Bund* and the *Länder*, are interwoven, or interlinked. German experts speak of *kooperativer Föderalismus*, in which compromises offering a clear delineation of functions between the *Bund* and the *Länder* are continually sought. Co-operative federalism aims to ensure effective utilisation of public resources. This involves a three-stage process of distributing financial resources between the sixteen states horizontally.

First, VAT in Germany is distributed among the *Länder* according to the respective size of population. Other taxes, but not VAT, are paid to the federal state or local authority in which the taxpayer is a resident. This is usually known as the local yield principal. In the case of VAT, up to one-quarter of the federal states' share of VAT revenue may be given to the financially 'weaker' *Länder*. This became problematical when the five reconstituted states of the former GDR, together with a reunited Berlin, joined the new Germany in October 1990.

Second, the system of equalisation payments (*Finanzausgleich*) is a key feature of German federalism. The level of finance required for a *Land* to provide public services for its citizens, corresponding to a national average, is ascertained and compared with its allocation. If necessary, equalisation payments are made. Between 1983 and 1990 three states regularly contributed to the equalisation process: Baden-Württemberg, Hamburg (both areas with very strong economies) and Hesse. Bavaria, also a region with comparatively low unemployment and high productivity, has since become a net contributor too, as have others. With Unification in 1990 the system was thrown into confusion. Small western states, such as the Saarland and Bremen, which used to benefit from funds via the equalisation process, now find themselves contributing towards supporting the new eastern states. Financial equalisation arrangements for the five new *Länder* were delayed until the end of 1995 (by Article 7 of the Unification Treaty) but are now in force. Financial assistance from the federal government and the western states will be necessary for much longer than originally envisaged.

Third, financially weaker states also receive aid grants from the federation. These federal grants were fixed at certain maximum amounts in 1974 by the Federal Equalisation Law (Paterson and Southern 1991: 156) and benefited all the poorer states, which sometimes included Bremen, the smallest of the German states. In a way, Bremen could be seen as a special case. It is, like Hamburg and Berlin, a city-state (Stadtstaat) which includes both the city of Bremen and Bremerhaven. The state parliament (Landtag) also doubles as Bremen city council (Stadtbürgerschaft).

The renewed system of equalisation in the 1990s aimed at maintaining a fair financial balance between the *Länder*, bringing each of the sixteen states up to 95 per cent of the average financial level of all the states, as was the case in the West before Unification. Before 1990 this had always been achieved by inter-state transfers. However, the dire financial straits of the new states in the east (they were struggling even to reach half the financial capacity of the average of the western states) made this impossible.

The problem was solved by a huge redistribution of VAT receipts. From 1995 onwards the percentage distribution between *Bund* and *Länder* was changed from 65:35 to 55:45. This resulted in boosting the money available for transfers between the federal states, which meant that the five new states plus Berlin – Berlin was really also a special case (see Chapter 2) – had around 92 per cent of the *Länder* average, so that the states in the west did not have to dig too deep into their own 'pockets' to make the figure up to 95 per cent.[3] The equalisation exercise for 1995, including VAT redistribution, inter-state transfers, federal grants, German Unity Fund annuities, etc., meant that the massive total of nearly DM 58 billion was transferred to the eastern states (Smith *et al.* 1996: 85). Three areas of administration are important here.

First, government administration is an area where the *Bund* looks after anything concerning the Office of the Federal Chancellor (Bundeskanzleramt) and the federal ministries, as these are the highest federal authorities. They belong to the administrative apparatus at the disposal of the Federal Chancellor and his government, assisting with the implementation of government decisions and the execution of legal matters. Second, the federation accepts responsibility for administering the following specific areas: foreign affairs, the federal railways, the federal post office, the German armed forces, the federal border police, national waterways and internal shipping, air traffic and federal finance. In these areas the federation has its own support network of embassies and consulates, customs offices, etc. Third, the federation administers a special area (*Sonderverwaltung*), which includes high federal authorities such as the federal patents office, the federal employment office and the federal central bank (Bundesbank).

The *Länder* take responsibility for administering a great deal of federal law, as well as any specific *Land* matters. The latter include laws relating to schools, municipal organisation, broadcasting, forestry and agriculture, data protection and the collection of church taxes. More than half the civil servants in Germany are *Land* officials, around a third are employed by the municipalities and just over 10 per cent by the federation.[4] The *Gemeinden* play a predominant administrative role in the areas of local government, social and welfare services, public utilities and transport.

THE POLITICAL DIMENSION

As indicated at the beginning of this chapter, the German federal structure has always possessed an important political dimension, since the second chamber, or upper house of parliament, the Bundesrat, represents the interests of the *Länder*. The Bundesrat is one of the five permanent constitutional organs of the FRG, the others being the Federal Presidency, the Federal Government, the Federal Constitutional Court and the Bundestag. The second chamber is intended as both a counter-balance to the federal government and an essential link connecting the federal states to one other.

When the Bundesrat – an indispensable institution in the German federal system (see Chapter 4, pp. 49–51) – was increased in size in 1990, following Unification, the four states with both the largest populations and the largest territories (North-Rhine Westphalia, Bavaria, Baden-Württemberg and Lower Saxony) demanded the allocation of six votes each. These twenty-four votes, out of a total of sixty-nine (see Table 4.1), mean that together they have over a third of the votes, thus being able to prevent the required two-thirds majority in the second chamber, even if all the other states voted unanimously. According to Art. 79 GG, a two-thirds majority of both houses of parliament is required in order to change the constitution.

The role of the second chamber has been strengthened from one legislative period to the next, as the number of matters which impact on the interests of the federal states has increased. Nowadays around 80 per cent (Stammen 1994: 52) of laws passed require the approval of the body which represents the *Länder*, the Bundesrat. This is another clear indication of the crucial role of the federal component in the political system of the Federal Republic.

The celebrated German political scientist Theo Stammen has likened the political dimension of the German federal system to 'a large building with three separate but linked storeys' (1994: 52). The building consists of local government on the ground floor, representing the municipalities, towns and districts, then on the first floor the sixteen federal states, each with its own constitution and political institutions, and finally on the top floor the federation with its central organs of state. The edifice could now be extended to include a fourth floor representing the European dimension.

Political activity occurs simultaneously on all floors, with each floor or level having its own political tasks and areas of responsibility. Decision-making is devolved to the appropriate political institutions, which are democratically constituted. This means that there are four different types of election held in Germany: local (municipal), *Land* (state), federal (national) and European. These are held every four or five years. At local level a new town and district council (Stadtrat/Kreisrat) is elected, along with mayors (Bürgermeister); at state level a new state parliament (Landtag); at federal level a new national parliament (Bundestag) (currently still in Bonn); and at European level German representatives are elected to a new European parliament (Europaparlament). The political parties (see Chapter 4, p. 53) are active at every level in the FRG, offering the voters a variety of policies, programmes and candidates competing for political office.

Many prominent post-war German politicians, including Helmut Kohl and several former federal chancellors, first gained important political experience at local and state level, for example as minister president of a *Land* or as the mayor of a large city. This has worked in both directions, so that federal politicians have also frequently later 'stepped down' to political office at state and local level.

The various strata of state organisation in the Federal Republic represent the *double* distribution of power, referred to at the beginning of this chapter as the *horizontal* and *vertical* separation of powers in the decentralised federal framework. Art. 28 (2) GG states that municipalities, or communes, must be guaranteed the right to regulate their own affairs, within the limits set by law. The association of municipalities (Gemeindeverbände) also have the right of self-government in accordance with the law. This part of the constitution guarantees the independence and individual responsibility of local government at the lowest tier of the German federal structure.

In recent years, however, the tendency has developed for the municipalities and towns in Germany to be increasingly dependent, in financial terms, on the *Länder* and the *Bund*. This, in turn, has of course placed some restrictions upon the political capabilities and freedom for manoeuvre of the *Gemeinden*. Nevertheless it is at local level that the individual German citizen has the greatest say in influencing decisions which affect his immediate political environment. This is undoubtedly true, even though the turnout at local elections is usually considerably lower than at state and federal elections (but higher than at European elections), and even though state or federal issues often weigh more heavily with the voters than local ones.

THE EUROPEAN DIMENSION

It was often said that nothing lasted longer than the temporary in the FRG's political system. Until Unification in 1990 there was a certain amount of truth in that. It applied equally to the stability and constitutional structure of the German *Länder* after 1945, created for the most part haphazardly, almost by accident, against the background of the four zones of occupation. With the exception of the two Hanseatic cities of Hamburg and Bremen, Thuringia and the Free States of Bavaria and Saxony, the other eleven federal states were artificially created constructions, known in German as test-tube creations (*Retortenländer*), which did not really reflect historical tradition.

Whilst the Unification process has thrown up tremendous problems of integrating the eastern states, which has already been referred to, further problems are arising from the additional question of the current European integration process. Although bringing the new states of the former GDR into line with the old ones as political entities within a democratic federal framework was not really problematical, the alignment of the eastern *Länder* in the financial equalisation process certainly was. The continuing economic reconstruction of East Germany, after the original gross underestimates of the scale of the problem by the federal government, is relevant to the European dimension, since the new eastern states are now of course part of the EU.

Indeed, the concept of subsidiarity, embodied in the Maastricht Treaty, has placed greater emphasis on the co-ordination of European regional policy. This is an area where the German *Länder* have a leading role to play, since they were developed as free-standing political entities with independent and constitutional status; they have gathered a wealth of experience of devolved decision-making, whilst nevertheless remaining a significant constituent part of a central unit. Such a principle could make an essential contribution to the future development of an ever-closer union in Europe, integrated politically and economically.

Many observers think that such plans are more likely to be realised via a federal European structure, although a lot depends on the precise definition of federalism. Certainly a federal structure along the lines of the German system has a lot to recommend it. Perhaps the EU membership of Austria, another country with a federal system, might have an influence.

Despite some disagreement of approach amongst the different nations in Europe, there is a widely accepted view that countries structured along more centralist lines (e.g. Great Britain, France, Italy) are not always in as good a position to solve the challenges presented by the European ideal as are those, like Germany, with a decentralised structure. The differing political developments in the individual countries of the European Union, the prevailing socio-economic conditions, the cultural idiosyncrasies and the wealth of languages hardly favour real European political and economic integration via a unitary, centralist approach.

In today's world it is paradoxically rich variety which is more likely to give free rein to the expression of human experience in Europe than uniformity. The German phrase 'unity in variety' (*Einheit in Vielfalt*) sums up not only the virtues of the German federal system but also those of a successful EU.

CONCLUSION

The federal system has clear advantages and disadvantages. On the positive side, a federal structure is said to bind together the constituent parts, or regions, of a country, offering them a genuine share in power. It should therefore combine external unity with internal diversity. In theory federalism promotes democratic values and encourages the commitment of individual citizens to democratic processes. Breaking down a large, often unwieldy system into smaller coherent units aims to increase interest and participation in the political process. It is claimed, for example, that the involvement of the sixteen German federal states fosters regional diversity and local pride. Citizens are usually less likely to feel remote from the centre of power if they have a say in matters which affect their daily lives. In Germany the capital cities of the federal states take on important roles, becoming a focal point for regional development.

On the negative side, it is frequently claimed that maintaining sixteen regional governments, on top of a national one, is too expensive. Some argue that a devolved structure is complicated and cumbersome, leading to one compromise after another. An ever more frequent criticism of recent years is that the German federal (i.e. national) level has been usurping more and more of the *Land* powers. Another concern is simply the number of *Länder* (see below). A reduction in the number of federal states, making them more equal in size, has been proposed more than once, although no serious suggestions for change have been forthcoming in recent years.

From time to time there have been proposals for reforming the federal structure. Both before and after Unification there were suggestions to reduce the number of federal states, making them more equal in size. There would be some justification for this, because a great imbalance exists between tiny units such as Bremen (0.7 million inhabitants), the Saarland (1.1 million) and Mecklenburg-West Pomerania (1.8 million), and large states such as North-Rhine Westphalia (17.8 million), Bavaria (11.9 million) and Baden-Württemberg (10.2 million). Various permutations were advanced for amalgamating the old *Länder* into either five or six units – for example with North-Rhine Westphalia, Bavaria and Baden-Württemberg approximately as they were, and Schleswig-Holstein, Hamburg, Bremen and Lower Saxony as one northern state, and Hesse, Rhineland-Palatinate and the Saar as another federal state. There have also been suggested changes in the east. For example, reducing the number of federal states there to three – namely Mecklenburg, Brandenburg (including Berlin) and Saxony-Thuringia – or even to just two new *Länder*: Mecklenburg-Brandenburg and Saxony-Thuringia.[5] More recently, however, there has been a general acceptance of the status quo.

Questionnaires amongst the German population reveal a high level of satisfaction with the federal system, despite a certain amount of general ill-feeling towards both Unification itself and the way in which it happened and this is referred to in the opening chapter. In the early 1950s opinion polls showed a high level of dissatisfaction with federalism amongst the West German population, who at the time apparently felt that the German federal system was a hindrance to prosperity and economic progress; it was seen then by many as expensive and outdated, creating too much duplication. This sort of reaction is no longer heard nowadays (Reuter 1991: 148).

There is now a new commitment by the majority of Germany's inhabitants to the federal framework, which, despite its minor drawbacks, provided a much-needed stable framework in the immediate post-war period when the FRG was so desperately seeking to establish a successful liberal parliamentary democracy. Federalism also enabled the former federal states of the GDR, via Art. 23 GG, to be re-constituted and assimilated into the new Germany in 1990 in the Unification process. It should be remembered, when considering the various aspects of German life and society dealt with in this book, that the federal framework plays a key role in so many of them, not least the political system, which is examined in the following chapter.

NOTES

1 This was confederative federalism, an association of states (*Staatenbund*), like the form practised in the USA from 1778 until 1787 and in the Swiss Confederation from 1803 until 1848. This was modified to a fully federalist state (*Bundesstaat*) and also adopted by the USA from 1787 onwards and by Switzerland from 1884 onwards.
2 Further explanation is given in Laufer (1991).
3 This point is explained in an excellent chapter by Charlie Jeffery, 'The territorial dimension', Chapter 5 in Smith *et al.* (1996).
4 Paterson and Southern (1991) refer on p. 149 to 11 per cent of German civil servants being employed by the federation, 54 per cent by the federal states and 35 per cent by the communes.
5 Maps outlining several proposed reform models are given in Laufer (1991: 334–340).

RECOMMENDED READING

Smith *et al.* (1996), Chapter 5.
Stammen (1994), a short article in English.
Watson (1995), Chapter 2.

BIBLIOGRAPHY

Laufer, H. (1991) *Das föderative System der BRD*, Munich: Bayerische Landeszentrale f. politische Bildungsarbeit (the standard work in German).
Paterson, W. E. and Southern, D. (1991) *Governing Germany*, Oxford: Blackwell, especially Chapter 6.
Reuter, K. (1991) *Föderalismus. Grundlagen u. Wirkungen in der BRD*, Heidelberg: Decker u. Müller.

Smith G. (1979) *Democracy in Western Germany; Parties and Politics in the Federal Republic*, London: Heinemann.

Smith, G., Paterson, W. E. and Padgett, S. (eds) (1996) *Developments in German Politics 2*, Basingstoke: Macmillan, especially Chapters 2 and 5.

Stammen, T. (1994) 'Federalism in Germany', *Regionalism in Europe*, EUROPA 1 (2/3): 51–67.

Watson, A. (1995) *The Germans: Who Are They Now?*, London: Mandarin, especially Chapters 2 and 5.

4 Government and the political parties

Peter James

The political system of the new Germany is a liberal parliamentary democracy, based on the rule of law and free elections, with (unlike in Great Britain) a written constitution. When the former territories of West and East Germany were merged in the autumn of 1990, it was the democratic polity of the old western federal states which prevailed. The political system of the former GDR disappeared on 3 October 1990, when that country ceased to exist. Fundamental concepts such as federalism,[1] a democratic republic, and a social state (one with an organised support network) with free and fair elections obviously take on a specific identity in the Federal Republic today, in the light of Germany's history and political past.

THE CONSTITUTION

The former Federal Republic – i.e. the old federal states in the west – had a written constitution from 23 May 1949 onwards. The Parliamentary Council met in Bonn from September 1948 until May 1949 to draw up a provisional constitution, which was to be valid until such time as a constitution adopted by a free decision of all the German people came into force (Article 146). This final article (usually referred to as Art. 146 GG) governing the duration of the validity of the constitution, the Basic Law (*das Grundgesetz*), was amended after Unification in 1990, as was the preamble. The original preamble stated that the German people in the western *Länder* had decided on the Basic Law, but it acted also for those Germans who had been prevented from participating. A post-1990 amendment refers to the German people in all sixteen federal states in the new Germany as having completed 'in free self-determination' the unity and freedom of Germany. With that the Basic Law became valid for the whole of the German people.

The more permanent-sounding German word for constitution (*Verfassung*) had deliberately been avoided in 1949, owing to the 'temporary' nature of the circumstances at that time. In 1989/90 there were those who argued in favour of drawing up a new constitution for the new Germany, particularly given that the constitution drawn up in 1949 was only provisional anyway.

A constitutional commission was formed, consisting of sixty-four members, thirty-two from each of the two houses of parliament, but few concrete proposals emerged. So in the event the Basic Law became valid for the whole of Germany. Some saw this failure to amend the content and name of the former West German constitution as a missed opportunity.

The very first article of the Basic Law – 'the dignity of man is inviolable' – immediately sets the tone of a German constitution which sought to distance itself from both the political instability of the Weimar Republic (die Weimarer Republik 1919–33), in which governments lasted only about eight months on average, and the disastrous dictatorship of Hitler's Third Reich (1933–45).[2] The Weimar Republic was Germany's first attempt at establishing a democratic political system. Unfortunately it failed badly. The social chaos which followed Germany's capitulation after the First World War in 1918 merely served to underline the fact that this was a country being asked to convert from a military dictatorship to a parliamentary democracy overnight. The Weimar Republic – the constitution was signed on 11 August 1919 in the city of Weimar in Thuringia – has been called a democracy with too few democrats and a republic with too few republicans, because the old structures and political attitudes were never completely swept away in 1918/19. As a result, it is often pointed out that the 1949 Basic Law was in many respects an anti-constitution, aimed at avoiding the pitfalls of its predecessor.

In fact, the whole of the first of the eleven sections of the current constitution[3] is regarded as fundamental, since it deals with basic human rights such as the liberty of the individual, equality before the law, freedom of religion, expression, assembly, movement, home and family, education, profession, privacy, etc. After twelve years of National Socialist tyranny, such fundamental rights were felt to be particularly important. It was a liberal, democratic constitution which aimed at, and in practice did actually achieve, a much more stable and successful political system than the Weimar constitution had done. In 1949 the Basic Law needed the approval of a two-thirds majority of the western *Länder*. Bavaria was the only *Land* to vote against, on the grounds that it was not federal enough. The essential elements of the Basic Law are unequivocally stated:

- The Federal Republic of Germany is a democratic and social federation.
- All of the state's power stems from the people.
- The legislative, the executive, and the judicial functions are exercised through separate institutions.
- This separation of powers guarantees a system of checks and balances in exercising power.

Any infringements of Germany's free, democratic, basic order (FDGO – Freie Demokratische Grundordnung), referred to in Arts 18 and 21 GG, are taken very seriously. The Federal Constitutional Court (Bundesverfassungsgericht) – see p. 52 – laid down strict regulations on free self-determination and the exclusion of violence and tyranny. There is to be 'no freedom for the enemies of freedom', and according to Article 20 (4) of the Basic Law all Germans have the right to resist (das Recht zum Widerstand), should anyone try to remove the constitutional framework governing the Federal Republic's democratic order *vis-à-vis* its executive, legislature and judiciary.[4]

THE EXECUTIVE

Federal Chancellor

The main executive power lies with the Federal Chancellor (Bundeskanzler), who lays down policy guidelines (*Richtlinien*), and chooses his cabinet ministers. The position of the Federal Chancellor in the new post-war system, compared with that of the Reichskanzler in the Weimar Republic, was considerably strengthened. The Chancellor and his ministers together make up the federal government (Bundesregierung); a German Chancellor, as head of government, is not only *primus inter pares* but also plays a dominant role. He therefore wields considerable authority and occupies a powerful position, comparable with that of a British Prime Minister. Following a federal election in Germany, the leader of the largest political party is usually elected as Chancellor for a four-year period of office by a majority of votes cast by the members of the Lower House of parliament, the Bundestag.

So far there have been only six chancellors since 1949: Konrad Adenauer (CDU 1949–63), Ludwig Erhard (CDU 1963–6), Kurt Georg Kiesinger (CDU 1966–9), Willy Brandt (SPD 1969–74),

Helmut Schmidt (SPD 1974–82); since 1982 the present office-holder, Helmut Kohl (CDU), has been in power.[5]

Federal President

The Chancellor is officially appointed by the Federal President (Bundespräsident), who is the head of state, comparable with a British monarch; a German president has representative and ceremonial functions but no real executive power. He (all the presidents so far have been men) does, however, have the right to dissolve parliament if the Chancellor loses a vote of confidence (*Vertrauensfrage*) in the Bundestag. The Federal President must be at least forty years old. He is elected for five years, in order to create an overlap with the Chancellor's four-year period of office, and may be re-elected only once, by a special assembly formed from both houses of parliament specifically for that purpose. This body is called the Federal Convention (Bundesversammlung).

It is important not to confuse the situation of the executive in Germany and Great Britain, where the offices of head of government and head of state are separated, with that of the USA, where the American President is both head of government and head of state. In Germany government ministers are also officially appointed and dismissed by the Federal President, but they are actually selected and proposed by the Chancellor, who is responsible for determining government policy. This again vests considerable power and authority in the office of Federal Chancellor. Within the limits set by the policy guidelines, each federal government minister conducts the affairs of his or her ministry autonomously and bears responsibility for decisions taken.

There have been seven Federal Presidents so far. The first one, Theodor Heuss (FDP 1949–59), was followed by Heinrich Lübke (CDU 1959–69), Gustav Heinemann (SPD 1969–74), Walter Scheel (FDP 1974–9), Karl Carstens (1979–84), Richard von Weizsäcker (1984–94) and the present incumbent Roman Herzog, all CDU. Although the President is a politician, he allows his party membership to lapse whilst in office and must be impartial. After leaving office he usually assumes the role of elder statesman.

The executive is strengthened by a crucial article of the German constitution, Article 67, which requires a *constructive* vote of no confidence if parliament wishes to remove the Chancellor from office. This means that it is no longer enough simply to pass a vote of no confidence in the Chancellor and remove him – as was the case under the Weimar constitution. It was far too easy to bring down a government in the Weimar Republic; and, since it was not necessary to elect a replacement chancellor, political chaos ensued. In the FRG the German parliament must have a majority for a successor, otherwise the incumbent remains in office. So far there have been only two attempts at using the constructive vote of no confidence since 1949. The first was the unsuccessful attempt to unseat Chancellor Willy Brandt in 1972; the second was the successful replacement of Helmut Schmidt by Helmut Kohl in 1982. The introduction of a constructive vote of no confidence was one of several elements which contributed to a more stable political system in (West) Germany's post-war history.

THE LEGISLATURE

The Bundestag

The passing of legislation is primarily the task of the first chamber, or lower house of parliament, the Bundestag, the equivalent of the British House of Commons or the American House of Representatives. The Bundestag is the organ of state which represents the interests of the German people. As such it is autonomous, not bound by any instructions or directives. It is also responsible for presenting the federal budget and keeping a check on the federal government.

After a federal election in Germany the lower house normally consists of 656 members of parliament, making it the largest in the democratic world – and also one of the most expensive, given the high salaries and generous allowances of German members of parliament (*Abgeordnete*). Half this number (328) are elected via single-member constituencies and the other half come from the party lists (see p. 63 on the electoral system). Between 1949 and 1994 no fewer than 7,500 bills, or draft laws, were put forward. Of these 4,900 were passed as laws by the Bundestag. Most of the proposals came from the federal government, some from the main body of the lower house or from the German second chamber, or upper house of parliament, the Bundesrat.

The Bundesrat

This is a very different body from the British second chamber, the House of Lords, and the American Senate. The German Bundesrat represents the interests of the sixteen federal states. It acts as a counterbalance to the first chamber and the government, as well as forming a link between the central/federal government and the regional ones. The federal, or decentralised, German political system, where the Bundesrat plays a vital role (see Chaper 3), is often described in German as one of unity in variety (*Einheit in Vielfalt*).[6] The political make-up of the second chamber is therefore a reflection of the strength of the parties in each of the *Länder*. Each *Land* sends delegates to the Bundesrat and one member acts as the 'vote-caster', voting in accordance with the agreement already reached by the state government. Voting is by a show of hands, not secret ballot, and the votes for each federal state must be cast *en bloc*.

The number of votes available in the second chamber, sixty-nine in total, depends on the population of each *Land* or federal state. This means that the four largest states, North-Rhine Westphalia, Bavaria, Baden-Württemberg and Lower Saxony, have six votes each. Hesse has five, the Rhineland-Palatinate, Schleswig-Holstein, Thuringia, Saxony-Anhalt, Saxony, Brandenburg and Berlin have four votes each, and the four states with the smallest populations, Bremen, the Saarland, Hamburg, and Mecklenburg-West Pomerania, have three votes each in the Bundesrat (see Table 4.1).

A significant aspect of Germany's present governmental system is the state of the majorities in the lower and upper houses of parliament. Since the upper house, the Bundesrat, reflects the strength of the parties in the federal states, it sometimes happens that the government of the day has a majority in the lower house, the Bundestag, but not in the Bundesrat. This was sometimes the case with Helmut Schmidt's social-liberal government (1974–82) and again more recently with Helmut Kohl's current conservative–liberal coalition. Consequently the results of *Land* elections in the German system can be very significant, because an opposition majority in the second chamber may permit it to approve or reject a bill, or draft law, which was not possible in the Bundestag, where the opposition parties are in the minority.

The Bundesrat also has an important right of veto on proposed legislation, some of which requires its approval (*zustimmungsbedürftige Gesetze*). These are laws which alter the constitution. According to Article 79 (2) GG, such laws require a two-thirds majority of the Bundesrat (i.e. 46 out of 69 votes) *and* a two-thirds majority of the Bundestag. This also includes any proposed legislation which affects the relationship between the federation and the federal states (*das Bund-Länder-Verhältnis*), for example anything on finance, territorial changes, judicial amendments, etc. Such changes require

Table 4.1 The strength of the parties in the *Länder* (Spring 1997)

CDU/CSU-led	Land	No. of votes in the Bundesrat	Next election by *
CDU rules alone	Saxony	4	9/1999
CSU rules alone	Bavaria	6	9/1998
CDU/FDP	Baden-Württemberg	6	3/2001
CDU/SPD	Berlin	4	10/2000
	Mecklenburg-West Pomerania	3	10/1998
	Thuringia	4	10/1998
	Total	27	
SPD-led			
SPD rules alone	Brandenburg	4	9/1999
	Lower Saxony	6	3/1998
	Saarland	3	10/1999
SPD/Greens	Hesse	5	2 /1999
	North-Rhine Westphalia	6	5/2000
	Saxony-Anhalt	4	6/1998
	Schleswig-Holstein	4	3/2000
SPD/Greens	Hamburg	3	9/1997
SPD/FDP	Rhineland-Palatinate	4	3/2001
SPD/CDU	Bremen	3	5/1999
	Total	42	
	Total number of votes in the Bundesrat	69	

Note: * Figures on election dates supplied by Simon Green at the Institute for German Studies, University of Birmingham

the approval of an absolute majority, i.e. over 50 per cent, of the Bundesrat, which means 35 votes.

There are other bills which do not require Bundesrat approval. In such cases it does not have the right of veto. However, if 35 of its 69 representatives are against the Bundestag's proposed law, the Bundesrat has the right to raise an objection (*Einspruch erheben*). The first chamber must then think again. If it rejects the objection by an absolute majority, the legislation goes ahead. The Bundesrat is also allowed to propose legislation. In practice it usually puts forward far less than the Bundestag or the government.

THE JUDICIARY

German law, which in part dates back to Roman law, is of course clearly subdivided into distinct legal areas, such as criminal law, labour law, procedural law, etc. These different areas of the law are usually dealt with in Germany in one of five types of court: labour court (*Arbeitsgericht*), administrative court (*Verwaltungsgericht*), social court (*Sozialgericht*), financial court (*Finanzgericht*), or in one of the 'ordinary' courts (*ordentliche Gerichte*).

There are several important courts at national or federal level in Germany, in addition to the Federal Constitutional Court (see below) in Karlsruhe. For example, the Federal High Court (also in Karlsruhe), the Federal Administrative Court in Berlin, the Federal Tax Court in Munich, the Federal Social Insurance Court and the Federal Labour Court, both in Kassel. The courts which operate in each of the federal states also play a crucial part in the German judiciary. Basically the courts work on four levels: High Court (*Bundesgerichtshof*), Court of Appeal (*Oberlandesgericht*), District Court (*Landgericht*) and Local Courts (*Amtsgerichte*).

The Federal Constitutional Court

According to the constitution (Art. 92 GG), judicial power in the German system is entrusted to the judges. A key feature is the Federal Constitutional Court (Bundesverfassungsgericht) in Karlsruhe, which is the highest court in the land. As such it is one of the five permanent federal institutions of the FRG, the others being the Federal President, the cabinet, the Bundestag, and the Bundesrat. The Federal Constitutional Court (FCC) is the guarantor of judicial independence and protector of the constitution; as such it can take binding decisions on the constitutional jurisdiction of areas of competence applying to the federation (*Bund*) and the federal states (*Länder*). Its far-reaching powers were a reaction to the disastrous experiences in the Third Reich, where the judiciary was under Hitler's personal influence. Everyone in Germany today has the right to a court hearing.

The FCC has banned political parties which it deemed unconstitutional (*verfassungsfeindlich*), for example the neo-Nazi SRP in 1952, and the Communist Party in 1956.

Its decision, in 1975, to overturn the ruling of the Bundestag on the abortion law (§218) was not without its critics. The GDR had given women the right to an abortion in 1972. The decision of the FCC rested on the grounds that the proposal to allow an abortion within the first twelve weeks of a pregnancy did not offer sufficient protection to the life of the unborn child (guaranteed by the constitution).

The Constitutional Court also plays a role as arbitrator between the Bundestag and the Bundesrat, if disputes arise which cannot be settled by the arbitration committee (Vermittlungsausschuß). The function of this mediation or arbitration committee is to submit compromise proposals, if differences of opinion concerning proposed legislation cannot be eliminated by the two parliamentary chambers. The committee consists of sixteen members of the Bundestag (one from each *Land*) and sixteen from the Bundesrat. Approximately every ninth bill requires the intervention of the mediation committee.

The Constitutional Court is broken down into two senates, each of which has eight judges elected for twelve years (no re-election possible); each senate has its own areas of authority. An independent administration and budget supports the FCC. Since there are eight judges in each senate, there may be a stalemate position with no majority on some decisions. In such cases there is no casting vote, and therefore no decision regarding a contravention of the constitution can be taken. In some cases – for example banning a political party – a two-thirds majority is needed.

POLITICAL PARTIES

In the early post-war years (1945–9) in West Germany it looked as if a multi-party system was developing, along the lines of a broadly four-strand Christian/liberal/social democratic/communist pattern. In German politics the term 'Christian' (*christlich*) has always meant conservative. This has sometimes been the subject of controversy, since the Catholic Church used to write a pastoral letter (*Hirtenbrief*) recommending Catholics to vote for a Christian party, to be read out from the pulpit of every Catholic church on the Sunday before a federal election. Religious denomination, though less relevant in today's more secular and pluralist German society, was always a reliable guide to electoral behaviour. Pre-1990 there was an approximately equal number of Catholics and Protestants in the former West Germany. (Today in the new Germany there are 28.1 million Protestants and 27.4 million Catholics.) One of the key factors determining voting patterns was the tendency for Catholics – especially regular church-goers – to support the 'Christian' parties, that is the CDU/CSU right-of-centre conservatives, with Protestants more likely to vote for the left-of-centre SPD (Social Democrats).[7] The other key factor which research surveys have shown to be relevant to voting behaviour is the urban/rural split. Broadly speaking, voters in urban areas tended more towards the SPD, whilst rural voters were more likely to support the CDU/CSU.

With eleven parties entering parliament after the first federal elections in1949, it appeared that a multi-party system, possibly along the lines of the Weimar Republic, was emerging, although that in fact did not happen. Some smaller parties represented specific interest groups, such as refugees and expellees, for example the BHE (Bund der Heimavertriebenen und Entrechteten). As the interests the parties represented gradually disappeared (in this case, as the refugees were assimilated), so did the parties. The larger, more successful parties soon realised that they would have to develop the concept of the 'catch-all' or people's party (Volkspartei), in order to widen their electoral appeal.

The two major parties which came to dominate the post-war political scene, and still do so today (though to a slightly lesser extent), did develop into people's parties. They were the newly formed conservative CDU (Christian Democratic Union), with its sister party the Bavarian CSU (Christian Social Union), and the SPD (Social Democratic Party of Germany), whose origins date back to 1875 and beyond.

CDU/CSU

The CDU exists in every federal state except Bavaria, whilst the CSU exists only in Bavaria. The CSU is a separate party with similar but somewhat different political traditions. Although the CSU was established as a new party in 1945/46, its political predecessors can be traced back to the Bavarian Patriots Party in 1869 and the Catholic Centre Party (Zentrum) from 1887 onwards. The CSU's immediate predecessor was the Bavarian People's Party (BVP), which represented political Catholicism in the Weimar Republic. After a federal election the CSU forms a joint parliamentary party (Fraktion) with the CDU when the two parties enter the Bundestag. The CDU/CSU are often referred to as the Union parties. In 1949 the CDU/CSU and the SPD emerged neck-and-neck; in fact the first Federal Chancellor, Konrad Adenauer (a Catholic and a former mayor of Cologne) of the CDU, was elected in the Bundestag by just one vote (Adenauer admitted voting for himself). Although he was seventy-three years old in 1949, Adenauer amazingly remained Chancellor until 'forced' to retire in 1963 at the age of eighty-seven. Even then he retained considerable influence as the chairman of his party, restricting the room for manoeuvre of his successor, Ludwig Erhard (the so-called 'father of the economic miracle'). Adenauer died in 1967.

Because Adenauer was the first incumbent, and also because he remained in office for fourteen years, he was able to stamp his own authority indelibly on the chancellorship. The strong constitutional position of the German Chancellor, together with Adenauer's dominance of both the executive and the wider political system, produced the term 'Chancellor Democracy' (*Kanzlerdemokratie*). The office of chancellor has since been shaped not only by the German constitution but also by its incumbents. Helmut Schmidt (SPD), for example, favoured the 'first among equals' approach. Many of his fellow-countrymen, as well as some British and American experts, consider that Schmidt was the most competent of the six chancellors so far.

Amendments to the electoral law for the second federal election in 1953 – federal or national elections are normally held every four years – reduced the number of parties entering parliament to six in 1953 and to only four in 1957. This was the year of the so-called Adenauer election; the election was widely regarded as a sort of referendum on the popularity of the first chancellor and his party, the CDU/CSU, which by then was presiding over the famous German economic miracle (*Wirtschaftswunder*), based partly on the extremely successful West German market economy (*soziale Marktwirtschaft*) (see Chapter 5, p. 70).

The 1957 federal election was the only one at which a party has ever gained an absolute majority of the votes (50.2 per cent). This meant that no coalition partner was required to form a government. By then, however, the (West) German liberal party, the FDP (Free Democratic Party), had already begun to establish itself as the largest of the small parties and the third force in German politics. From 1961 until the emergence of the Greens at federal level in 1983 the FRG had a stable three-party system. It was sometimes described as a two-and-a-half-party system, with the German liberal party as the small but influential 'half', adopting a pivotal role as coalition partner to either the right-of-centre Christian Democrats or the left-of-centre Social Democrats. The FDP switched sides in 1969, enabling Willy Brandt to become the first SPD Chancellor since 1930. In 1982 they switched back to the CDU/CSU in a coalition led by Chancellor Kohl.

The phenomenon of Helmut Kohl's political longevity is amazing. Indeed, it appears incomprehensible to some. Despite the fact that Kohl's ability as a public speaker could in no way be compared with the passion of a Brandt or the clarity of a Schmidt – he does not appear to have their intellectual gifts either – he just goes on and on, announcing in April 1997 his intention of standing as the CDU/CSU

Chancellor candidate for the 1998 federal elections. Kohl is apparently politically astute and a good party manager, despite being the butt of so many jokes concerning his gauche manner and clumsy image.

SPD

Whilst some German citizens, especially the older ones, may speak of the achievements of Konrad Adenauer (CDU) and the brash and unpredictable Bavarian leader Franz Josef Strauβ (CSU), others sing the praises of the SPD chancellors Willy Brandt and Helmut Schmidt, who exerted just as great an influence on the political system of the FRG. Although the Christian Democrats provided the Federal Chancellors for the first twenty years of the old FRG, the Social Democrats also contributed a great deal to the development of West Germany via their work in the Parliamentary Council in 1948/49, as well as in their achievements in the federal states. Kurt Schumacher, the SPD's first post-war leader, was a fierce defender of social justice and a proponent of the reunification of the two Germanys. The name of Willy Brandt will always be associated with the policy of *rapprochement* with the East (*Ostpolitik*). His SPD/FDP government (1969–74) made tremendous progress towards the Unification eventually achieved in 1990; this area had been completely neglected by CDU chancellors. Brandt's successor, Helmut Schmidt, displayed great ability in managing the economy and boosting (West) Germany's image abroad. In the 1980 federal election many CDU supporters conceded that Schmidt was 'the best Chancellor that Germany had ever had – just a member of the wrong party'.[8] A lot of CDU supporters in north Germany could not stomach the rough-and-ready, highly controversial style of the CDU/CSU chancellor candidate in 1980, Strauβ, even though he was treated like a king in his native Bavaria. The contrast in political style and image between the two candidates could hardly have been greater.

Since the change of power in 1982, the SPD has suffered from a leadership crisis – no one of the calibre of Brandt or Schmidt has been forthcoming. Oskar Lafontaine from the Saar, who has not been entirely uncontroversial, is back as SPD leader again, after the uninspiring Rudolf Scharping. If the German Social Democrats are to take over the government in 1998 – they came very close in 1994 – they need to regain some of their dynamic and decisive approach to key policy areas which they displayed so convincingly in the Brandt and Schmidt eras. They also need a reliable coalition partner. The most obvious course of action would be to team up with the Greens, but there are currently problems with SPD–Green co-operation within both parties.

The SPD gained its first opportunity to share power at federal level in Bonn when a Grand Coalition government, involving the two main parties, was in power as a 'stop-gap' between 1966 and 1969. The first real crisis for the Union parties began in the mid-1960s, when for the first time the FRG suffered a serious economic recession. There were street demonstrations by student groups and others, and strong political protest against press concentration and the passing of the controversial Emergency Laws (*Notstandsgesetze*) in West Germany. The formation of an extra-parliamentary opposition movement, APO (Außerparlamentarische Opposition), was influenced by American groups protesting against the Vietnam War. The movement tried to compensate for the lack of an effective parliamentary Opposition to the SPD/CDU/CSU government.

The Grand Coalition enabled the SPD to gain a higher profile in federal politics in Bonn, and in 1969 the first real change in power (*Machtwechsel*) came about, with Willy Brandt (SPD) as Chancellor and Walter Scheel (FDP) as Foreign Minister. The German Liberal Party, having formed its first federal coalition with the Social Democrats, remained with them until 1982, when Brandt's successor as Chancellor, Helmut Schmidt, was replaced by Helmut Kohl from the CDU. This second change in power was possible only because the FDP switched its support.

The pivotal position of the Liberals

Because of the way in which the German Liberal Party, the FDP, has been able to bring about major changes in power at federal level (see above), it has always played a key role in the German party system. Even in 1949 the Liberals received three out of fourteen seats in Adenauer's first cabinet, and in the Schmidt–Genscher social–liberal coalition governments of the 1970s and early 1980s they at times held four crucial ministerial posts out of sixteen. The Free Democrats have, owing to their essential role as coalition partner, spent more time in government than either of the 'big two'. This has provided an influence disproportionate to the party's real size, membership and electoral support, which has attracted discussion of what the party really stands for. With polls at federal elections of between only 5.8 per cent (its lowest in 1969) and 12.8 per cent (its highest in 1961), the FDP, whose hard-core support amounts to about only 3 or 4 per cent, has frequently been voted for more because of its role and function in the German party system than because of any clear political identity.

Essentially, there were four key functions performed by the Free Democrats: government *majority maker* for either the Christian or Social Democrats, *liberal corrective* (i.e. a sort of political watchdog, keeping the main government party in check on specific issues), *an agent of transition*, enabling a change in power at federal level, and *ideological/numerical balancer* in German coalition politics. In the current political climate in the new Germany the FDP is in serious danger of losing its special role and function in the party system. In the approach to the 1994 federal elections the Liberals' base in the *Länder* became weaker and weaker; yet every time a death sentence is pronounced the FDP somehow manages to escape. Survival has become its speciality.[9]

The Green Party shakes up the system

In 1983 the German Greens (die Grünen), Europe's most successful Green party, following substantial achievements at local and regional level in the 1970s and early 1980s, added a new dimension to the Federal Republic's three-party system, with its reputation for stability, continuity and moderation – terms such as 'boring' and 'stale' were also used by critics – by entering the federal parliament in Bonn for the first time. This produced a four-party system. It also heralded the advent of younger – and an increased number of female – Green politicians with a new environmentalist and anti-nuclear political agenda, defending the rights of minorities. They wore pullovers, jeans and trainers in parliament, often causing a stir amongst a predominantly male, middle-aged Bundestag population, normally dressed in suits, white shirts and ties. The rapid rise of a new dynamic political force was followed by an equally rapid decline. There were disagreements over the rotation principle, whereby the Greens themselves stipulated that their members of the Bundestag had to relinquish their seats after two years, so that Green MPs would not become part of the Establishment. There was also a damaging split into the fundamentalist (*Fundi*) and realist (*Realo*) wings. In 1989/90 the Greens in the West did not embrace the concept of German Unity. It was a mistake not to unite with the East German Green movement, and they paid the price at the first all-German elections in December 1990.

In 1993 the Greens in the East and the West finally joined forces to form Alliance '90/the Greens (Bündnis '90/die Grünen). As a result of not having amalgamated earlier, the West German Greens were not represented in the Bundestag between 1990 and 1994. At the 1994 federal election the new party polled just over 7 per cent, slightly more than the FDP.

Parties on the right

Given Germany's past, the emergence of any right-wing extremist parties has of course always been viewed with deep suspicion (see Chapter 8). It should be remembered, however, first, that the amount of support such parties receive from German voters is really extremely small and, second, that even those few votes are often protest votes. The SRP (Socialist Reich Party) (see Chapter 8 – p. 133) was founded on 2 October 1949, when the Allies' permission to found a party was no longer required. It was a blatantly neo-Nazi party founded on National Socialist principles. The Federal Constitutional Court ruled that the SRP should be banned as unconstitutional in 1952, and the party disappeared. No such ban was applied for in the case of the right-wing NPD (Nationaldemokratische Partei Deutschlands), founded in 1964. This neo-Nazi party had some limited but significant success at regional level between 1965 and 1969, during a time of economic recession and political uncertainty in Bonn. The NPD still exists today. Although it occasionally puts in a sporadic appearance in local and/or regional politics, its support is negligible.

The Republican Party

In 1983, Franz Schönhuber, a Bavarian journalist and popular media presenter, left the CSU following a disagreement with Franz Josef Strauβ, and formed the far-right Republican Party (die Republikaner). The party gained a lot of publicity, due largely to the persuasive appeal amongst very limited sections of the population of their demagogic leader, who drew large and often unruly crowds wherever he went, not just in Bavarian beer halls. Even though the Republicans in Germany were supported by fewer voters than Le Pen's National Front Party in France, and despite the fact that there was a string of similar right-wing extremist parties right across Europe at the time, the mass media both at home and abroad were quick to draw parallels between Franz Schönhuber and Adolf Hitler.

The new party undoubtedly encouraged anti-foreigner feeling – it played on this *Ausländerfeindlichkeit*, and demanded that German territory in the east be returned to Germany. However, Unification in 1990 took the wind out of the party's sails. Internal leadership struggles and the euphoria of German Unity left the Republicans very weak. At the 1994 federal elections they polled only 1.9 per cent. In their home territory of Bavaria the Republican Party appears to be a spent force, as CSU hegemony has returned, following a temporary loss of influence after the death of its most dynamic post-war leader, Franz Josef Strauβ, in 1988.

German People's Union

Another extreme right-wing party, the German People's Union (DVU – Deutsche Volksunion), chaired by the Munich publisher Gerhard Frey, was originally founded as a movement in 1971 to mark the hundredth anniversary of the establishment of Bismarck's Reich. In 1987 the DVU became a political party; it scored two small successes in Bremen in 1991 and again in the Schleswig-Holstein state elections in 1996. Frey has always been a strong proponent of restoring Germany to its 1937 borders. As with the Republican Party, however, it is important not to exaggerate the appeal of the DVU and to remember that a handful of fanatics and small, disillusioned sections of the electorate will always cast a protest vote for such parties. Exploratory talks by Schönhuber and Frey, attempting to merge their parties before the second all-German elections in 1994, not only came to nothing but also caused much friction within both camps. As a result Franz Schönhuber was removed as federal leader of the Republicans in December 1994 and replaced by Rolf Schlierer.

Parties of the left

It is frequently forgotten now that in the immediate post-war period being able to prove that you had been, or were, a communist was not necessarily anything to be ashamed of. At that time it was often taken by the occupying forces as proof that you were not a Nazi. Communists participated in several state governments in the early years.

KPD/DKP

In 1956 the German Communist Party (KPD) was banned by the Federal Constitutional Court. The ban remained in place until 1968. With hindsight this was seen by many observers as an unnecessary ban, given that the party was rapidly losing support anyway, particularly since the policies of the East German regime 'next door' were viewed with increasing animosity in West Germany. In 1969 a 'new' Communist Party (DKP) – based on a very orthodox Moscow-orientated communist ideology – was founded in Essen. The DKP itself, and many of its associated groups, was often directly or indirectly supported and financed from the GDR.

As well as the ruling SED (Sozialistische Einheitspartei Deutschlands), the Socialist Unity Party of Germany, in the GDR, there were numerous Marxist–Leninist and Trotskyist parties, such as the Communist League (KB), the Communist League of West Germany (KBW), etc. Some of the left-wing splinter groups joined with the Green/Alternative scene. None of them had any success in state or federal elections in the western states.

In 1972 a decree against radicals (*Radikalenerlaß*) was issued in West Germany by the Office for the Protection of the Constitution, a sort of internal intelligence service, whose task is to monitor right- and left-wing extremism. Civil servants in Germany (*Beamte*) enjoy a high level of status, privilege and salary, including excellent pensions, and have to pledge support to the state and its free democratic basic order. The extremely controversial *Radikalenerlaß* implied that membership of an organisation or party with aims hostile to the constitution (e.g. the Communist Party) could prevent someone from being a civil servant. Since not only Chancellery officials and teachers but also train drivers and postmen are civil servants in Germany, the directive became known as the *Berufsverbot*, a kind of professional debarment on political grounds. It was passed by Brandt's SPD/FDP government as an attempt to co-ordinate the approach of the various federal states to dealing with extremist infiltration. Critics, however, strongly resented its authoritarian overtones. For some people it even recalled memories of fascist policies. It was also felt at the time that the left wing was being targeted more than the right.

The PDS – a 'new' party in a 'new' party system

Since unification in 1990, and especially since 1994, the 'new' German party system (not really vastly different from the former western one) has been a five-party system, owing to the appearance of a new party, the PDS (Party of Democratic Socialism). The East German party system did clearly change in 1990; it is now really a three-party system consisting of the CDU, SPD and PDS. The PDS has added a new dimension, as the East German successor to the former SED (Socialist Unity Party), which was in charge in the days of the former GDR. The new party originally named itself the SED/ PDS in December 1989, under the chairmanship of Gregor Gysi, who is still an influential politician today. It represents almost exclusively East German interests. At the second all-German elections in 1994 the party polled nearly 20 per cent in the east, but only 1 per cent in the west.

Whilst many young East Germans applauded the demise of the GDR's political system and headed west, immediately exploiting the new freedom to travel, there is still a hard core, particularly amongst the older generation, who long for the return of law and order, full employment, fixed prices and rents, etc., refusing to embrace the 'virtues' of western, capitalist society with its high unemployment, inflation, lack of discipline and perceived social problems. There are, however, also younger citizens of the former GDR who feel disadvantaged in the new Germany, and who see the PDS as the only party which can represent their specifically East German political, socio-economic and cultural aspirations. It should also be pointed out that, although the membership of the PDS tends towards the older age bracket, its voters are predominantly in the younger one.

The PDS, under the leadership of Gregor Gysi and Lothar Bisky, sees itself as following in the traditions of Marx and Engels, but *not* Lenin, Ulbricht (the first Stalinist GDR leader) and Honecker (the last GDR leader). Its main challenge now is whether it is willing or able to make the transition from an almost exclusively East German to a German party.[10]

A disillusionment with politics?

A disillusionment or disenchantment with politics, and with politicians generally (*Politikverdrossenheit*), has been a recent feature in Germany. The German term *Staatsverdrossenheit* (the state gone stale) was used in the 1980s to imply that some of the major parties and politicians had carved things up according to their own vested interests. Once the initial euphoria of German Unity had subsided and the huge political, economic, social and cultural problems became apparent in the cold light of day, renewed disenchantment quickly set in, especially in the east. Nevertheless the turn-out at German elections, even though voting is not compulsory, is still high (federal election 1990: 77.8 per cent poll; 1994: 79.1 per cent).

THE GERMAN ELECTORAL SYSTEM

The electoral system used to elect the lower house of parliament (Bundestag) in Germany is based on the principle of proportional representation (PR), explained below. However, it has been described as a 'personalised' system of PR, since the German voter in a national, i.e. federal, election is able to vote for both a candidate as well as a party. This is because each voter has two votes. The first vote (Erststimme) is cast for a constituency candidate; the winner is chosen on a simple majority or 'first-past-the-post' system, as in Great Britain or the United States. The second vote (Zweitstimme) is cast for a political party. Here, however, the voters have no way of influencing which candidates will actually represent them, as it is the parties who select the candidates and place them in order on the party lists (Landeslisten) in each of the sixteen *Länder* in the FRG. The parties are allocated seats in parliament on the basis of strict proportional representation. That means that, if 40 per cent of those who voted in a particular *Land* voted for the SPD, that party, the SPD, must receive 40 per cent of the Bundestag seats allocated to that *Land*.

Only parties which gain at least 5 per cent of the second votes are eligible for seats. The 5-per-cent clause, or hurdle (Fünf-Prozent-Klausel/Hürde), was intentionally introduced in 1949 as a stabilising factor, after the negative experiences of Weimar, which had an electoral system based on pure PR with no cut-off clause. The result was chaotic, producing unstable government, with too many splinter parties in parliament. There is an alternative to clearing the 5-per-cent hurdle. If a party wins three or more first-vote constituency seats, as happened with the PDS at the 1994 federal election, it is allocated parliamentary seats on the basis of its share of second votes. The PDS gained only 4.4 per cent of the second votes, but won four constituencies, all in East Berlin. The party was therefore allocated 4.4 per cent of the total number of Bundestag seats, giving them thirty seats.

In allocating parliamentary seats, it is the second votes which are counted first. This determines the number of deputies (Abgeordnete), or members of parliament due to a particular party from each *Land*. If there are one hundred seats to be allocated, and the SPD gains 40 per cent, via the second votes, then it will be allocated forty seats. Then the number of candidates from that party who won their constituencies, via the first votes, is subtracted from forty, so that, if ten constituencies were won, only thirty list seats would be allocated.

It sometimes happens that a party wins all, or nearly all, the constituency seats in a *Land*. Since a constituency seat must always be retained, it could be the case that a party has already gained more (first-vote) constituency seats than it is, strictly speaking, entitled to according to its proportion of (second-vote) list seats. If this happens, as it did again at the 1994 federal elections, then extra or additional mandates/seats (*Überhangmandate*) are created, and the size of the Bundestag is increased. In 1994, for example, the CDU won twelve extra seats and the SPD four, rather unusually, with the result that the present German parliament contains not 656 deputies, as prescribed, but 672. The reason why in the new Germany there are normally 656 seats in the Bundestag is that before a federal election the whole country is divided into 328 constituencies. One deputy is elected for each constituency, via the first votes, and an equal number via the second votes. Since, as we have seen, the second votes are based on PR the voter's second vote is more important than the first, although, according to research, quite a large number of German voters incorrectly think that either the two votes are of equal value or that the first vote is more important.

Any German citizen over the age of eighteen is eligible to vote. Because of the list system, if a German deputy dies or retires, he or she is simply replaced by the next candidate on that party's list. There are no by-elections, as in Great Britain for example.

An interesting feature of the German system is that voters may 'split their ticket' (*Splitting*), by giving their first vote to a candidate from one party and their second vote to a different party. About 10 per cent of German voters have done this at some federal elections. The FDP in particular, and also the Greens, sometimes benefit from this; it means that a voter may register a preference for a coalition government, if he or she wishes. The most common way of doing this in practice has been to cast a first vote for a constituency candidate from either the SPD or the CDU/CSU, combined with a second vote for the FDP or possibly the Greens.

PARTY FINANCE

The question of how the political parties are financed has often been the subject of controversy in Germany, as in other countries. They are funded from two main sources: private and state finance.

Private finance comes from four areas: party membership contributions (in Germany, unlike in Britain, there is a sliding scale of membership fee according to income), donations, income from party funds and miscellaneous income. State finance comes from three areas: the reimbursement of election expenses to the tune of DM

1.30 per vote for the first 5 million votes and one DM each for the remainder, for parties which gain over 0.5 per cent at federal and European elections or over 1 per cent at *Land* elections, annual subsidies of DM 0.50 for every DM of contributions or donations from private individuals (maximum of DM 6 per person) and tax breaks for private contributors and donors. The SPD and the CDU/CSU benefit most, of course, from membership fees, with around 900,000 and 700,000 members respectively. The most controversial aspect of party finance is the area of donations from individuals and companies. The CDU, the CSU and the FDP, with their influential connections in economic circles, are usually the main beneficiaries of donations.

CONCLUSION: A STABLE FUTURE?

The political scientist Alfred Grosser said after the 1994 federal election that the process of German unity was clearly not complete, and it will be some years yet before the old and new states, and their inhabitants, come together and solve all their political problems, including the differing political cultures of east and west. A nation's political culture relates to the opinions, attitudes and value judgements of the population towards its political system, leaders and institutions. Although research has shown that this is a complex area, there is no doubt that the political cultures of the former FRG and the GDR were very different. It could hardly have been otherwise, given the diametrically opposed polities of the two states up until 1989/90. The changes which were introduced on paper in October 1990 could not possibly have been accepted overnight in a practical sense by the German people. There clearly have been major problems, and will continue to be for a number of years yet, in attempting to merge two distinct political cultures.

Despite these difficulties, Germany's tradition of coalition governments at both federal and regional level has, of necessity, usually led to a political atmosphere of consensus and compromise, since agreement usually has to be reached between two or three parties. The two main changes of power (in 1969 and 1982) have underlined the fundamentally democratic and stable nature of the German polity. This proven stability should do much to allay the fears expressed by Germany's European partners prior to Unification (see Chapter 12).

NOTES

1 Federalism is a decentralised system where political power is divided between the central government and a number of regional ones, in the case of Germany the sixteen *Land* governments. For further details, see Chapter 3.

2 For a concise summary of the main influences on political life in the Weimar Republic and under National Socialism see Paterson and Southern (1991: 26–39).

3 For an up-to-date copy of the constitution in English or German (Basic Law – *Grundgesetz*) write to the German Information Centre, 34 Belgrave Square, London, SW1X 8QB. Another very useful source of information in German on all aspects of the political system is die Bundeszentrale für politische Bildung in Bonn.

4 Such matters became an issue during an extremely controversial time in the early 1970s when the Baader–Meinhof Gruppe (RAF – Rote Armee Fraktion) carried out a series of terrorist attacks. For a time there was talk of political anarchy in the Federal Republic. See Chapter 8 (pp. 138–9) and note 4 of that chapter.

5 For an excellent analysis of the role and powers of the Federal Chancellor, as well as a study of the different political styles of leadership of the six incumbents, see Padgett (1994).

6 The *Bundesrat* publishes a valuable information booklet, available in English or German, from their Public Relations Office, D-53106 Bonn.

7 It is important not to exaggerate this denominational factor in today's secular German society. Nevertheless there has been in the past – and there still is today in some circles – a definite link between the Protestant and especially the Roman Catholic Churches in Germany and political parties. In Bavaria, for instance, a Concordat (*Konkordat*) was signed between the Vatican and the Bavarian State in 1583 and again in 1817. Even today gifts are still sent to the Pope in Rome from the CSU government headquarters in Munich every Christmas.

8 'Helmut Schmidt war der beste Kanzler, den wir je gehabt haben – er war bloß Mitglied der falschen Partei.' Franz Josef Strauß had to speak from behind a bullet-proof screen during his election tour of North Germany, and although he was the candidate of the CDU/CSU parties, many CDU members and supporters felt he would not have presented the right image of the FRG either at home or abroad.

9 See P. Lösche and F. Walter (1996) *Die FDP*, Darmstadt: Wissenschaftliche Buchgesellschaft for a recent account in German, and Paterson and Southern (1991), Chapter 7, especially pp. 207–211, for a summary in English of the FDP in the party system.

10 For more details on the PDS see H.-G. Betz and H. Welsh, 'The PDS in the new German party system', in *German Politics* 4(3), Dec. 1995.

RECOMMENDED READING

Anderson/Woyke (1995), a very useful reference work in German.
Braunthal (1996), for a thorough examination in English of the political parties.

Smith *et al.* (1996), especially Chapters 2–4.
Watson (1995), especially Chapter 5.

BIBLIOGRAPHY

Andersen, U. and Woyke, W. (eds) (1995) *Handbuch des politischen Systems der BRD*, Bonn: Bundeszentrale für politische Bildung.
Braunthal, G. (1996) *Parties and Politics in Modern Germany*, Boulder, Colo. and Oxford: Westview Press.
Dalton, R. (ed.) (1996) *Germans Divided*, Oxford and Washington: Berg.
German Politics. Journal of the Association for the Study of German Politics. Various.
Lewis, D. and McKenzie, J. (eds) (1995) *The New Germany. Social, Political and Cultural Challenges of Unification*, Exeter: University of Exeter Press.
Mintzel, A. and Oberreuter, H. (1992) *Parteien in der BRD*, Opladen: Leske und Budrich.
Padgett, S. (ed.) (1993) *Parties and Party Systems in the New Germany*, Aldershot and Brookfield USA: Dartmouth.
—— (1994) *Adenauer to Kohl. The Development of the German Chancellorship*, London: Hurst.
Parkes, S. (1997) *Understanding Contemporary Germany*, London and New York: Routledge.
Paterson, W. and Southern, D. (1991) *Governing Germany*, Oxford: Blackwell.
Pulzer, P. (1995) *German Politics 1945–1995*, Oxford and New York: Oxford University Press.
Smith, G., Paterson, W. and Padgett, S. (eds) (1996) *Developments in German Politics 2*, Basingstoke and London: Macmillan.
Von Beyme, K. (1991) *Das politische System der Bundesrepublik Deutschland nach der Vereinigung*, Munich: Piper.
Watson, A. (1995) *The Germans: Who Are They Now?*, London: Mandarin.

5 Investing in Germany: *Standort Deutschland*

Hanna Ostermann and Ute E. Schmidt

INTRODUCTION

On 16 June 1996, 350,000 people from all over Germany followed the trade unions' call and congregated in Bonn to demonstrate against the government's proposed reforms of the German welfare system. The immense costs of unification, recession or slackening economic growth in many export countries and increasing globalisation of economies have plunged the state into deficit. The economy which up to the late 1980s had gone from strength to strength now faces a serious crisis. Economic growth has remained below that predicted, unemployment has been rising, and public debt has increased to such an extent that Germany may be in danger of not meeting the criteria for the European Single Currency. While some experts warn of structural problems and others point to the ever-increasing involvement of the state in the economic process, both groups agree that far-reaching reforms in the public and the private sectors are the prerequisite for a successful way out of the crisis.

Unemployment is probably the most visible economic problem. Since 1991, one year after German Unification, the number of unemployed has risen from 2.6 million or 6.7 per cent of the civilian working population (*Globus Kartendienst* Kb-3881), passing the 4.5 million mark in January 1997. The new *Länder* are especially hard hit with an unemployment rate of 14.9 to 17.7 per cent in 1996. In West Germany the regional variations are wider (14.2 per cent in Bremen, 6.8 per cent in Bavaria) (*Globus Kartendienst* Kb-3893). According to a survey by the ifo Institut for the magazine *Wirtschaftswoche* (Klusmann 1996a: 16–26) nearly three-quarters of employers and managers were pessimistic about the prospects of an economic upturn in 1996. Only one in ten companies was planning to expand in Germany; twice as many may even decrease their operations there.

In this context the debate about *Standort Deutschland* (Germany as a location for industry) has come to the forefront of political and economic discussion in Germany. The implication is that Germany is losing its attractiveness as a location where industry would invest and produce – with all the negative results for the labour market and the country's financial affairs.

THE *STANDORT* DEBATE

Fears about Germany's future as an attractive location for investment are caused partly by increasing economic globalisation, by the opening of Eastern Europe, and by the Single European Market, which offer firms, especially those with an international clientele, more options as to where to invest. Factors which determine their decision include not only labour costs but also productivity, general economic performance, efficiency of management, capital costs, political and social stability, a skilled workforce, tax levels and state intervention. Based on a total of 378 criteria, the Geneva Weltwirtschaftsforum and the Institut für Management-Entwicklung in Lausanne produced a list of the thirty most competitive countries in the world in 1995. Germany ranked in sixth place behind the USA, Singapore, Hongkong, Japan and Switzerland (Great Britain was in eighteenth place) (*Globus Kartendienst* Va-2921).

Germany is still among the top locations for industry, but decreasing foreign investment, high unemployment and cheaper imports are causes for concern. This concern is reinforced by the growing trend of German firms to expand or even relocate their production abroad. The general *Standort*-debate in Germany focuses mainly on the industrial sector rather than on the service sector, with particular reference to:

- labour costs and labour relations;
- the burden of high taxes and bureaucracy;
- lack of innovation combined with a dependence on traditional manufacturing industries;
- the cost of environmental protection.

The following section examines the above points after a brief introduction to post-war German economic history.

FROM THE SECOND WORLD WAR TO UNIFICATION

The systems that existed in the GDR and the Federal Republic of Germany before Unification were of a very different, even contradictory nature in the political, economic and social sense. The Germans on the opposite sides of the Wall lived in two fundamentally different worlds. When the two sides were unified, the Communist command economy was abandoned in favour of the democratic social market economy. Although the GDR economy was the most successful in the Eastern bloc, the gap between it and the West German economy was considerable.

West Germany's economic success has generally been attributed to the country's export strength. As Germany lacks the raw materials it needs for its industrial production and energy demand (apart perhaps from coal) it has always had to rely on foreign trade partners. In 1990 for the first and only time, unified Germany could boast the title 'World Export Champion', having exported goods amounting to 421 billion dollars or 12.3 per cent of world exports (*Globus Kartendienst* Eb-1948). In fact, only because of the continuously rising export figures has Germany been able to build such a stable economy, balancing the books against an increasing number of imports from America and Japan. According to E. Owen Smith exports are vital for the German economy (Owen Smith 1994: 11).

The event that has generally been seen as a catalyst for Germany's ascent from rags to riches is the currency reform of 1948. In 1990 this event repeated itself in the form of the German Monetary and Social Union (GEMSU). Both events emerge as strikingly similar in German economic history. In 1990, with the economy on a downward trend in both parts of the country, politicians and population alike were hoping that Unification and the repetition of an event that had proved to be the stepping stone into a 'golden age' would spark off another economic miracle (*Wirtschaftswunder*). As we know now, this dream has not come true. Instead of increasing industrial output, maintaining the level of employment and extending the export markets in Eastern Europe, joining the social market economy has led to deindustrialised regions and mass unemployment. Some experts now speak of the detrimental effect that the market economy has had on East Germany (Klinger 1994: 3).

However, this single factor alone does not seem to be a plausible explanation for the fact that the expectations of a second 'miracle' did not materialise. The following discussion will contrast the different developments that took place in 1948 and 1990 by focusing on three areas:

● political background;
● psycho-social factors;
● economic development.

The **political background** suggests more similarities than differences between 1948 and 1989 as both German currency reforms occurred in the aftermath of major global events – the end of the Second World War in the first instance and the ideological and institutional changes in the Eastern-bloc countries in the second. In both cases, the introduction of the DM coincided with the departure from a totalitarian system. However, whereas the currency reform in the three Western sectors manifested the formal divide between the two German states for the first time, GEMSU had the opposite effect by restoring German unity.

From the **psycho-social point of view**, however, the picture reveals more discrepancies. In both periods the direction of the migration movement was east to west, which meant that the West experienced a huge influx, whereas the East was depleted of people. Up to the building of the Wall in 1961 the GDR workforce was bled by a constant stream of highly skilled workers. As soon as the borders between East and West weakened, this migration resumed. After the war, the rebuilding of West German industry benefited greatly from the human capital of skilled workers, engineers, accountants and business people who arrived daily as refugees, expelees or returnees without a home in the tidal wave of war. The only possessions they had were those they carried with them. They were determined to make a new start and put all their energies into work in order to be accepted. However, they carried the most important prerequisites for success in their heads: the knowledge of competition and personal initiative in a capitalist system.[1]

Many people who queued up in East German banks to exchange their money on 1 July 1990 lacked this knowledge. Since the majority of the East German labour force had spent their working lives under a Socialist regime, they had integrated into its ideological system, which left the main economic decisions to institutions, favoured more informal problem-solving techniques and, most importantly, provided each individual with the constitutional right to a job. So, even when they were willing to adapt to the new system, most East Germans did not have the techniques and methods to be successful in a market economy. Klinger (1994: 4) points out that it is not enough to introduce competition into a system hoping that this will generate a market economy. As there was only a small pool of people with entrepreneurial skills – an estimated 360,000 people at the end of 1989 – the expected surge of successful new businesses failed to appear. It also has to be assumed that many who wanted to determine their lives actively had done so earlier in 1989 by taking their competitive methods to the west of the country. The others who had stayed saw their old culture of co-operation and dependence clash with the new demands that competition and independence made on them. This makes evident one major factor in the differing developments: the post-war period benefited from a huge intake of highly motivated people – approximately 10 million at the end of 1950 (Abelshauser 1982: 38) – into West Germany, whereas the East Germany of the post-unification era had to cope with a decrease in its entrepreneurial potential.

These discrepancies in attitudes are quite symptomatic of the general *economic picture* of the relevant periods as well. In 1948 two different systems existed side by side in the Western sectors. One was strictly regulated by rationing and coupons, the other was a market economy functioning rather primitively in the form of bartering on a black market. This means that the introduction of the DM meant a *reform* of an existing system. The GDR, on the other hand, had been organised as a planned economy, prices were set solely by the government as were the amounts of products to be manufactured. The means of production were owned by the state rather than by individuals. GEMSU in 1990 therefore meant for East Germans a *transition* from one economic system to another.[2] Additionally, the young Federal Republic had benefited from a more level playing field at the end of the Second World War, when the economies of European states, whether winners or losers, had suffered equally, whereas the new German *Länder* had to compete with their more highly developed neighbours straight away.

Marshall Aid,[3] capital formation and the currency reform are mainly seen as the factors that sparked off the economic miracle in West Germany. Exports were another important factor. In particular, the Korean War contributed to the first economic boom and a decline in the unemployment rate of 10 per cent (Giersch *et al.* 1992: 10). The situation after the currency union in 1990 was different. The new *Länder* did and still do receive financial transfer payments from West Germany which are invested directly, or paid as subsidies or as social contributions. An export boom, however, has not ensued. This is partly due to the negative effect the currency union had on the former export markets of the GDR. Forced to pay in hard currency, most of its former East European customers were faced with an impossible task and placed their orders elsewhere. In Western markets, however, the quality of East German products was not competitive. In fact they could not even compete on the home market, as everybody was initially determined to buy West German goods. Thus only the West German economy boomed.

With a total of 6 million unemployed (Hickel and Priewe 1994: 18), an artificial second labour market and a level of deindustrialisation in the East that beats that of underdeveloped areas in Western Europe, Germany's economy is facing the worst crisis since the Second World War. The reasons for this 'false start' are manifold: the rushed, mainly politically motivated date of the currency union that revalued East German assets, and the hasty privatisation process by the Treuhandanstalt, the agency responsible for selling off state-owned companies in the former GDR to private bidders, without paying too much attention to the future needs of industry. Most importantly, the 'German model' is now transposing its structural problems (as discussed in this chapter) to the new market economy in the East.

LABOUR COSTS AND LABOUR RELATIONS

Labour costs are an important factor in investment decisions, and the high wage level in Germany is often presented as the country's most negative *Standort* factor. The cost of one hour's work (wages plus additional costs such as the employer's national insurance contributions, holiday pay, etc.) in West German industry, according to the Institut der deutschen Wirtschaft, was the highest in the world with DM 45.50 in 1995. In Japan and the USA it was DM 35.50 and DM 25.20 respectively. The rate in Great Britain by comparison was DM 21.00 (*Globus Kartendienst* Mb-3570). West German wages are even higher when compared with the Tiger States (e.g. Singapore: DM 9.90 in 1993) (*Globus Kartendienst* Mb-2544) or Eastern Europe (e.g. the Czech Republic, which attracts more and more investment from Germany: DM 3.36 per hour in 1994; West Germany by comparison in 1994: DM 43.97) (*Globus Kartendienst* Ve-3223). These figures, however, must not be seen in isolation from productivity. The hourly rate in industry may be high in Germany but so is productivity, the result of that hour's work. If one takes productivity in 1995 in West Germany as a baseline and calls it 100 per cent, the figures for the USA and Great Britain were much lower, reaching 71 per cent and 55 per cent respectively of the West German productivity level. Some other important competitors, however, achieved higher levels of productivity at lower labour costs – for example, Japan (104 per cent productivity), Belgium (109 per cent) or France (106 per cent) (*Globus Kartendienst* Mb-3570).

It is especially the additional costs which push up the wage bill. In 1995 employers in West German industry had to pay an additional DM 80.10 for each DM 100 of direct wages (*Globus Kartendienst* Mb-3275). However, more demands on the social benefit system (partly due to rising unemployment), as well as high expectations regarding living standards, will make it unlikely that demands for reductions in labour costs can be easily met.

A survey by the ifo Institut in 1995 of 151 German and 107 foreign firms showed that a major reason for investing in a foreign country is to enter or expand in a foreign market. Cost considerations are important but often secondary to market-entry considerations, depending on the type of firm. However, the survey also showed that in recent investment decisions, especially in industry, firms have become more cost-conscious, particularly with regard to the cost of labour (Wilhelm 1996: 9–18). Investing in production facilities abroad enhances a firm's chances of entering that market and establishing the firm's name, which may well promote exports from its factories in Germany. On the other hand, investment abroad could represent an additional threat to German jobs, especially if differences in wage levels remain high and differences in productivity and skills levels decrease. While the company may thrive as a result of increasing globalisation, *Standort Deutschland* may suffer.

Since the post-war years, wages and working conditions have been settled through a process of collective bargaining whereby trade unions and employers' associations negotiate contracts for pay (once a year) and conditions (normally once every five years). During the running time of these contracts changes are normally not possible and strikes or lockouts are illegal. The system of industrial relations was shaped by the Western Allies after the Second World War. Employers and employees were encouraged – and were largely successful – to act as partners (*Sozialpartner*) who can operate within a framework of labour laws, free from direct state interference (*Tarifautonomie*). The state is only allowed to participate in negotiations on wages and working conditions for the public services where it is the employer. This system of social partnership and consensus has its origin in the political and economic situation of the post-war years, when employers and employees had the same aim of rebuilding the German economy. The strength and productivity of this economy allowed constant improvement of income and conditions for the workforce including co-determination at company level, *Mitbestimmung* (representation on the supervisory boards of firms with more than 2,000 employees), and at plant level, *Betriebsräte* (works councils). These provisions entitle the workforce to information and consultation in the decision-making processes of their firm.

German trade unions are organised on the basis of industries, *Industriegewerkschaft*, i.e. there is only one trade union representing the workforce in a particular branch of industry. Negotiations are carried out generally at regional or federal level and are accepted as binding. With regard to wages, it effectively means negotiating a minimum wage for that industry. In times of constant growth and economic strength, this system worked to mutual benefit, strikes were rare, and firms could operate in a stable environment. However, with increasing globalisation of the economy, the introduction of the Single European Market and competition through cheaper products from low-wage countries, many employers feel this stability is turning into a strait-jacket. Negotiated wage levels do not take into account the situation of individual firms. For those struggling for survival, industry-wide or regionally agreed wage increases may ultimately mean cutting jobs or closing down altogether.

Calls for a reduction of labour costs are therefore often coupled with calls for a change in the collective bargaining system in order to improve investment conditions in Germany. Employers argue that rather than negotiating collectively agreed contracts, *Flächentarife*, which are binding for whole regions or industries, the system should be decentralised. They would like to introduce a more flexible system whereby trade unions and employers' associations would negotiate a general basic framework for wages, working times and conditions, but leave it to individual firms and their works councils to negotiate firm-specific contracts. The four-day week introduced at VW in 1995 in order to safeguard jobs in times when orders are down is only one example of how more flexible, firm-based contracts might be envisaged.

This demand for flexibility applies not only to labour costs, but also to how and when that labour can be used. Regulations concerning working hours, holiday entitlements, shift work at night and at weekends are strict, resulting in lower factory running times in West Germany than in other countries. Here, too, changes are emerging. The new law regulating working hours of 1994 enables firms to apply for the re-introduction of the seven-day working week if increased machine running time keeps them internationally competitive. Working on Saturdays and Sundays is still the exception in many industries. Increasing the length of the working week should not affect the workload of individual employees, which in 1995 was 37.71 hours a week on average (Great Britain: 43.7). The 1,602 hours worked in

West German industry per year is less than in any other industrial country in the world (Harenberg 1996: 35). Employers would also like to make Saturday a regular working day, but here they have run into strong opposition from trade unions (ibid.). How difficult it is to change established working patterns is shown by the long time it took to liberalise shop opening times, which had been among the most restrictive in Europe until they were reformed in 1996.

In spite of higher labour costs, shorter working hours and still comparatively short machine running times, Germany has kept its position of economic strength with productivity remaining relatively high. However, this productivity has been retained through substantial job losses.

TAXES, DUTIES AND BUREAUCRACY

Another aspect of the cost factor is the high level of taxation. Taxes and duties are the state's way of generating income.[4] In the last decade of the twentieth century, demands on the German budget have been high: financial transfers to encourage investment and economic growth in the East, rising unemployment figures that require benefit payments, and contributions to the EU funds are only some of the areas that raised the state deficit of 1994 to 60.1 per cent of the GDP (*Globus Kartendienst* Ta-3428). With a deficit that is a hundred times higher than in the 1950s and required DM 114 billion in interest payments in 1994, fiscal policy had to make amends for the shortfall, raising the demands on private and commercial taxpayers to record heights. Of around forty different taxes, seven accounted for 85 per cent of the overall sum, the biggest contributor being income tax (see table 3.2, p. 35). Equally lucrative were VAT, commercial tax, the solidarity contribution (revived in 1995) and corporation tax (*Globus Kartendienst* Tb-3443). It is estimated that in the financial year of 1995 the tax burden for private households and commercial ventures including social contributions amounted to an equivalent of 48.5 per cent of GNP – the highest figure ever (*Globus Kartendienst* Tb-2593).

With a system that operates on three tiers, companies often find themselves taxed by federal, *Länder* and *Gemeinde* administrations (for more in-depth information see Chapter 3 on federalism). Moreover, German tax rates were traditionally higher – even before the introduction of the *Solidaritätszuschlag*, an additional duty raised to support the economic restructuring of East Germany. Now that the government has reintroduced this duty income tax and corporation tax have become even higher. In 1993 the Federal government passed the *Standortsicherungsgesetz*, which was intended to raise Germany's image as a location for industry, but it has not yet succeeded in reducing tax rates substantially. Therefore it is not surprising that a company like Siemens decided to establish a subsidiary in Great Britain where corporation tax – a tax levied on the profits of a company – is half the amount of that in Germany.[5] On the other hand German book-keeping principles allow companies to calculate their profits in a different, more favourable way. Certain items do not have to be declared, so the 'damage' can be limited legally. However, the legislation is very complicated, and often a firm's accountants and tax inspectors do not agree in their interpretation of the law, as statistics show: in 1995, DM 15.6 billion was retrieved after company audits in which tax officers interpreted the balance sheets differently (*Globus Kartendienst* Tb-2961).

A simplification of the tax laws seems essential. Moreover, tax cuts have been suggested by experts for a long time. However, the plans fielded by the government so far are not very promising for either private households or businesses. The devastating effect of a mis-guided tax policy is illustrated by the current plans of almost all *Länder* ministers of finance who are planning to impose higher taxes on the branches of foreign banks in Germany. International bankers concerned have indicated that a step like this could easily jeopardise *Finanzplatz Deutschland*, Germany as a financial centre, as they would strive to avoid the financial disadvantage such a step would impose on them, by locating their branches elsewhere and conducting their German business via computer technology (Bauer 1996: 52).

On the other hand, there is the effect that the high taxation of private income has on the spending power of the German consumer. Increasing deductions have left private households with less money to spend. Social contributions included, an average earner saw 48 per cent of his/her gross income dwindle away on direct and indirect taxes in 1995 (Harenberg 1995: 396). The Federal Constitutional Court (see Chapter 4, p. 52) is also concerned about this develop-ment; it ruled that a minimum amount of money covering the basic needs of a person to exist (with amounts varying according to marital status – *Existenzminimum*) has to be left untaxed. It also called for a reform of the tax system for 1996.

Like the tax system, German bureaucracy needs reorganisation, as it puts the customer at a disadvantage. Many aspects of business require detailed permission (patents, building applications, etc.), which takes a long time to obtain because the system is organised in many different layers of administrative responsibility. Understaffing and a lack of modern technology in offices dealing with the general public slow down procedures. It takes only three months to apply for the concession to build a chemical plant in the United States, compared with between eight and fifteen months in Germany (Bundesministerium für Wirtschaft 1996). On the other hand the administrative structure at ministerial level has been deemed overstaffed, unmanageable and resistant to change (*Der Spiegel* 27/1996: 40–42). While the explanations for this phenomenon vary, the general consensus is that deregulation – a simplification of existing rules – is essential to make Germany more attractive to investors.

INNOVATION

High quality and a high level of technological achievement have been the hallmark of German products for a long time. Even before the Second World War, German engineers and scientists competed with their American counterparts for world leadership in product design, scientific acclaim and Nobel prizes. At the end of the war, when the German economy was at an all-time low, many of the research organisations no longer existed, decimated by death, emigration or exile, and research could have come to an end simply owing to a lack of personnel.

With some of the production base destroyed, new ideas and innovative thinking were required if Germany was not to end up an agricultural society. This had originally been envisaged by Henry Morgenthau, US Minister of Finance under Roosevelt, but was then superseded by the Marshall Plan. The German education system provided its students with a strong basis in scientific and technical knowledge throughout the war, and this is often given as one of the reasons for the speedy recovery of German industry and its depleted research laboratories. From as early as the end of the nineteenth century innovation did not stop at the three Rs; pupils and students in all areas of education were introduced to a certain level of science and technical subjects.

After the rubble had been cleared, those parts of the factories that could be salvaged had to be put to productive use. For this reason, owing to the relative lack of resources, mechanics and engineers often had to be more inventive and imaginative, employing alternative ways of thinking, thus developing the German passion for puzzling over problems (*tüfteln*). The second pillar in post-war innovation was the fact that American investors often insisted that their money be channelled into the latest technology America could offer. This meant that some of the new German factories were soon better-equipped than those of their competitors in other European countries. Not hindered by having to use outdated technology, these new plants also helped to cement Germany's image as a producer of quality goods. In due course, German engineers started to develop their own technologies, and established Germany as a leader in mechanical and electrical engineering, the automotive and chemical industries.

However, innovation and inventiveness are not qualities that only have their place in a post-war era. As new ideas can mean new products, new customers and new markets, both are a key to maintaining and improving the level of sales and thereby the wealth of a nation. If no efforts are made to encourage research a country will soon lag behind its competitors. For this reason, research foundations like the Max-Planck-Gesellschaft or the Fraunhofer-Gesellschaft were set up by the state to institutionalise co-operation between scientists and industrialists.

Nevertheless, Germany seems to have an innovation problem which has manifested itself in the development of a technological gap. Whereas inventors paved the way to success in the post-war period, establishing Germany as a superpower in the manufacturing sector, it appears that the German ideals of stability and reliability now hinder innovative thinking. Young inventors and innovators are leaving the Federal Republic in droves either because their efforts are not taken seriously (Hofinger and Nielsen 1995: 15) or because they feel limited by the inflexibility and arrogance of their compatriots (Reischauer *et al.* 1996: 103). Looking at the effects this has had on the German labour market, one cannot help but think that German management has displayed a certain amount of self-absorption and complacency, and that for once the strategy of long-term planning has backfired, leaving them trailing the competition.

The technological gap arises as a result of deficiencies in the following areas:

- structural change;
- Germany's standard of innovation;
- investment into research;
- education;
- attitude.

It was high-tech mechanical engineering and car engineering that won Germany accolades in recent decades. Now, however, such expertise is not enough when we are on the brink of the information and service society – a fact that seems only too obvious when we look at the statistics. Recent figures of service-sector contributions to economic growth show that, whilst the average of other OECD countries amounts to 2.3 per cent, Germany lags behind with 1.5 per cent, whereas the United States leads with 3.3 per cent (Klusman 1996b: 39). According to figures produced by *Globus Kartendienst* (Wa-3187), Japan, the USA and Germany are at the top of high-technology exporters, with 21 per cent, 19 per cent and 16 per cent of the world market share respectively. However, this superficial glance at the figures hides the fact that, whereas Japan's and the USA's exports contain a high proportion of future technology (semiconductors, computers and other consumer electronics), Germany relies mainly on its old strengths: chemical, machine and automotive products. The fact that the rest of Europe is equally dependent on Japan as the supplier of microelectronic components is only a small consolation. German employers are also reluctant to explore other opportunities, such as the biotechnical industries as well as the service sector. This not only has repercussions on export figures but can ultimately also mean losing jobs.

Spending money on future technologies in order to catch up with the competition would therefore seem to be a prime objective. But by comparing figures it becomes quite clear that this has not been the case. It was still predominantly private enterprise that funded research investment in 1995 with DM 49 billion, rather than the state with only DM 32 billion. Overall this represents 2.4 per cent of GDP, which is 0.4 per cent less than in 1990 (*Globus Kartendienst* Ic-3461). In 1994 Germany ranked fourth in a global comparison of research spending. Sweden took the lead with 3.1 per cent of its GDP, followed by the USA with 2.7 per cent and Japan with 2.8 per cent (*Globus Kartendienst* Ic-2527). An explanation could be that, faced with cost-cutting exercises, the state, as well as many German companies, reduced their research and development activities first.

One way of assessing the standard of innovation of different countries is to compare their output of patents. In 1993, Japan led the race for new inventions in four out of five categories, registering the highest number of patents in the fields of micro and consumer electronics, medical and aerospace technology; while its competitors, the USA and Germany, only scored highest marks in mainframe computing and the automotive sector respectively. Taken on their own the bare figures reflect badly on Germany, because with one exception it seems to monopolise the third position (Harenberg 1995: 183). However, as they stand, these results do not make any reference to the quality of the patent registered, registration practices or the bureaucratic process in the different countries, and therefore they are not really comparable. What can be said is that the slogan 'Vorsprung durch Technik' (one step ahead through technology) still rings true, when German inventiveness is focused on cars, whereas it seems to avoid electronics and computers. And even in the old domain of mechanical engineering Germany has lost out to the Japanese competition where new technology combines mechanical components with microchips. As electronic products date fast, catching up should prove difficult.

The German system of education and training (see Chapter 7), although in many ways highly acclaimed, has not done enough to close the technological gap. Initiatives like Hubert Frenzl's inventors' course, which he started as part of the youth research initiative 'Jugend forscht', are exceptional. Under his supervision, pupils won more than a dozen prizes in national and international competitions and fifteen registered patents. Unfortunately, most young inventors decide to leave Germany because industrialists tend to see them as a threat rather than a source of innovation (Hofinger and Nielsen 1995: 14).

Apart from the bureaucratic obstacles, the way in which established businesses, administration and the general public perceive the innovative process is significant. Clinging to their traditional manufacturing background, banks and financial services do not leave enough room for creativity and new ideas. For that very reason, potential business-owners are turning their backs on Germany. Interviews with young German entrepreneurs who have established their businesses elsewhere (Reischauer *et al.* 1996: 102–108) reveal that, apart from cost factors, reasons for not staying in Germany are lack of dynamism and flexibility, no space to develop and the fact that everything had to be done by the book.

THE COST OF ENVIRONMENTAL PROTECTION

Germany is often seen as one of the leading countries in environmental protection. The creation of vociferous pressure groups and the establishment, in 1980, of the German Green Party (Die Grünen) (see Chapter 4, p. 58), the politically most successful environmental party in Europe, have put pressure on the established political parties and successive governments to concern themselves with environmental questions. Above all, worries about the widespread damage to forests in Germany led the federal parliament in 1983 to introduce the most stringent restrictions in Europe for the emission of air pollutants by industry. The accident at the nuclear power station in Chernobyl in 1986 resulted in the creation of the Bundesministerium für Umwelt, Naturschutz und Reaktorsicherheit (the Federal Ministry for the Environment, Protection of Nature and Reactor Safety). As a ministry in its own right, it joined the Umweltbundesamt (Federal Agency for the Environment), established in 1974 as a department within the Ministry for the Interior. During the last thirty years, a number of measures have been taken in Germany to combat environmental damage, and in many fields the country has taken the lead.

The majority of measures have taken the form of legally enforced restrictions and regulations, such as emission and product norms, to a lesser extent taxes and duties for environmentally damaging production processes. Complying with these regulations, for example by installing special filtering systems or using prescribed technology, such as catalytic converters in cars, adds – at least initially – to the production costs. For many firms, environmental costs (together with high energy costs) are yet another negative aspect of *Standort Deutschland*. These additional costs make German products less competitive in international markets. Firms are forced to make savings elsewhere, which can mean reducing production and cutting jobs, investing in labour-saving technology, or even relocating part or all of their production to countries where the costs are lower. While the need for environmental protection is not disputed, the extra costs this may incur for producers and consumers are less widely accepted. Especially in times of recession or economic difficulty, ecology is mostly seen as secondary to economy.

While environmental policy may pose certain threats to firms in Germany, it also offers many opportunities. Forced by legislation, firms have developed new products and technologies for the protection of the environment, for example in the chemical and the steel industry or for power stations, as well as technologies for the cleaning up of polluted environments (soil or water). A whole new industrial sector has developed; in 1994, 8,500 German firms were involved in the production of environmental technology, and about 680,000 people were employed in jobs related to the environment. The number of jobs in the production of environmental goods and technologies, in direct environmental tasks and in the public sector has risen steadily in West Germany alone from 428,000 in 1984 to 546,000 in 1990, with 785,000 predicted for the year 2000 (*Der Spiegel* 26/1994: 82–84). With unification, the national market for environmental technology expanded dramatically. East Germany is heavily polluted, and local councils as well as private firms are now legally obliged to clean up polluted soil and water and to prevent further damage by upgrading existing factories and power stations. It is estimated that DM 220 billion are needed to make water, air and soil in East Germany as clean as in West Germany by the year 2000. The Deutsches Institut für Wirtschaftsforschung in Berlin predicts yearly growth rates of 6 per cent for the environmental industry (Heckel and Weidenfeld 1994: 47–48). In this sector, German firms were also very successful internationally. By 1995 they were leading the world market for environmental technology, with 21 per cent of the market share, ahead of the USA and Japan, with 16.9 per cent and 13.1 per cent respectively (Great Britain 7.1 per cent) (*Globus Kartendienst* Dc-2995). In 1996, however, the situation looked slightly less positive. In spite of continuing world-wide demand, German firms lost orders, and it was predicted that Germany's exports would be overtaken by the USA (Kutter and Röhrlich 1996: 110). Two reasons given are the high price of very sophisticated German technology and increasing competition, especially in the Far East.

Also, environmental legislation in Germany has been more focused on repair and limitation of environmental damage, which has encouraged the development of so-called end-of-pipe technology. This technology deals with environmentally damaging by-products of production processes rather than with the avoidance of these substances in the first place through changes in production processes and resources. It is these technologies which are believed to be the market of the future. As already pointed out in the context of innovation as a *Standort*-factor, German firms are often accused of not being innovative and forward-looking enough. Industry, on the other hand, blames the government for lack of financial support. Research into alternative energies, and in particular their commercial application, is not subsidised as much as in the United States, for example. Most major German firms in the solar industry have moved their production abroad, where subsidies may be higher and labour costs lower (*Der Spiegel* 26/1995: 103).

However, environmental aspects have already become a factor of competition. According to a survey among 200 managers from private industry for the magazine *Wirtschaftswoche*, environmental considerations play 'a large or very large part' in the production and marketing of their products for 56 per cent of them (Kessler *et al.* 1995: 15). Textiles and household goods are a good example. Looking at the whole life cycle of a product from production to disposal, some major retailers and textile producers have developed minimum ecological standards. Only suppliers who can comply with these standards will be accepted. These developments are not the norm yet, but they highlight the beginning of a new important trend. The restriction of the use of CFC gases has led to the development, for example, of CFC-free fridges. The combination of consumer demand and state legislation for the use and disposal or recycling of certain substances is enforcing a change in production processes which has given producers who reacted quickly a competitive edge. However, in most firms environmental strategies so far have been a reaction to legislation concentrating on production processes rather than to product innovation. The number of true pro-active 'eco-pioneers' is still relatively small (Birke and Schwarz 1996: 24).

In 1994 the Deutsches Institut für Wirtschaftsforschung (DIW) published a study with suggestions for restructuring the German tax system using ecological considerations. Based on the principle that the polluter pays, the *Verursacherprinzip*, a system of taxation was envisaged which would penalise heavy use of energy, the emission of environmentally damaging substances and environmentally damaging products and production processes. Such a system involves punishment and incentive at the same time. It is expected that as an incentive it would encourage innovation in environmentally friendly products and production processes, as happened to a certain extent after the oil crises in the late 1970s and early 1980s, when high petrol costs forced car manufacturers to design cars which were more economical in their petrol consumption.

The reaction to suggestions for an ecologically orientated tax system has been mixed. The Confederation of German Industry (BDI) is worried about the implications of ecological taxes, particularly an energy tax, for the *Standort Deutschland*. Energy-intensive industries would be disadvantaged through higher costs, especially as the proposal for a standardised European energy tax failed to get the consent of all EU member states in 1994. A national CO_2/energy tax would add substantial extra costs to an already high tax burden for firms. They see such a tax as detrimental to *Standort Deutschland*, as many firms would relocate production to cheaper countries. The necessity of environmental protection is not disputed but the methods are. The BDI is in favour of, for example, voluntary self-control by industry and suggests fiscal incentives, such as tax reductions for investment into modernisation of plants to encourage more environmentally friendly production processes (Henkel 1995). The *Wirtschaftswoche* survey of 1995, on the other hand, showed that over two-thirds of managers who were interviewed would support an ecological tax reform in return for lower employers' national insurance contributions. The DIW study suggested this reduction so that ecological taxes would not affect the competitiveness of German goods through increased prices. But there are also voices among employers asking for more stringent measures to speed up the ecological restructuring of German industry. They see ecological orientation as essential for future competitiveness.

Such a restructuring of the economy will inevitably mean that there will be winners and losers, especially in the short term. As far as product development and marketing are concerned, environmental issues have already proved themselves as a business opportunity. Environmental protection will become one of the major issues world-wide. German firms may then find themselves in a better position than their competitors because German legislation has forced them along an environmental path earlier. Even though stringent legislation combined with extra costs may still be a threat at the moment, in the long run other countries may well be forced to follow suit and then Germany should have a *Standort*-advantage again as the structural changes have been made there already. This hope in a future along an environmental path is highlighted by the theme of Expo 2000, 'Man – Nature – Technology', to be held in the German city and trade-fair centre of Hanover (Head 1992: 154).

CONCLUSION

Randlesome describes the main values of German business culture as 'conservatism and strength' (Randlesome 1994: xi). Stability was of paramount importance, and for four decades Germany's economy has thrived on it. A clearly regulated business environment and a stable political system have allowed long-term planning and have made Germany a reliable trading partner. In an economic climate of globalisation and rapid technological development this stability may, however, hinder quick adaptation to changing circumstances. The *Standort* debate as a whole is characterised by this ambivalence; the workforce is expensive but well qualified, and the standard of work is high. The system of labour relations may be felt to be a strait-jacket, but it has guaranteed social peace. Environmental protection adds cost, but is an investment in the future. High taxes and social contributions increase costs, but provide a high standard of living.

Germany is still among the most competitive countries in the world. Its geographical position at the centre of Europe, reinforced by Unification, and its excellent infrastructure both remain stable positive *Standort*-factors, but there is rising unemployment, more frequent signs of social unrest and the possibility that Germany may not meet the criteria for European Monetary Union. All these indicate that the country has entered a new, more unsettled phase in which the economic miracle has lost its magic.

NOTES

1 For further details see von Krockow (1992: 282).
2 For further details see Bryson (1992: 119).
3 It seems to be agreed that the financial effects of Marshall Aid were negligible. Abelshauser (1982) sees its beneficial effects in the 'public relation' effect for Germany; as one of the recipients it was accepted in the international trade community. For von Krockow (1992) it presents a boost for German self-confidence after the loss of the war.
4 Both taxes and duties are collected by the state. The difference between them is how their revenues are used: whereas the tax revenue is not dedicated to a specific purpose, duties are collected for a specific purpose, for example the *Müllabfuhrabgabe* (the duty paid for waste management) can only be spent on the waste management budget.
5 According to Rauscheder (1994: 75) Germany led the world's corporation tax league tables in 1994 with a rate of 62 per cent, followed by Japan (59 per cent), France (52 per cent), the United States (45 per cent), Canada (44 per cent) and Great Britain (33 per cent).

RECOMMENDED READING

Rauscheder (1994).
Smith (1994).

BIBLIOGRAPHY

Anon. 'Die Macht der Häkchen', *Der Spiegel* 27/1996: 40–42 (1996).
—— 'Forsche Schrittmacher', *Der Spiegel* 26/1994: 82–84 (1994).
—— 'Wahnsinn in Wedel', *Der Spiegel* 26/1995: 103 (1995).
Abelshauser, W. (1982) 'West German economic recovery 1945–1951: a reassessment', *The Three Banks Review* 135: 34–53.
Bauer, S. (1996) 'Helle Aufregung', *Wirtschaftswoche* 23: 52.
Birke, M. and Schwarz, M. (1996) 'Umweltschutz im deutschen Betriebsalltag: Eine Bestandsaufnahme in mikropolitischer Perspektive', *Aus Politik und Zeitgeschichte*, Beilage zur Wochenzeitung *Das Parlament*, B 7: 23–29.
Bryson, P. (1992) 'The economics of German unification: a review of literature', *Journal of Economics* 16: 118–149.
Bundesministerium für Wirtschaft (ed.) (1996) *Standort Deutschland: Die Herausforderung annehmen*, Bonn: BMWi.

Giersch, H., Paqué, K. and Schmieding, H. (1992) *The Fading Miracle: Four Decades of Market Economy in Germany*, Cambridge: Cambridge University Press.

Globus Kartendienst (1995) Dc-2995, 30, 10.

—— (1995) Va-2921, 18, 9.

—— (1994) Eb-1948, 30, 3.

—— (1995) Mb-2544, 13, 3.

—— (1995) Tb-2593, 10, 4.

—— (1995) Tb-2961, 9, 10.

—— (1996) Mb-3570, 5, 8.

—— (1996) Ve-3223, 19, 2.

—— (1996) Ic-2527, 17, 6.

—— (1996) Ic-3461, 17, 6.

—— (1996) Kb-3833, 14, 12.

—— (1996) Mb-3275, 11, 3.

—— (1996) Ta-3428, 28, 5.

—— (1996) Tb-3443, 3, 6.

—— (1996) Wa-3187, 29, 1.

—— (1997) Kb-3893, 20, 1.

—— (1997) Kb-3881, 13, 1.

Harenberg, B. (ed.) (1995) *Harenberg Lexikon der Gegenwart: Aktuell '96*, Dortmund: Harenberg.

—— (1996) *Harenberg Lexikon der Gegenwart: Aktuell '97*, Dortmund: Harenberg.

Head, D. (1992) *'Made in Germany': The Corporate Identity of a Nation*, London: Hodder & Stoughton.

Heckel, M. and Weidenfeld, U. (1994) 'Gruben säubern', *Wirtschaftswoche* 5: 47–48.

Henkel, H.-O. (1995) 'Mehr Umsatz durch weniger Steuern', *Frankfurter Rundschau* 4(7).

Hickel, R. and Priewe, J. (1994) *Nach dem Fehlstart: Ökonomische Perspektiven der deutschen Einigung*, Frankfurt am Main: Fischer.

Hofinger, T. and Nielsen L. (1995) 'Die Erfinderschmiede', *PZ Wir in Europa* 82: 14–15.

Kessler, M., Kowalewsky, R. and Peter, M. (1995) 'Von alleine', *Wirtschaftswoche* 25: 14–27.

Klinger, F. (1994) 'Aufbau und Erneuerung: Über die institutionellen Bedingungen der Standortentwicklung in Deutschland', *Aus Politik und Zeitgeschichte (Beilage)* 17: 3–13.

Klusmann, S. (1996a) 'Bangen und Hoffen', *Wirtschaftswoche* 10: 16–26.

—— (1996b) 'Grenze erreicht', *Wirtschaftswoche* 16: 36–39.

Kutter, S. and Röhrlich, D. (1996) 'Keine Hilfe nötig', *Wirtschaftswoche* 19: 110–114.

Owen Smith, E. (1994) *The German Economy*, London: Routledge.

Randlesome, C. (1994) *The Business Culture in Germany*, Oxford: Butterworth-Heinemann.

Rauscheder, W. (1994) *Wirtschaftsstandort Deutschland*, München: Heyne.

Reischauer *et al.* (1996) 'Drang nach drauβen', *Wirtschaftswoche* 23: 102–108.

von Krockow, C. (1992) *Die Deutschen in ihrem Jahrhundert 1890–1990*
  Hamburg: Rowohlt.
Wilhelm, M. (1996) 'Motive deutscher und ausländischer Direktinvestoren'
  Ifo Schnelldienst 16: 9–18.

6 Social provision

Sue Lawson

After looking at the history and basic principles of the German welfare state, this chapter considers three issues which are bringing changes in social provision in Germany. These are (1) the effects of Unification, with particular reference to women, (2) the demographic changes since the inception of the welfare state, and (3) the advent of the global economy and its influence on employment in Germany. Finally a brief look will be taken at suggestions for possible reform.

HISTORY AND BASIC PRINCIPLES

The German welfare state was founded in 1881, making it one of the oldest in the world. The first old-age pensions were paid at age 70 – 'habitual drinkers' (*gewohnheitsmässige Trinker*) were paid theirs in food and drink only, just to be on the safe side! (*Der Spiegel* 6/1996: 22). By the late 1970s, nearly a hundred years after its founding, the social insurance system covered 90 per cent of the German population.[1] The original social legislation introduced by Bismarck, Imperial Chancellor of Germany from 1871 to 1890, was brought in partly to prevent the Socialists gaining too much power. On the positive side, however, it made providing for old age and against illness, accident or poverty into a common rather than an individual or family responsibility (Rink 1994: 11). The constitution of the Weimar Republic (1919–33) explicitly gave its citizens certain social rights. These are not the same as human rights; you can have the one without the other. Human rights, such as equality before the law, are intended to prevent the state from encroaching too far into the province of the individual. Social rights mean that the individual can expect more from the state than simply law, order and defence. They include the right to work, to housing, education, state support when in need,[2] co-determination[3] in the workplace, and the right to form trade unions. However, when we talk about the welfare state and social provisions we normally have in mind how the country in question makes provision for its citizens when they need help.

The underlying principle of the German welfare state has always been *insurance* against the basic risks of work, to which employer and employee pay *equal* contributions. It has traditionally also been one of the most generous states as regards benefits. However, conditions today are stretching some aspects of social provision to their limits, and it may be that radical change is the only solution.

Before looking at the current problems it is useful to know something about how social welfare is organised in Germany. It is based on compulsory insurance: when someone is working, they and their employer pay contributions; when they stop work, they receive benefits. Insurance can be state-run or private, or a mixture of both, just so long as you are insured.

As in other areas of life, Germany's federal structure shows through in its social provisions. While social *legislation* is almost exclusively a Federal responsibility, its realisation may vary with the different *Länder*. The *Länder*, however, may only legislate on additional provisions; they cannot affect what is legally prescribed. Unemployment insurance is the only unified central scheme; other insurance may be organised at *Land* level or privately. Supplementary benefit (*Sozialhilfe*) is means-tested and normally provided at *Land* level. Health services are provided by voluntary agencies or the private sector, this last particularly in the case of residential care. All benefits are still relatively generous compared with most other countries.

SOCIAL INSURANCE

Anyone working in Germany, and their employer, must make contributions in three areas: towards a pension (*Rentenversicherung*), health insurance (*Krankenversicherung*, which is paid to a *Krankenkasse*, a statutory health insurance agency) and unemployment benefit (*Arbeitslosenversicherung*). In 1995 a fourth area was added: care insurance (*Pflegeversicherung*), for anybody unable to look after themselves in old age or through illness. Employees do not pay industrial accident insurance (*Betriebsunfallversicherung*). Should someone have an accident at work, any benefits will be funded entirely by their employer.

Pensions

Provided employees have an unbroken record of contributions, and depending on occupation, they would get about 40–60 per cent of their former income in retirement pension (*Altersrente*). Benefits depend on prior insurance contributions and are also earnings-related. Thus income differentials while working are reproduced in retirement. Widow(er)s' and orphans' benefits also vary according to occupation; a general's widow would get DM 4,500 per month. Civil servants have a non-contributory scheme.

Health insurance

Helmut Kohl's well-publicised regular visits to 'health farms' to keep his weight in check are merely a high-profile example of something most West Germans can do. Health insurance will pay for people to spend time every few years taking a 'cure' (*Kur*) at one of the 185 health spas (*Bäder*) in Germany. Until 1996 sick pay was 100 per cent of earnings for the first six weeks; since 1996 it has been 80 per cent. Health insurance schemes are either state-run but organised locally through the AOK (Allgemeine Ortskrankenkasse), or they are occupational (*ständisch*) using a variety of state-regulated private insurers. For this Germans pay about 13.4 per cent of their earnings.

Unemployment insurance[4]

Having paid your contributions (for a minimum of 360 days in the past three years) in Germany you are entitled to three levels of unemployment pay, depending on how much you earned, how long you were working and how long you remain unemployed. *Arbeitslosengeld* may be drawn for a year to eighteen months, and this amounts to around 60–67 per cent of the last net earnings. After that there is a step down to *Arbeitslosenhilfe*, which is 53–57 per cent of the last net earnings. This may be drawn for a maximum of two years after *Arbeitslosengeld* runs out. Both are paid out of the employee's *Arbeitslosenversicherung* share by the Federal Employment Agency (Bundesarbeitsanstal). The final stage, *Sozialhilfe*, is a *Land* responsibility. It is not specifically for the unemployed, but for all those who have no other means of support or whose other means of support are inadequate. It is non-contributory and can be paid in money and/or in kind. It is based not on what was earned but on the statistical minimum necessary to support a life worth living (*ein menschenwürdiges Leben*). Incidentally, as well as food, rent, heating, clothing, and furnishings, this also includes a daily paper and a monthly visit to the theatre or cinema (*Wegweiser für die Sozialhilfe*: 11.) Even the least well off are allowed the opportunity to take an interest in politics and culture.

Care insurance

This additional provision was hotly debated before becoming law in 1996, partly because it appeared to discriminate against the old. Of course people do not have to be old to be disabled and in need of care, but you are statistically more likely to need care when old. Like *Sozialhilfe*, *Pflegehilfe* can be paid in cash and/or in kind. The *Pflegekassen* are organised as part of the *Krankenkassen*. Provided someone needs at least 90 minutes of care per day, they may receive a monthly allowance, on a sliding scale which depends on the degree of disability. People can get a grant towards converting accommodation if necessary. From July 1996 the *Pflegekasse* will pay for hospital treatment, but patients pay for their 'board and lodging' whilst there (Harenberg 1996: 328).[5]

THE SOCIAL BUDGET

The benefits mentioned above have been described as generous – they are, and that of course means that they are also expensive for the state. They cost more than the contributions bring in. On the other hand, as we shall see later on, the German social budget is not clearcut, and also finances some elements (*versicherungsfremde Leistungen*) which are not strictly speaking *social* benefits.[6] At present benefits are financed by a combination of employee and employer contributions, and general taxation. In 1996 the social budget amounted to 29.1 per cent of GDP.[7] About 30 per cent of this comes from general taxation. Social insurance contributions account for 70 per cent, 40 per cent from the employer and 30 per cent from the employee. Together these contributions account for about 21 per cent of German labour costs, and in 1996 the employee's contribution rose to over 40 per cent of earnings (Harenberg 1996: 327).[8]

EFFECTS OF UNIFICATION

The citizens of divided Germany had widely differing expectations of what and how the state would provide for them. In the old GDR housing, energy, basic foodstuffs, public transport and other essential services were subsidised, so that even the lowest earners could manage a reasonable, if modest, standard of living. Poverty, homelessness and dependence on benefits hardly existed. Generous support from the state towards combining a career and a family – known as the second wage packet – was taken for granted. Taking child benefit, the low cost of child care and other allowances together, a parent with two children could supplement any wages by about 50 per cent. Since full employment was guaranteed by the state, unemployment benefit was not needed. In the old West Germany, there was, for example, much less state support for combining employment and children, but then again, unemployment benefit was both necessary and relatively generous.

Before Unification it might have appeared possible somehow to merge the two systems, taking the best from both. In the event the East had to accept the West German welfare system, plus a few measures intended as temporary to ease the pain of transition. All ex-GDR citizens were of course affected by this transition, but its effects are arguably most clearly seen in the case of women.

Differing attitudes to women

Since the GDR disappeared there has been a nostalgic tendency to view its social provisions through rose-tinted spectacles (*ostalgie*), particularly in the area of women's emancipation. However, there was some hard-headed economic thinking, not merely ideology, behind the GDR's generous provision for mothers. No state supports its citizens out of pure altruism. Every citizen of every state is potentially an economically active participant, as employer, employee, consumer or all three. At a certain stage in their lives, women are also producers of, and a primary influence on, the next generation of the economically active, and different societies have different ideas on how this period should be accommodated in their economy.

After the creation of two German states in 1949, both East and West Germany had a low birth rate and an acute labour shortage. They tackled this problem in different ways according to their different circumstances. East Germany did all it could to enable women to combine motherhood with being more or less permanently members of the full-time workforce. Interest-free loans (*Ehekredite*) were available for those under thirty marrying for the first time (Justizminister-ium der DDR 1987: 2.1#4). With each child the couple were released from some of the repayments (ibid.: no. 5). Full-time motherhood, and part-time working by mothers who would have been working full time were it not for their children, were both frowned upon by the state on ideological and economic grounds. This led to the so-called 'baby year' (see below) and a pretty well universal system of state crèches and kindergartens.

West Germany tackled the labour shortage in the first instance by recruiting foreign workers, intending that they should return home when no longer needed. There was no concerted effort to redefine women as permanent full-time economically active members of society. Thus child care provision remained patchy. East German mothers were normally back at work full time once their youngest child reached eighteen months or so, while West German mothers would generally be working part time or not at all until their youngest child reached sixteen or so.

Maternity and child care

Both East and West Germany had a statutory period of paid maternity leave of about six weeks before and eight to twelve weeks after the birth of a child. After that, child care provisions differed, and were both more generous and more consistent in the old East Germany than in the West. From 1976 onwards all East German mothers had the right to one year's paid child care leave (*Babyjahr*) for the second and subsequent children, with the right to return to their old job or to one of similar status. By the late 1980s this leave had been extended to eighteen months, covered the first child as well, and could be taken by the mother, the father or by another relative. In practice it was most often taken by the mother herself or the grandmother. Sometimes it was shared.

West German women were entitled to four months' paid child care leave, with the right to return to their old job or one of similar status, and continued membership of the health, old-age and pension insurance schemes. After that it depended on their occupations and – owing to West Germany's federal system – their *Land*. Some *Länder* and occupations were more generous than others. Female civil servants, for instance, could take unpaid child care leave until the child started school, and then return to a similar job.

East German women therefore, and mothers especially, were hard hit by the post-Unification change from the East German to the West German model of social provision. It made immediate and permanent changes to their daily life. In the GDR, almost all children except those needing special mental or physical care had been looked after during the day either in the state-run crèches and kindergartens or at school. Most women of working age in the old GDR had therefore been able to combine a job with children. This does not mean that they could necessarily have a career, or that the jobs they did were all fulfilling and interesting, or that they were all emotionally better off as a result. They worked long hours, as did all GDR citizens, and had the added burden of family responsibilities as well (*Doppelbelastung*).[9] However, the 'baby year' for each child and the system of state-run crèches and kindergartens had made it relatively straightforward, if hard work, for mothers to earn their own living, with or without a husband or partner.[10] As members of a united Federal Republic their economic position was much less secure.

Working is, however, still much more common among women in the East than in the West (see Table 6.1), especially between the ages of 30 and 50. Note how sharply the participation rate drops for the over 55s, to less than in the old *Länder*. This reflects the fact that early retirement, one of the main weapons used after Unification to reduce overstaffing, was more frequently offered to women than to men. You might therefore think that gainful employment, though falling slightly, remains as normal for ex-GDR women as it always was, and in a sense you would be right. Eastern German women, who have grown up in a Socialist *Arbeitsgesellschaft*, a society of working people, have lost neither their psychological nor their economic need to work. What has gone is the security. Once a normal area of life that women took for granted, employment is

Table 6.1 Labour-market participation of women by age groups in the old and new *Länder* (%)

Age group	*Old* Länder		*New* Länder	
	1992	*1993*	*1992*	*1993*
15–20	34	33	43	37
20–25	73	71	85	83
25–30	73	72	95	94
30–35	68	68	97	96
35–40	70	70	97	97
40–45	73	73	97	96
45–50	69	70	96	95
50–55	61	62	90	91
55–60	46	47	27	27
60–65	12	12	3	3
65–70	4	4	—	—

Source: Datenreport 1994: 80 (in Kolinsky 1996: 279)

now not only a psychological and economic necessity, but a source of anxiety as well.

Unemployment

Market-based economies have unemployment openly. Command economies do not. This is of course a gross simplification, but Americans or Britons, while they may fear being unemployed, do understand what it is and have some idea what to do in that situation. In the old GDR you were never unemployed. After finishing their education, citizens would be allocated a job by the relevant authorities. Individuals might have had little choice in where or what, but they knew they would have work. Thereafter, provided people were fit to work, they were either working, or were being educated or trained, or on maternity or child care leave, or else retired. Anyone not fit to work drew the appropriate pension.[11] The extension of West German unemployment benefit to the old GDR did very little to mitigate the psychological shock of realising that jobs were no longer secure. Losing your job and having no prospect of another was something new and frightening for the East Germans.

An expensive system

Unfortunately, the take-over of the Eastern by the Western system happened just as the latter was proving too expensive to sustain. By 1996 sick pay alone was costing employers around DM 90 million a year. In 1950 about a quarter of the state budget was spent on welfare; in 1994 it was nearly half. Ironically, one reason for the expense was the take-over itself. Throughout the 1980s West Germany had experienced a long period of relative growth of around 3 per cent per annum. In 1991 the unemployment rate was 6.3 per cent, its lowest since 1981. The share of the budget spent by the state fell in 1989 from over 49 per cent to around 45 per cent. Unification changed all that. Suddenly the social security system was responsible not for 62 million inhabitants but for nearly 80 million. Simultaneously unemployment in the East rose from virtually nil to 37 per cent, while productivity declined by nearly 40 per cent between 1990 and 1992. When the Wall fell there were 9 million jobs in the GDR. By 1992 this number had fallen by one-third. Since 1990 the West has transferred about DM 1 billion to the East; in 1996 the 'new' *Länder* were still living mainly on transfers from the West. The social and economic difficulties had been seriously underestimated, and the time-scale envisaged for the East to become self-supporting proved far too short.

However, the problems discussed below were merely highlighted, not caused, by Unification, and are not passing away with the GDR. Demographic changes happen relatively slowly; the 'greying' of Germany began before the First World War. German unemployment is now largely structural, and is not falling but rising.

AN AGEING POPULATION

When the welfare state system was created, 4 per cent of the German population lived to 65. In 1901, 48 per cent reached 60. Nowadays 88 per cent reach 60, and 14 per cent surpass the age of 80 (Roloff 1996: 6). This alone indicates one reason why, even without unification, the German welfare state could not continue as it had been. Figure 6.1 illustrates the problem. You can see it most clearly not in the details but in the general shapes. It was assumed that pensions for the older generation would be financed by the younger working generation (*Generationenvertrag*). The demographic state of affairs that made this assumption reasonable in 1901 is illustrated top left in Figure 6.1. The German for this diagram is the *Lebensbaum*, or 'life tree'. A 'normal' or 'healthy' distribution of the generations looks like a healthy, if stylised, conifer, and would – indeed, did – support such a system. Germany's 'life tree' now looks much more like the picture on the right, and by 2030, when 35 per cent of Germans will be over 60, will be even more top-heavy (Figure 6.1, bottom left). If the tree is 'sick', the system falters and eventually collapses. The number of younger people in work cannot support the number of older retired people.

One reason for an ageing population is a decrease in the birth rate. This can be caused by a number of factors. One factor is the many options other than, or as well as, motherhood open to educated women. Another is the growth of welfare provision itself. In terms of the population as a whole, once people no longer need to have children to look after them in old age, because provision is made for this either by the state or through insurance, the number of children born to each woman does gradually fall. Once this has begun to happen, it is difficult to reverse. In Germany recently other factors have caused a sharp drop in the birth rate, particularly in East Germany. This was due partly to uncertainty about the future in general, partly to the collapse of the system of child care and allowances. Part of the fall may also be due to individual women simply

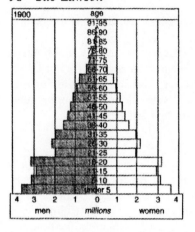
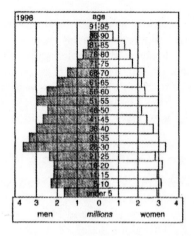
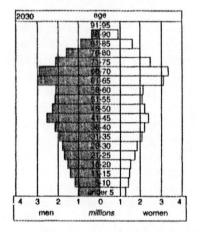

Figure 6.1 Life tree (*Lebensbaum*) showing the distribution of the generations.
Source: Statistiches Bundesamt

postponing a family. One of the effects of the East German child care system was that women had their children relatively young, since they did not have to wait while they established themselves in a career to return to afterwards.

Germany is, of course, not alone here. Most developed countries, including Britain and the USA, have an ageing population and a low birth rate; the 'sick tree' demography is no longer abnormal. The problem is what to do about it. Looking briefly at Britain might help to clarify things here. Most pension schemes in Britain are funded;

the contributions paid while earning are invested, and, in most cases, earn interest. On retirement, the pension is paid out of these funds. State pension rates in Britain have been linked since 1970 to prices rather than to earnings. That portion of the pension which depends on actual earnings is paid for by the occupational or private pension scheme, which is normally funded.[12] Even so, Britain is looking at ways of economising on its pensions bills.

In Germany, pensions are not normally funded. They are paid from current contributions, not out of money invested in pension schemes in the past. In other words, the contributions paid do not go into consolidated funds, but directly to the older generation who have retired. When you retire, your pension is paid directly by those still in work. Thus each working generation is 'taxed' to pay directly the pensions of the previous ones. Since 1957, German pension rates have been linked to earnings rather than to prices.[13]

This system is clearly based on having a 'healthy' life tree. Once there are many more retired people than workers, either those in work must pay higher contributions, or the retired be content with less. Otherwise the cost will grow until it becomes unmanageable.[14] But the healthy conifer is not the only factor. You need to ask not only how many younger people versus how many older people there are, but also how many people in work have to support how many people not in work. In other words, unemployment is an important factor in the equation. Germany's unemployment figure passed the 4.5 million mark[15] at the beginning of 1997 (see Chapter 5), and the future outlook on the employment front is not rosy.

THE GLOBAL ECONOMY

Pensions policy in Germany was based on the assumption that people would be employed lifelong to build up sufficient contributions to finance a relatively short period of retirement. We have already seen what impact an ageing population has had on this assumption. However, the *Generationenvertrag* has proved difficult to keep to in other ways as well. National economies are losing ground to multinational firms, who no longer need to invest in high-cost countries with comprehensive welfare states. German multinational firms are therefore no longer confined to investing and working in their own country. They are not yet deserting Germany in droves. They are, however, choosing foreign locations for new investment (see Chapter 5). Electronic technology applied to production methods, communications and banking means that Siemens (for example) can manufacture software in Bangalore, lightbulbs in South and Latin America, and silicon chips in the north-east of England. The products and advertisements of Mercedes Benz and Siemens no longer say 'made in Germany' but 'made by Mercedes Benz', 'made by Siemens' (*Der Spiegel* 39/1996: 80) (see Chapter 5).

Last time trade 'went global', during the colonial period and at the turn of the nineteenth century, the colonies were seen merely as a source of raw materials rather than as a market to sell to, and certainly not as a location for the manufacture of sophisticated technological products. Globalisation was driven by transport – railways, shipping – and telegraphy. Nowadays it is production which has 'gone global'. Western economies and welfare states, Germany again among them, must therefore compete against cheap-labour countries in Eastern Europe and non-welfare states in Asia. The Single European Market is also beginning to have a psychological effect as German investors begin to see the EU, rather than simply Germany, as their home market. Even within the EU there are higher-cost and lower-cost countries.

As a high-cost welfare state, Germany thus finds itself in a cleft stick. If (in order to avoid paying German social costs for their employees) German companies now manufacture in countries where these costs are lower, Germany then suffers a net loss of jobs. It has been estimated that since 1991 around 1.2 million such potential jobs have been 'exported'. Manufacturing outside Germany not only does nothing to bring down German unemployment, which in January 1997 reached its highest level since the Second World War,[16] it also removes from the country the wages which could be taxed to provide benefits or create jobs.

How much longer can Germany afford its present level of social provision? What alternatives exist?

MAINTAINING THE STATUS QUO

Is leaving the system as it is an option? Will, for instance, the recent immigrants of foreign and of German origin, the *Ausländer* and *Aussiedler*, help to correct the demographic imbalance and to provide employment? The former tend to have larger families than Germans, and the latter have brought in able and qualified potential workers and employers to Germany. However, this argument only stands up if these people do actually get jobs (Rink 1994: 90). They are only potential workers; unless and until they find jobs, they will not contribute to the welfare state.

Adjusting the present system

The pragmatic course is to make the social state less expensive: cut rates and make savings as and where possible. For instance, since 1992 pensions have risen with average *net* incomes rather than with average *gross* incomes, as part of the austerity measures (*Sparpaket*). Another example of this approach is the savings package introduced during 1996 (Harenberg 1996: 182). This included a cut in sick pay (*Lohnfortzahlung*) from 100 per cent to 80 per cent of average earnings, and arrangements were set in train to raise the age at which unemployed men can receive a retirement pension in stages from age 60 to 63, and thence to 65. Women's pension age will be raised in monthly stages from the year 2000. The maximum length of a spa visit (*Kur*) was cut from four to three weeks, and the minimum interval between such visits increased from three to four years.

There is a danger that such measures will appear opportunistic rather than pragmatic, and they were bitterly opposed by the SPD (*Das Parlament* 1996). In the event, however, some of the austerity measures proved relatively acceptable. According to a *Spiegel* survey (*Der Spiegel* 18/1996: 72–73) most of the general population were in favour of tightening up the sick pay system. Almost one-third (in the old GDR, 11 per cent) knew colleagues who abused it (*krankfeiern*).

Der Spiegel also commented later that year on Helmut Kohl's continued popularity despite what might have proved very unpopular suggestions for reform, and suggested that the insecurity consequent on rising unemployment meant that the population were more prepared to make sacrifices to keep their jobs (*Der Spiegel* 30/1996: 24).

Even with the reforms mentioned above it remains difficult to balance the budget. Every proposal means raising taxes or contributions somewhere (*Der Spiegel* 30/1996: 22–24). For example, the pressure on the pension budget would be somewhat relieved by interpreting *Rentenversicherung* more narrowly, and transferring costs such as provision for the East to general taxation. This would mean, however, that an extra DM 580 million or so would have to be found from either direct or indirect taxation – and Kohl's government intends lowering direct taxes. The unemployed pay no direct tax anyway. They do, however, mean higher social costs, which in turn mean higher taxation or wage costs, which drive companies who can do so to invest outside Germany, resulting in more unemployment (*Der Spiegel* 16/1995: 101). Thus the system as a whole may not function much longer, and alternative methods of provision have to be found.

More radical reform

Two possibilities for the future are being discussed. One model envisages a two-tier system – a basic rate of provision financed by the state, and an additional enhanced rate financed through private arrangements made by individuals (*Der Spiegel* 16/1995: 102).[17] Taxes would have to rise to pay for the basic rate, but employer contributions would fall, so that wage costs would be reduced.

The principles of the welfare state mean ensuring that all citizens and their families have at least a basis for livelihood and access to health services and education so that they can live independently and responsibly (*eigenverantwortliche Lebensgestaltung*). The costs of this, however, must be kept within bounds, which probably means some form of private provision will have to be introduced. In the short term this may be politically difficult, since the present working generation will have to pay both higher taxes *and* higher contributions. The long-term danger here is that the introduction of any privately financed element may break the consensus on which the welfare state has relied for so long. Without this general agreement on the principle of solidarity the welfare state may disappear altogether (*Der Spiegel* 7/1996: 36). Therefore the other model assumes that the present system cannot be maintained, and that people must be encouraged to make their own arrangements as soon as possible. The choice will not be an easy one.

NOTES

1 One hundred per cent coverage is not regarded as possible; 90 per cent is therefore very high.
2 The GDR lacked some human rights (freedom of movement, freedom of speech) but had all these four social rights.
3 German *Mitbestimmung* (participation in decision-making) is one manifestation of the right to negotiate working conditions.
4 Data from 1996. The rates quoted are of course always subject to change, and are tending to decrease.
5 Rates for 1996 were DM 400 to DM 1,300 per month, and DM 2,500 to DM 3,300 per month for hospital treatment. DM 5,000 could be granted towards conversion of accommodation for disabled use.
6 For example, compensation for victims of Nazism.
7 The EU average was 27.8 per cent.
8 See also Chapter 5. UK employees pay about 30 per cent of earnings.
9 The average working week in the GDR was 43.75 hours, reduced to 40 for mothers with three or more children under 16 at home.
10 '*Gleichberechtigung*' for women in the GDR meant the right and the duty to work.

11 This had important social and economic effects. It militated against rationalisation and investment in technology, even where that could have been afforded, since it was important to find people jobs.
12 There are exceptions, e.g. some university teachers' schemes.
13 As a result, pension rates rose between 1957 and 1990 by 650 per cent (*Der Spiegel* 6/1996: 23).
14 One alarmist forecast (*Sunday Times*, 5 November 1996) is 139 per cent of GNP over the next seventy-five years.
15 Or 10 per cent of the workforce. In Eastern Germany the official unemployment rate is 15 per cent, and there is still a great deal of hidden unemployment. Before Unification it was hidden by overmanning; now it is hidden by early retirements, special training schemes and educational courses.
16 The figure was 12.2 per cent of the population.
17 The basic rate would not be dependent on either previous occupation or previous salary, but a flat rate of 40 per cent of the average net income. The enhanced provision would of course vary.

RECOMMENDED READING

Aus Politik und Zeitgeschichte 35/1996. (Supplement (*Beilage*) to the magazine *Das Parlament*.) The whole of this edition is devoted to the problems of a social state and an ageing population. The language is difficult, but the graphics are useful.
Harenberg, B. (1996) *Lexikon der Gegenwart Aktuell '97*, Harenberg Lexikon Verlag Dortmund. A very useful source of brief up-to-date information on a wide variety of topics. It is regularly updated and deals therefore only with developments in the last year. The publication date is always the year before the date in the title.
Kolinsky, E. (1996) 'Women in the new Germany'.
Mangen, S. (1996) 'German Welfare and social citizenship', in Smith, G., Paterson, W. and Padgett, S. (eds) *Developments in German Politics 2*, Basingstoke and London: Macmillan, pp. 250–266.
Rink, S. (1994) A useful introduction in German. Being updated at present, therefore temporarily out of print.

BIBLIOGRAPHY

Anon. (1996) 'Allein der Markt regiert', *Der Spiegel* 39: 80–95.
Anon. (1995) 'Ausbeutung der Jungen', *Der Spiegel* 16: 100–103.
Anon. (1996) 'Der blaue Virus', *Der Spiegel* 18: 72–73.
Anon. (1996) 'Erbittetes Ringen um das "Sparpaket"', *Das Parlament* 46/28.
Anon. (1996) 'Jedes Sicherungssystem wird teuer', *Spiegelgespräch* with Prof. Winfried Schmähl, *Der Spiegel* 6: 25–30.
Anon. (1996) 'Lohnfortzahlung: Desaster in Sicht', *Der Spiegel* 39: 22–24.
Anon. (1996) 'Renten: Bergwacht in Not', *Der Spiegel* 6: 22–24.
Anon. (1996) 'Sozialstaat: Das ist eine klare Kante', *Der Spiegel* 18: 36–38.
Anon. (1996) 'Späne im Kraftfeld', *Der Spiegel* 30: 22–24.

104 *Sue Lawson*

Harenberg, B. (1996) *Lexikon der Gegenwart Aktuell '97*, Harenberg Lexikon Verlag Dortmund.

—— (1994) *Lexikon der Gegenwart Aktuell '95*, Harenberg Lexikon Verlag Dortmund.

Justizministerium der DDR (1987) *Familiengesetzbuch der DDR*, Staatsverlag der DDR.

Kolinsky, E. (1996) 'Women in the new Germany', in Smith, G., Paterson, W. and Padgett, S. (eds) *Developments in German Politics 2*, Basingstoke: Macmillan.

Noack, H.-J. 'Sozialstaat: Der kleine Fels', *Der Spiegel* 7/1996: 34–36.

Rink, S. (1994) *Stichwort Sozialstaat* (Heyne Sachbuch 19/4056), München: Heyne.

Roloff, J. (1996) 'Alternde Gesellschaft in Deutschland', *Aus Politik und Zeitgeschichte*, 23 August, pp. 3–11.

Senatsverwaltung für Soziales Berlin, *Wegweiser für die Sozialhilfe* (regularly updated pamphlet).

7 Education, training and the workplace

Hanna Ostermann and Ute E. Schmidt

In his book on the state of German universities, Peter Glotz refers to Germany as a country of few natural resources, a low birth rate and a costly social security system. He therefore sees the quality of education and research as paramount (Glotz 1996: 23). At the same time employers voice their concern that the education system does not prepare its graduates adequately for the world of work. Article 7 of the German constitution identifies the state as the main organisational and supervisory body of education, with the responsibility of organising and financing the primary, secondary and tertiary sector including further education and parts of vocational training. In this, the *Länder* enjoy cultural sovereignty (*Kulturhoheit*). Within their boundaries they provide most of the funding and decide about types and organisation of schools, curricula, examination procedures, training and appointment of staff (see also Chapter 3). In other aspects there is nation-wide uniformity: for example, the civil servant status of teachers – they are employed by the *Land*, not by individual institutions – or the minimum compulsory school attendance of twelve years, of which the last three can be part time.

Between 1965 and 1976, the education sector experienced a massive expansion (Arbeitsgruppe Bildungsbericht 1994: 653). However, this expansion, coupled with the restructuring of some sectors of the education system, has also created problems which have led to a renewed discussion about aims and organisation of education and its ability to provide the workforce the country requires in order to hold its own in a rapidly changing economic environment. This chapter therefore gives a brief overview of the school system before examining the sectors of vocational training and higher education in detail.

THE SCHOOL SYSTEM

The German school system has three tiers, the *Hauptschule*, the *Realschule*, and the *Gymnasium*, one of which children enter after four years of primary education in the *Grundschule*, where they start at the age of six. They attend the *Hauptschule* for five to six years, and on successful completion receive the *Hauptschulabschluß*, the most basic qualification, which enables pupils to apply for an apprenticeship. At the *Realschule*, the *Realschulabschluß*, originally called *Mittlere Reife*, is awarded after year six. This certificate allows the options of further school education and entry into vocational training for a wider range of jobs. The *Gymnasium*, grammar school or high school, offers the qualification of *Mittlere Reife* after successful completion of year six, and after year eight or nine the *Abitur*, the entry qualification for higher education. All these qualifications can also be gained in the *Gesamtschule*, comprehensive school, which combines all three tiers. It exists in various forms in most *Länder* but is less common than the three-tier system. In theory, this system allows sideways moves for those pupils who have chosen an inappropriate type of school or who decide to gain a higher qualification at a later stage than in the last year in primary school. In practice, there has been little mobility between the different types of school, but opportunities to study for a higher qualification after completing the first one have increased.

Progression is generally based on regular assessment. From year two in any of the three tiers onwards, a student who fails two or more subjects without being able to make up for it with very good marks in others has to repeat the year (*sitzenbleiben*). It is not possible to repeat a year more than once; in case of a second failure on the same level a pupil would be sent to a different (lower) type of school.

Legislation also leaves room for private institutions, which in 1994 comprised 5 per cent of schools. They often have a complementary function, such as special needs or vocational training, but they also include *Gymnasien*. They have to be approved by the minister of education in each state, and are then entitled to supplementary state funding, but this does not automatically exempt parents from fees. Most private schools are run by the Catholic and Protestant churches. Also important, but smaller in number, are *Weltanschauungsschulen*, such as the Waldorf schools, which represent alternative education philosophies.

Since the expansion in education in the 1960s/70s the three-tier system has developed an imbalance, exposing both the *Hauptschule* and the *Gymnasium* as problem areas. As most parents prefer their children to achieve a higher qualification, the numbers at the *Hauptschulen* have dwindled. Attracting almost 70 per cent of a year group, the *Hauptschule* was the most widely attended school in the early 1960s. In the 1990s this figure has decreased to an average of about 30 per cent (Etzold 1996). Some experts explain this with the restructuring of the former *Volksschule* into the *Hauptschule* in the early 1960s. By adopting a more science-based curriculum and employing subject teachers, its profile became more similar to that of the *Realschule*. While this worked for some pupils, those of lower ability struggled with the raised standards, thus creating an increased potential for frustration and violence. Unpopular with parents, pupils and employers, the *Hauptschule* has become a *Restschule*, a collection point for those pupils who were not encouraged to attend or failed at other schools. The proportion of pupils from a socially disadvantaged background is high, and more pupils have learning and/or behavioural difficulties. These problems have resulted in the discussion as to whether the three-tier system should be changed into a two-tier system with the combined *Haupt-/Realschule* and the *Gymnasium*. This system already exists in some of the new *Länder*, and one of the old *Länder*, the Saarland, has decided on the reorganisation of its school system, abolishing the *Hauptschule*. This approach, however, may not solve the problem of under-achievers and may also increase the pressure on the *Gymnasium*.

With the expanding intake of pupils into the *Gymnasium*, the *Abitur* qualification has been criticised for lowering its standards. Passing this examination entitles the student to entry into higher education. In view of complaints about gaps in knowledge and skills the question has been asked, however, whether the *Abitur* really attests the ability of the candidate to proceed to higher education. Reasons for the alleged drop in standards are seen partly in the fact that examinations are not centralised and that demands vary between *Länder*.

Despite differences of opinion, a return to an elitist education system is unlikely. An enforced reduction of the number of pupils taking the *Abitur* could prove counter-productive to Germany's needs, because the international trend is towards more education rather than less. In order to meet the market's demand for well-qualified people, a proportion of 30–40 per cent of students in higher education in any one year group is considered the necessary average for industrialised western societies (*Der Spiegel* 29/1996:

64). While the aim of expanding higher education has been fulfilled in Germany, the result has not been an unqualified success. Similarly, the system of vocational training has been criticised for not keeping pace with the changing demands of the job market. Much of the current debate focuses on the balance of academic and vocational training and how well the education system is facing the challenge of preparing the country's workforce for the future.

VOCATIONAL TRAINING

For school-leavers who prefer a non-academic route when training for a job, the *Duales System* (dual system of qualification/training) provides an alternative to become qualified for the job market via an apprenticeship scheme (*Ausbildung, Lehre*). The minimum entry requirement is the school-leaving certificate awarded by the *Hauptschule*. As the name indicates, training in the *Duales System* consists of two components: practical instruction in a trade or industrial company, a workshop or a public-sector firm on the one hand and theoretical training in a *Berufsschule* (vocational school) on the other. After an apprenticeship that typically lasts between two and a half and three and a half years, trainees are awarded a certificate.

The tradition of vocational training in Germany dates back a long time. In its hierarchical structure of apprentice–journeyman–master craftsman (*Lehrling–Geselle–Meister*), as it still exists in industry and the trades, it evolved from the apprenticeship schemes of the medieval guilds. Each profession would set its own guidelines for length and content of training. In the late nineteenth century, supplementary theoretical instruction was introduced. However, professional and regional variations and discrepancies persisted until 1969 when a specific law, the *Berufsbildungsgesetz*, was passed in order to regulate professional training for all professional groups, to co-ordinate the responsibilities of all bodies involved and to set nation-wide standards.

The *Duales System* combines the benefits of education with those of a job: apprentices are paid wages or a salary while on training. Remuneration during the apprenticeship varies according to the chosen occupation and the level of expertise. Also, trainer and trainee sign an *Ausbildungsvertrag*, a contract that specifies the rights and duties of both sides, before training commences. On-the-job training is linked with periods of attendance at the regional *Berufsschule* (vocational school), but as more time is spent at the workplace than at college it is the practical side that receives the main emphasis.

There is no automatic right to a *Lehrstelle* (training place); aspiring apprentices may have to go through a tough application process if their chosen career is in demand. There are currently 373 occupations registered with the Bundesinstitut für Berufsbildung, the overseeing body for vocational training in Germany. Based on the assumption that every sector of the economy needs qualified employees, training opportunities span different areas, and even shop-assistants, filling-station attendants and professional drivers can train under this scheme. As new technologies open new fields of employment, the Bundesinstitut publishes a list of registered jobs and their job descriptions every year.

The other component of the scheme is theoretical instruction at the regional vocational schools (*Berufsschulen*). Depending on the local arrangements, either apprentices spend up to two days per week at college or the classes take place in blocks of weeks (*Blockunterricht*). Year groups for each occupation are taught in job-specific classes, so that the theoretical background information can be adapted to their needs. The schools' syllabus comprises three areas: practical vocational instruction relevant to the job (for instance, typing, laboratory exercises), theoretical background information (such as mathematics, accounting, drawing) and further education in general subjects such as German, Sport, Politics, and RE. After compulsory full-time school attendance, part-time attendance at a vocational school is obligatory until the eighteenth birthday or until training for a job has been completed. In the event of school-leavers not finding a training place, it is possible to complete school attendance by spending a year at a vocational school full-time (*Berufsvorbereitungsjahr*). Students may attain their *Hauptschulabschluß* in this time, if they left school without it.

The achievements in the theoretical and practical field are assessed in two examinations at the end of the training period: the final exam at the college and the examination before the professional body (*Kammer*). The successful trainee is awarded a certificate: trainees in industry receive the title *FacharbeiterIn* (skilled worker), those who have qualified in an administrative environment become *Fachangestellte* (qualified clerk), whereas apprentices in the traditional trades are awarded a *Gesellenbrief* (journeyman's certificate). Particularly in the areas of industry and the trades, there is – after sufficient work experience – the opportunity of attending courses to obtain a master craftsman's certificate (*Meisterbrief*).

The organisational structure of this educational route gives more evidence of its dual nature, as the private and the public sectors are responsible for different parts of the operation. Whereas the ministers of education of the Federation and the *Länder* set and control the framework and provide the finance for school education, on the vocational side the professional organisations, the Chambers (*Kammern*), trade unions and employer organisations have a more direct input into the scheme. Although it is the task of the relevant federal minister to approve new training occupations (*anerkannte Ausbildungsberufe*), it is the chambers that vet firms or companies as training agencies[1] and staff the examination committees for the qualifying examinations. The Bundesinstitut für Berufsbildung (Federal Institute for Vocational Training), in which all groups are represented, coordinates the day-to-day running of the nation-wide scheme.

Full-time vocational colleges

One can also qualify for a job by attending a full-time vocational college (*Berufsfachschule*). Offering courses with a mixture of general and vocational subjects, these institutions were originally introduced in the 1980s, when there were not enough training opportunities in the private sector. As a rule, they were for registered training occupations (*anerkannte Ausbildungsberufe*) in fields such as business, commerce, domestic science or technical assistance in the medical field (*kaufmännische, hauswirtschaftliche Berufe oder medizinisch-technische Assistenten*) as qualifications in these areas can normally not be obtained in the *Duales System*. Generally, a *Hauptschulabschluß* is the minimum entry qualification. The ministry of education of each *Land* supervises all of these colleges, some of which are private.[2]

The *Duales System* – to be continued?

Despite the fact that the German vocational training scheme is widely praised abroad, the voices inside Germany calling for change and/or reform are growing ever louder. The problematic issues are:

● an imbalance of training places and applicants;
● the employers' attitude to the problem;
● the vocational colleges' role;
● the organisational structure of the system.

A lack of training places seems to be the most prevalent issue. At the beginning of 1993 the total figures for supply and demand of training places (*Lehrstellen*) in Germany indicated an excess of 202,995 training vacancies (Harenberg 1996: 235), and critics voiced their concern about the training scheme's seeming lack of attractiveness for school-leavers. However, a closer look at more recent figures reveals that the focus of the problem has shifted. Since 1993 about 100,000 training places have been cut. Employers named lack of demand for skilled workers in the short term and high cost of the training scheme as reasons for the cuts. Since Unification there has been a lack of places in the eastern part of the country, whereas vacancies outnumber applicants in some areas of the west.[3] While the eastern dearth of training facilities is due to the fact that there are simply not enough enterprises to offer jobs, let alone training facilities, only some areas like northern Germany, the Ruhr and Berlin suffer the same fate in the west. In Baden-Württemberg, where the number of training vacancies (16 per cent) equals the percentage of unsuccessful applicants (16.1 per cent) (Harenberg 1995: 262), the problem is more of a structural nature. In this case the places on offer did not correspond with the applicants' chosen careers. Research has shown that school-leavers opting for an apprenticeship do so mainly because they want a secure job (Braun 1996). Against a background of job cuts in the manufacturing sector, however, many school-leavers think twice before sending off an application for a blue-collar job (*Der Spiegel* 39/1995: 130). Consequently, some jobs like those in the area of technologies of the future are over-subscribed whereas other branches of the economy cannot fill their vacancies.

With an increase in school-leavers for September 1995 and a lack of skilled workforce forecast for the year 2005, Chancellor Kohl appealed to all sectors of the economy to provide 10 per cent more training places. Trade unions and members of the SPD simultaneously put forward two more suggestions. They wanted to make it obligatory for employers to train new staff (*Ausbildungspflicht*) – and link to that the right of school-leavers to be trained (*Ausbildungsrecht*). As these provisions would be very expensive, a special levy, the so-called *Ausbildungsabgabe*, was suggested. This proposal works on the assumption that every firm can offer an apprenticeship scheme. The unions suggest that firms that do not provide training would have to pay a duty depending on their size and potential training capacity. The proceeds of this would finance *überbetriebliche Ausbildungsstätten* (training facilities not at company level).

The employers rejected this plan. In recent years they have come to see the *Duales System* as a burden rather than a boon. Complaints about high cost for little return are commonplace. Before monetary pressures restricted firms financially, they were happy to take on contingents of trainees that exceeded their own demand, thereby providing the market with a trained workforce. Now, however, faced with the need to remain competitive, tens of thousands of jobs have been cut, which has affected training more than any other area. According to *Der Spiegel* (39/1995: 130) big firms like Siemens reduced their intake of apprentices by two-thirds, whereas other firms – small and medium-size companies in particular – have abandoned training altogether.

At its best, training new staff can have many positive side-effects for an employer. Assuming that training communicates the latest know-how and technology, it can be a vital source of innovation, and firms can combine research and development with grooming new staff. The actual cost of training, however, is not the only factor in the decision to miss out on that source of innovation in the long run. Employer criticism is directed at three main points: time spent in the *Berufsschule*, the complicated regulations for training and the high wage level for apprentices. As mentioned before, apprentices have to attend school, which means that they spend almost half of their working time separated from the workplace. Considering the length of training and the restrictions on working hours for younger apprentices, employers hardly get their wages' worth and it is virtually impossible to integrate an apprentice into the working process in a meaningful way (*Der Spiegel*, 33/1996: 68).

Employers do not stand alone in their criticism. Experts have discussed the function of the *Berufsschule* (vocational school) for a long time (Geissler and Harney 1992). Introduced as a continuation of the mainstream school, it was to supply the more general element in the training scheme by combining general education with instruction relevant to the job. However, in an age when jobs are becoming more specialised, and *Ausbildungsberufe* provide too general a basis for the jobs people will eventually take up, an even more general level of instruction is not only out of date but also a luxury that does not make sense. Quite often large companies set up their own *Lehrwerkstätten* (training workshops) to mould new staff according to their needs. Apprentices receive tailor-made training that introduces them to relevant techniques and processes, backed up by the latest theoretical know-how (Schmidt 1994). An increasing number of smaller firms send their trainees to *überbetriebliche Ausbildungsstätten* in order to provide more balanced training than they would be able to provide themselves. Following another trend, trainees in some professions spend the first and/or second year of their training in a full-time vocational college (*Berufsfachschule*) or in fact complete their whole course in a college (*Berufsvollzeitschule*). As the places of learning diversify, the function of the *Berufsschule* is undermined. The value of its leaving certificate is negligible, because it does not have any impact on the process or the final result of the training. The *Berufsschule* is now being pushed to the periphery for various reasons: there is a lack of staff, the technology and rooms used for teaching are not up-to-date and, worst of all, the teaching methods used have been described as passive and irrelevant to the practice of the job. As co-operation between teachers and trainers in the firms is left to personal initiative, a general improvement is not in sight.

The reasons for this are seen in the organisational structure of the system. The *Berufsschulen* in their present form are an add-on feature without a formal body of representation in the committees that make the decisions. Hence the suggestion that they involve their representatives more by creating local educational networks whose functions could extend into areas like further vocational training (*Weiterbildung*), general adult education or even into mainstream schools (Geissler and Harney 1992). Furthermore, it is argued, if both vocational schools and firms were involved in designing the curriculum, the result would not be determined by a layperson's assumptions, but could be based on a needs analysis for the firms in one particular area. By changing the legal structure of the *Duales System* – i.e. by allowing experts who are not civil servants to teach in a state school – theoretical background information could be made available in a modular system in which both state-employed teachers and professionals working in a particular field could explore more innovative ways of teaching.

Ultimately, however, the whole system needs reforming in order to make the *Duales System* more flexible and attractive. Since the 1970s an imbalance between academic and vocational learning has developed. In 1990 the news that there were more students (1.5 million) than apprentices (1.4 million) made headlines. Although this news story slightly misrepresents the facts,[4] it bears testimony to a trend that has been described as *Bildungsinflation* (educational inflation). With the *Mittlere Reife* and the *Abitur* becoming increasingly common, many future employers are hesitant to train school-leavers with 'only' a *Hauptschulabschluß*. Many attractive jobs, particularly those involving technologies of the future, are only open to those with higher qualifications. On the other hand, a number of *Abiturienten* are choosing a two-level education: they train in the *Duales System* first, and then go on to university, thereby depleting the training firms of highly skilled staff.

One solution could be to improve the profile of the *Hauptschule*. Other models have started to offer *Abiturienten* an option to continue their training in the *Duales System* on a higher level, thus setting them on an equal footing with graduates of polytechnic business courses who enter a firm on a trainee basis (Schumann 1994: 14–16). A model like this could be the way forward, because, unlike in Great Britain, where some higher education institutions will consider relevant job experience as an entry qualification to certain courses, this is still not common practice in Germany. The inference that vocational training is of less value than a university degree has filtered through to school-leavers, as the problems in the university sector show. If everybody receiving a *Facharbeiterbrief* were awarded the *Fachhochschulreife* (entry qualification for *Fachhochschule*) at the same time, training schemes would become more attractive, more pupils would choose this route as opposed to the *Gymnasium*, and the profile of a whole education sector could be raised. These changes would have to go hand in hand with the provision of equal grants (BAföG) for pupils, students and *Meister* trainees.

HIGHER EDUCATION

There are over 300 higher education institutions in Germany including universities, art colleges and *Fachhochschulen*, of which all but a few are state-run. The *Länder* provide up to 90 per cent of their resources and control their staffing levels. But even though the *Länder* are the trustees of higher education institutions, their author-ity is not as far-reaching as in the primary and secondary education sector. Science and research, provision of grants for education and the financing of extension and building of universities are matters for the *Bund*, the central government. An important task for the *Bund* is also the setting of a general framework for higher education policy, the *Hochschulrahmengesetz*, which is binding for the *Länder* (Arbeits-gruppe Bildungsbericht 1994: 634).

Since the *Öffnungsbeschluß*, the opening of higher education, in 1977 at the end of the expansion period in education in the 1960s/70s, the number of students has nearly doubled. At the same time, funding for universities has not risen in line with the increase in student numbers. Even federal and *Länder* ministers for education and finance have calculated that higher education institutions now have an annual shortfall of a minimum of 6 billion marks (*Bundestag*

Report 1996: 6). In the winter semester 1995/96, 1.86 million students had to share 970,000 places (Harenberg 1996: 187). Some universities are catering for between 30,000 to 60,000 students. Between 1977 and 1992 the number of first-year students in West Germany rose by 73 per cent, whereas the number of places increased by only 11 per cent and the number of academic staff by just 6 per cent (Arbeitsgruppe Bildungsbericht 1994: 679). The ideal of opening up higher education has been realised, but at the same time it has been said that the increase in student numbers without adequate funding for universities has also resulted in a decrease in the quality and the value of a university education.

The large majority of students are enrolled at traditional universities, including colleges of education (1,405,378 students in the winter semester 1994/95). The second most important providers of higher education are *Fachhochschulen* (400,656 students – Harenberg 1995: 213). They were established in the late 1960s to introduce an element of training and vocational orientation often involving practical experience into higher education. Many *Fachhochschulen* concentrate on few subjects or subject areas and are therefore smaller than traditional universities. Because of the high number of students, applicants cannot always choose the institution they want to attend or have free access to the subject they want to study. For some very popular subjects, and some which depend on laboratory places, limited access, the *Numerus Clausus* (NC), has had to be introduced. A central office, the Zentralstelle für die Vergabe von Studienplätzen (ZVS), deals with admissions for all institutions. Places for NC subjects are allocated on the basis of – among other criteria – *Abitur* results and waiting time. Admission to non-NC subjects is generally automatic, but places are allocated according to the distribution of student numbers in these subjects in the individual institutions.

Higher education institutions, unlike schools, enjoy academic autonomy – with the exception of academic appointments – which has its roots in Wilhelm von Humboldt's (1767–1835) ideal of independence in research, teaching and learning for an academic elite, and the unity of research and teaching. This allows university teachers freedom in the choice of content and methodology in their research and in the courses they offer. For students, freedom in learning means that they have a degree of choice as to how they organise and structure their degree course (Arbeitsgruppe Bildungsbericht 1994: 121).

For all degree courses the number of semesters is specified (*Regelstudienzeit*), but in many institutions, especially the traditional universities, these specifications are treated as a guideline only and are not strictly enforced. The curriculum of a degree course generally offers students a core programme complemented normally by quite a wide range of options for which the type (seminar or lecture etc.), minimum number, and possibly the subject areas are prescribed. Students are therefore free to follow their own interests within a given framework. German undergraduate courses are not organised on the basis of yearly progression. Within the prescribed framework the decision is often left to the students themselves in what semester to take particular seminars or lectures. As a result there are students of different levels in the same class and younger students can benefit from the experience of the more advanced ones. This is particularly relevant because a tutoring and guidance system, as it is known in British or American universities, does not exist in Germany. In many cases students can also decide when to register for final examinations and which examiner to choose. This has led to a very loose structure of university courses – particularly in the Arts and the Social Sciences, less so in the Sciences – which differ widely from institution to institution. It has also contributed to two of the major problems in German higher education: the length of time students need to graduate and the overcrowding of universities. At the *Fachhochschulen* the situation is slightly different. Their courses are shorter and more structured but they are also filled to capacity.

Higher education in the state sector in Germany is free; tuition fees were abolished in the early 1970s. The cost of subsistence, however, is not covered, and the large majority of students are forced to earn money, in term time as well as during the holiday periods. Financial support from the state is available depending on parental income, the number of siblings and the student's own income. In 1994, 28 per cent of West German students and 88 per cent of East German students received state subsidies (Gruber 1994: 41). BAföG (named after the law determining state subsidies for pupils and students, *Bundesausbildungsförderungsgesetz*) is paid over a limited period of time, 50 per cent in the form of a grant, the other half as an interest-free loan repayable, depending on income, over a maximum period of twenty years. Since 1996, students who do not graduate within the specified time limit are only eligible for 100 per cent loans at market rates for the extra semesters they need.

In the 1990s the number of first-year students dropped slightly, by 2.8 per cent between 1993/94 and 1994/95. Reasons for this decrease are costs and poorer job prospects for graduates (Harenberg 1995: 214). In spite of this recent fall in numbers of first-year students, overcrowding has reached crisis point. As well as being a cause of current difficulties, it is also a symptom of inherent structural problems. Concern focuses on four main aspects:

- the staff–student ratio and the resulting quality of tuition and supervision;
- the average length of degree courses and course structures;
- the content of courses and demanding examination requirements;
- the reputation of German higher education abroad.

Overcrowding has led to a high student-to-staff ratio in West Germany, which means little personal contact between students and staff and often inadequate supervision of students. This has resulted – it is claimed – in the general decline of the quality of tuition. A survey among students and lecturers conducted for the magazine *Der Spiegel* in 1993 tried to establish a ranking of universities in Germany. Results for West Germany showed that the picture of overcrowded and chaotic mass institutions which has regularly been portrayed in recent years is not true across the board. But they indicate a strong link between the size of the institution and the degree to which students are content with the tuition they receive. This includes adequate access to books and equipment in their subject area. According to this survey criticism focuses particularly on the large traditional universities (*Spiegel Spezial* 1993: 23).

In 1993 the magazine *Focus* also conducted a study to establish a ranking of German universities based on the publication records of the institutions (Jurtschitsch and Gottschling 1993) which showed a rather different result. In this study the large traditional universities of Berlin (FU Berlin, 54,316 students), Munich (60,106 students) and Bonn (36,866 students)[5] were at the top of the list. However, the assumption that a good research record also means quality in tuition – as perceived by students – is not confirmed by the *Der Spiegel* findings. The top research universities rank eleventh, thirty-sixth and last, respectively, as far as the students' evaluation of tuition is concerned. The Humboldt ideal of unity of research and teaching does not seem to have proved itself in modern mass universities.

Overcrowding has also contributed to the increased length of university courses: thirteen to fourteen semesters on average. Students may have to wait for a semester or more before there is a place for them in a seminar they wish to or have to attend. German graduates, on average 28 years of age, are the oldest world-wide. National service or equivalent for the male population and the need for some pupils to repeat a year at school means that German first-year students are generally between 18 and 21 years old. Flexible course structures and the necessity to earn money during term time are other reasons for the long period spent at university.

Overcrowding and a poor student–staff ratio may also help to explain the high drop-out rate. Twenty-seven per cent of students leave without a qualification, and the figure is even as high as 37 per cent in the Arts, Economics and Business Studies (Groothuis 1994: 9). According to a survey carried out in 1993/94 by the Hochschul-Information-System, Hanover, other reasons why students leave university prematurely are non-identification with content and aim of the course, the offer of a job, or poor job prospects in that field as well as financial problems and the feeling of inadequacy (Kempcke 1996: 102).

There seems to be a growing consensus that these problems can be solved only by re-examining how higher education is provided, that only a reform of the system itself can improve the situation. Politicians and academics seem to agree that the majority of students take a degree in order to gain a qualification for a professional career rather than to become academics. A highly specialised and often very theoretically orientated university course does not always provide the necessary preparation for the world of work. It has therefore been suggested that study programmes consisting of a foundation course of three to four years and a postgraduate course should be introduced. The foundation course is intended for the majority of students. It would lead to a qualification that is recognised on the job market and is also an entry qualification for those, a minority, who want to take a postgraduate course and concentrate on academic research, comparable to the British and American Bachelor and Master degrees. Stipulating a maximum number of years for a foundation course would require a clearly structured, prescriptive course programme. This has been criticised as *Verschulung* of universities – making them more like schools by taking away the flexibility that students have been used to – but it would reduce the time wasted by students because of loose course organisation.

Enabling students to concentrate on their studies full time also depends on reforming the grant system so that more students would qualify for financial support. One step in the opposite direction was the proposal to reintroduce tuition fees per semester in order to solve the funding problem of higher education institutions. Tuition fees, it is argued, would also weed out those who are not wholly committed and generally encourage students to graduate within the suggested time limit. The *Hochschulrahmengesetz* (framework legislation for higher education) (see Chapter 3, p. 33) leaves the decision about tuition fees to the individual *Länder*. For the time being this proposal has found little positive response. Tuition fees would constitute social selection unless coupled with a thorough reform of the BAföG system. Present conditions at universities can also make it difficult for students to complete their studies in less time.

The length of degree courses and the corresponding age of graduates is only one aspect influencing students' chances of finding employment after graduation. With increasing numbers of graduates, a university degree has ceased to be a guarantee of finding work. Jobs have been cut in all areas of life – in public services, the traditional destination for graduates, as well as in industry, which has become another very important area of work. Even though employment among graduates is still higher than among groups with lower qualifications, economic recession has had its effect on them as well. Another question is whether the kind of employment they find is appropriate to their qualifications. According to two studies by the Technical University Berlin, as reported in *Handelsblatt* (1996), 25.3 per cent of those students who graduated after 1990 are either unemployed or overqualified for the work they carry out in comparison with 17.9 per cent of those graduating before 1990. Employment prospects vary according to subject area. Hardest hit are the arts (36.8 per cent of university arts graduates), the social sciences and economics/business studies (30 per cent), and engineering and agronomy (25 per cent). There are no problems in mathematics and the sciences. Figures for *Fachhochschule* graduates are: 25 per cent in non-technical subjects compared with only 3 per cent in technical subjects. According to the Institut der Wirtschaft in Cologne only 25 per cent of graduates working in the private sector were carrying out work that required an academic education (Groothuis 1994: 9). This not only suggests that the degree course may have been a wasted investment in effort, time and money, it also has serious implications for those with lower qualifications who without competition from graduates would have been the obvious recruits for those jobs.

This situation raises the question as to whether either higher education produces more graduates than are needed or the education offered by universities produces graduates who are not easily employable. Many graduates lack practical experience. The *Absolventenreport 93*, a yearly graduate survey, stated that up to 75 per cent of graduates in economics, business studies, sciences and computer studies felt inadequately prepared for the world of work (Roth 1993: 30). Specialist knowledge and excellent examination results alone are no longer sufficient for finding appropriate employment. Employers are increasingly looking for practical experience, creativity, flexibility and social skills, including the ability to work in teams. In a global economy larger firms in particular are also interested in foreign languages and international experience as welcome extra qualifications – but study periods or work placements abroad are not compulsory even on modern language degree courses.

The suggested reorganisation of university courses into undergraduate (foundation) courses and postgraduate courses would also have to address the question of course content. University education has traditionally been understood as education in the broadest sense, without the element of training. It has been pointed out by politicians, employers and also academics that universities have a service obligation to society. Independence in teaching and research cannot be carried out in a vacuum. The question is where to draw the line between academic freedom and the needs of society or the market. The number of places and the range of subjects in the *Fachhochschulen* are scheduled to expand. It has been suggested that more interdisciplinary courses in higher education should be considered and also that greater emphasis should be placed on non-academic skills such as social competence, *Schlüsselqualifikationen* (key qualifications), as Jürgen Rüttgers, Secretary of State for Education, Science, Research and Technology, calls them (Rüttgers 1996).

Lack of international orientation in universities is another area of concern. Internationally recognised degrees such as Bachelor are not offered in Germany. This shortcoming, together with the well publicised problems of German universities, seems to have deterred students from other countries from coming to Germany, especially students from the industrially powerful or potentially powerful states of the Pacific Rim who prefer to complete their education in the USA or in Great Britain. For an economy that is dependent on exports, this means a wasted opportunity to open doors in potential export markets and reinforce existing contacts. Compared with Great Britain, for example, where universities actively try to recruit students from abroad and where many degree courses have placements in other countries built into the curriculum, Germany seems to have missed the boat. On the other hand it may be a little unfair to blame just the tertiary sector. The language barrier – English is after all the world language – as well as acts of hostility towards foreigners and changes to the immigration and asylum laws may also have something to do with the low proportion of only 4 per cent of students from other countries in German higher education (Peter 1996: 30–9).

Some *Fachhochschulen* seem to be ahead of universities in the area of internationalisation, offering programmes which include a study period or work placement abroad or acting as partner institutions for international degrees. In order to increase internationalisation the Federal government and the *Länder* have made money available for the introduction of bilingual international degrees as part of a programme for improvements in higher education, the Sonderprogramm III for the years 1996–2000.

Suggested reforms described so far have addressed the content and delivery of courses. Other proposals concern administrative and managerial changes. Universities are supposed to have more autonomy not only in academic but also in financial matters so that the institutions can decide for themselves how to spend the money allocated to them. At the same time it has been suggested that institutions should be exposed to market forces. This includes quality controls for universities and teaching staff and the abolition of automatic tenure and civil servant status for professors/lecturers. Data which allow students to compare universities and make an informed choice do not exist. Quality control mechanisms, it is claimed, would provide these data with a view to improving the universities' performance through competition for students. At present, universities cannot select their students, but new selection procedures are being discussed.

To conclude, suggestions for reforming the education system have been discussed for many years but few measures have been put into practice. This is particularly true for vocational training and higher education, partly due to opposing political and academic views. While nobody disputes the importance of education for the country's economic future, the question has been raised, for example, to what extent economic needs should define academic freedom. It must also be remembered that, in spite of its shortcomings, the system as it exists has also provided many benefits for all groups involved. Changes are a matter for each individual *Land* governed by different political parties, and developments so far, if they have happened at all, have been slow and varied.

NOTES

1 One of the prerequisites is that the trainers are qualified as master craftsmen/women or have similar qualifications.
2 In 1991 26 per cent of all full-time vocational colleges in West Germany were private (*Arbeitsgruppe Bildungsbericht* 1994: 588).
3 Latest figures from the Bundesanstalt für Arbeit indicate that in 1994/95

there were 478,383 applicants and 512,811 vacancies in the West, but 191,692 applicants for only 120,129 places in the East.
4 These figures were based on the number of registered *Ausbildungsverträge* of that year. However, as Braun (1996) points out, this view was based on a misconception. Apart from not comparing like with like (on average, students spend twice the amount of time being educated as apprentices) four factors can lower the number of registered *Ausbildungsverträge* for one year: a discrepancy between the jobs school-leavers choose and the jobs on offer, demographic trends, the economic climate and its effect on companies, recruitment practice of different companies.
5 Figures for winter semester 1994/95 (Harenberg Lexikon 1995: 213).

RECOMMENDED READING

Arbeitsgruppe Bildungsbericht am Max-Planck-Institut für Bildungs-forschung (1994).

BIBLIOGRAPHY

Anon. (1996) 'Quo vadis universitas?', *Bundestag Report* 7–8: 4–11.
—— (1996) 'Schlechter Start für Studierte', *Handelsblatt* 9(7).
—— (1993) 'Ein heilsamer Schock', *Spiegel Spezial 'Welche Uni ist die beste?'*, 3: 14–29.
—— (1995) 'Das stille Sterben', *Der Spiegel* 39: 126–130.
—— (1996) 'Apathie im Hörsaal', *Der Spiegel* 29: 53–64
—— (1996) 'Enttäuscht aufgegeben', *Der Spiegel* 33: 68–69.
Arbeitsgruppe Bildungsbericht am Max-Planck-Institut für Bildungs-forschung (1994) *Das Bildungswesen der Bundesrepublik Deutschland – Strukturen und Entwicklungen im Überblick*, Reinbek: Rowohlt.
Braun, W. (1996) 'Duales System im Auf und Ab', *Süddeutsche Zeitung*, 14.2.
Etzold, S. (1996) 'Die Hauptschule. Ein Nachruf', *Die Zeit* 2.2.
Geissler, K. and Harney, K. (1992) 'Man macht sich Sorgen um die Berufsschule: Zur Krise einer Institution des "dualen Systems"', *Frankfurter Rundschau* 3.12.
Glotz, P. (1996) *Im Kern verrottet? Fünf vor zwölf an Deutschlands Universitäten*, Stuttgart: Deutsche Verlags-Anstalt.
Groothuis, U. (1994) 'Zum Leben zu wenig', *Wirtschaftswoche-Sonderheft Beruf und Studium*, 1: 8–9.
Gruber, C. (1994) 'Rabatt für Überflieger', *Wirtschaftswoche-Sonderheft Beruf und Studium* 1: 40–41
Harenberg, B. (ed.) (1995) *Harenberg Lexikon der Gegenwart: Aktuell '96*, Dortmund: Harenberg Lexikon Verlag.
—— (ed.) (1996) *Harenberg Lexikon der Gegenwart: Aktuell '97*, Dortmund: Harenberg Lexikon Verlag.
Kempcke, H. (1996) 'Rechtzeitig die Notbremse', *Spiegel Spezial 'Karriere durch Bildung?'* 11: 100–102.
Jurtschitsch, E. and Gottschling (1993) 'Die besten Universitäten', *Focus* 39: 129–131.

Peter, M. (1996) 'Macht der Provinz', *Wirtschaftswoche* 25: 30–39.
Roth, M. (1993) 'Kaltes Grausen', *Wirtschaftswoche* 16: 30–34.
Rüttgers, J. (1996) 'Nur gute Köpfe entwickeln vermarktbare Technik', *Handelsblatt* 17(4).
Schmidt, S. (1994) 'Von der ausgehöhlten Funktion der Berufsschule: Über die äußeren und inneren Ursachen der Krise der dualen Ausbildung', *Frankfurter Rundschau* 6.1.
Schumann, H. (1994) 'Doppelt hält besser', *Wirtschaftswoche Sonderheft Beruf und Studium*, 14–18.

8 The Nazi legacy
Coming to terms with the past

David Kaufman

VERGANGENHEITSBEWÄLTIGUNG

Coming to terms with a difficult past is necessarily a burden. For the Germans this burden is so great that they have coined a word for it: *Vergangenheitsbewältigung*. The term has broad connotations since it implies the removal of Nazi influences, and the pursuit and punishment of criminals, and it implies the need and readiness to accept responsibility for the past, and to keep the memory of the past alive in the generations succeeding that which lived through the Third Reich. In all these aspects the German people are still compelled to examine themselves and their society. The crimes committed in Germany's name by a minority of the population remain a mark of Cain on the national psyche, accepted by some and resented by others. There is, as we shall see in this chapter, constant confrontation with the Nazi period and neo-Nazis on the one hand, and with the witness of the people and peoples who suffered for the Nazi ideology on the other.

Hans Frank, the Governor-General of Poland throughout its occupation by the Nazis, said, before his execution for war crimes at Nuremberg in 1946, when he appeared to take some responsibility for his actions: 'A thousand years will pass without taking this guilt away from Germany' (Wistrich 1987: 92). (Previously, at the height of his power, he had said with pride: 'If I were to have a poster put up for every seven Poles who have been shot, then Poland's woods would not be sufficient to produce paper for such posters' (Smelser and Zitelmann 1989: 47).) While most of the Nazi leaders at the Nuremberg Trials were at pains to make Hitler and Himmler solely responsible for the crimes that were committed during the Third Reich, Frank, while in essence doing the same thing, was also perceptive and predictive in his assessment of future attitudes to Germany: even now, more than fifty years after the end of the Second

World War, the Germans are constantly reminded both at home and from abroad that they still have to deal with their past, regardless of Chancellor Kohl's assertion of the alibi provided by what he called *die Gnade der späten Geburt* ('the good fortune to have been born too late [to be involved]'). Kohl indeed seemed in 1985 to wish to use the fortieth anniversary of the end of the war in Europe as a moment at which the suffering of all its victims could be shown to be of a similar quality, regardless of the historical context. In taking President Reagan to a war cemetery at Bitburg, where ordinary soldiers but also SS were buried, the German Chancellor provoked a national and international scandal, while also finding a very positive response amongst certain sections of the German population. In addition, so-called revisionists, not only in Germany, deny the Holocaust, while some historians accept that it took place, but declare it to have been not a singularly German crime (see *Historikerstreit*, p. 130).

The fiftieth anniversary of VE Day and the almost weekly anniversaries of the liberation of the concentration camps in the early months of 1995 were at first seen as the psychological moment finally to draw a line beneath the era of historical burden and for a reunited Germany to enter the next century having come to terms with its recent past. But the problem of collective guilt and responsibility, exacerbated by the frequent appearance of neo-Nazis in the news through their involvement in acts of racialist violence, continues to exercise Germany's collective conscience and intellect. The legacy of Hitler remains, so that a book such as *Hitler's Willing Executioners* (Goldhagen 1996) presents a view of such anti-German conviction that it has brought new controversy to the Germans' role in the Holocaust, the greatest of the country's burdens from the past.

THE EARLY POST-WAR YEARS AND THE PROBLEM OF DENAZIFICATION

In the immediate post-war years, the Allied occupation forces wanted, initially, to proceed against the perpetrators of war crimes and to 'denazify' Germany. By the end of 1945, the trials of the major war criminals were taking place in Nuremberg, and it seemed both just and logical to remove Nazis from all positions of influence. This was, however, problematical: there had been 6 million members of the Nazi party itself, and even people who had never joined the party had been members of its many affiliated associations. It had required a great deal of civil courage to resist the pressure to join the Nazis' professional organisations, so that few teachers stayed outside the

NS Teachers' Association, few doctors outside the NS Doctors' Association, few civil servants outside the German Civil Servants' Association, and so on. It thus quickly became clear in all the zones of occupation that the country could not be run without recourse to people who had been politically or otherwise professionally active during the Third Reich, even if this had been under the auspices of the Nazi party. By the end of the 1940s and the beginning of the Cold War, the Western Allies were concerned with this ideological conflict with the Soviet Union rather than with the pursuit of war criminals, so that many Nazis with a dubious past, especially in West Germany, were able to resume their interrupted careers.

As far as the German population was concerned, there was understandably a desire to forget the twelve years of the Third Reich and to get on with rebuilding the country. This was the perceived way of coming to terms with the past in the Federal Republic. In the German Democratic Republic, memories of the period and of political martyrs were kept alive, but the responsibility for the crimes was interpreted purely as a Western German one: the culprits – all of them apparently – were living in the Federal Republic. Certainly it is a matter of record that by the mid-1950s many deeply culpable Nazi bureaucrats and functionaries, doctors, lawyers, judges, and economists were back in place, notably but not exclusively in the FRG, having been able to move effortlessly from their employment in the Third Reich to similar if rather more innocuous post-war activities, their past catching up with them either much later – or not at all. Perhaps the crassest example of this can be seen in the career of Hans Globke, a high-ranking official in the FRG's Ministry of the Interior, who was a major contributor to the work on the Nuremberg Laws, which among other things prohibited sexual relations between Aryans (in the Nazi 'philosophy' people of Germanic and thus non-Jewish descent) and Jews, except in marriages which already existed, and was thus the first major step towards the outlawing of Jews from German society. It was also Globke's idea to compel all Jews to adopt the middle name Israel for men and Sara for women on all official documents, in case their given names did not sound Jewish. From 1953 until 1963 Globke was Chancellor Adenauer's State Secretary and major adviser in the appointment of personnel; in the mid-1950s two-thirds of the personnel in the West German Foreign Office were former Nazis: as we have seen, the ministry needed people with experience (Friedrich 1984: 294–98). Only after Globke was sentenced *in absentia* in the former GDR in 1963 to life imprisonment for his complicity in the implementation of the Nuremberg Laws was his resignation accepted.

None the less, Globke was able to live out his retirement unmolested and on a full pension. Hanging judges, doctors who, using Nazi legislation, during the Third Reich practised euthanasia on people they considered unworthy of life (the mentally and physically handicapped), industrialists who had wittingly used slave labour – most of them were able to survive and prosper in the Federal Republic with the connivance of helpers in high places.[1]

In the late 1950s and 1960s there was much mud-slinging between the two German states and there were frequent revelations about Nazis in high places in both countries. The GDR, while proclaiming its hostility to Nazis and Nazism and the affront caused by the presence of ex-Nazis in high-profile positions in the FRG, was no stranger to this phenomenon in its own state. In response to the many GDR reports of Nazis in public office in the FRG, Western German sources revealed in 1958 that there were seventy-five ex-Nazis in leading positions in the GDR (Assheuer and Sarkowicz 1994: 114), fifty of them in the East German Parliament (Farin and Seidel-Pielen 1993: 69), and in 1968 Simon Wiesenthal, head of the Documentation Centre in Vienna, provided evidence for the presence of several dozen former Nazis in highly influential positions in the GDR media. It turned out, for example, that Hans Aust, who had worked on the SS newspaper *Das Schwarze Korps* (The Black Corps), a violently nationalistic, virulently racist newspaper, was the chief editor of the government's main foreign affairs newspaper (Farin and Seidel-Pielen 1993: 69). The fact was that although in the Soviet zone half a million Nazis were removed from their posts by 1948 thereafter it became easier for smaller (and some bigger) fish to find a place in the GDR hierarchy.

VERJÄHRUNG

By the end of the 1960s attitudes in the Federal Republic had changed. In 1965 twenty years had passed since the end of the Third Reich, and there was a controversy regarding *Verjährung* (statute of limitations, the period within which proceedings against a criminal must be initiated and at the end of which he or she may no longer be pursued), which would at that time have come into force for crimes committed during the Nazi period. This public debate on the *Verjährung* of war crimes in the FRG led to a change in the law so that – at least theoretically – the perpetrator of a war crime may be tried regardless of the number of years that have passed since the crime was committed. Since then, the German central office for the investigation of war crimes at Ludwigsburg has prosecuted a fairly large number of criminals, but with the passing of so many years the search for surviving and ageing witnesses and the equally ageing murderers has become more and more difficult so that the last trials in Germany for crimes committed during the war have probably already taken place.[2]

EDUCATION, AND ATTITUDES TO THE HOLOCAUST

As far as the presentation of recent history is concerned, in West German schools coverage of the period was sparse for a long time after the war, while in East Germany the history was treated in depth – but tendentiously. From the 1960s the post-war generation of children in the FRG were confronted more and more in their schooling with Third Reich studies, which were covered in much greater depth than hitherto, often several years running and with much emphasis on Nazi anti-Semitic policies and legislation and the Holocaust, with the result that schoolchildren began to object to having to shoulder the blame for their parents' apparent support of Hitler: sympathy fatigue set in. However, in 1979, an American television serial based on the Holocaust was broadcast in Germany. It was a dramatised, sanitised version of events, whose victims it was easier to identify with than the piles of emaciated and dehumanised bodies the population were used to seeing in television documentaries. Young people asked their elders why there had been such acquiescence to Nazi racial policies; there was much public debate of the issue, which has continued sporadically ever since and has recently been renewed with the Goldhagen controversy (see p. 136).

The concentration camps as memorials and museums

The sites of the major concentration camps in Germany, such as Dachau, Buchenwald, Bergen-Belsen and Sachsenhausen are national memorials to the victims; buildings and barracks have been made into museums, and their historical context and the crimes committed there are explained in the plainest of language. Guided tours and lectures, films produced by the Allies after the liberation give graphic and horrific detail of the conditions which obtained there and the treatment meted out by the guards to their victims. Many schools organise visits to these places, so that nowadays young people have often been given a very clear impression of what took place there.

There is some controversy regarding the way in which the camps in the former GDR were used by the SED government as monuments to the communist resistance to fascism: clearly, very many communists *were* murdered by the Nazis in the camps, but there was a tendency for the victims of the Nazis' atrocities to be portrayed almost exclusively as communists, and this modification of the truth is being corrected. In addition, for some years after the war the Soviets took over and continued to use the concentration camps in their zone of occupation for Nazis or people who displeased them, but this was never admitted by the GDR regime – indeed, it was concealed. This historical distortion is now being rectified, so that, for example, after the recommendations of a government commission (Röll 1992: 11, 19) the administration in Thuringia now demonstrates in an exhibition at Buchenwald that the camp continued to be used as a means of abuse after its liberation. Likewise controversially, such actions by the Soviets, which despite their relative brutality still do not compare with the tortures inflicted by the SS, are also used as evidence of the non-singularity of the Nazi crimes by right-wing historians (see p. 130).

MEDIA

As far as the media are concerned, the press, publishing in general, and television have made a great contribution to keeping the past present in the minds of the population. With each anniversary of events that took place between 1933 and 1945 many articles and books are published (a many-volumed series on the Nazi period under the Fischer imprint for example), and on television scarcely a week passes without some programme on the Third Reich in general, on the concentration camps, the treatment of those conquered by the Nazis, or a chat show in which the views of representatives of German Jewry are sought. Often they are referred to as *unsere jüdischen Mitbürger* (our Jewish fellow citizens), which on the one hand is clearly meant to embrace them (in contrast to the exclusion practised by the Nazis), but which on the other is characteristic of a philosemitism[3] (in contrast and as a reaction to the anti-Semitism practised by the Nazis) which can sometimes appear patronising or embarrassingly obsequious.

The newsworthiness of fascist gatherings means that a vocal minority of extremists often receives more media publicity than it should warrant, but at the same time the moral outrage demonstrated universally by the German news commentaries properly places such groupings beyond the pale. It is, however, the Germans' misfortune that such publicity raises the spectre of resurgent Nazism in the mind of the world, so that the foreign reports of neo-Nazi activity often give a false impression of its size and influence.

HISTORIKERSTREIT

In the mid-1980s some respected historians, politically on the right, began to question the place of National Socialism in German history, to question the singularity of the atrocities committed in that period, and to place the Holocaust in a global context, in which Stalin, for example, might be considered to be responsible for just as many crimes against humanity as Hitler, if not more. In 1986 Ernst Nolte, a history professor in Berlin, wrote in an essay in the *Frankfurter Allgemeine Zeitung* (6 June) that everything which the Nazis did, with the sole exception of the technical procedures used in the gassings, had already been done by other peoples. Clearly, Germany's preoccupation with its burdened past, its painful memories, would be lightened should the crimes of the Nazi period be re-examined and seen to be an aberration – which had been experienced elsewhere and similarly before. This view was opposed by equally respected historians of the left. The so-called *Historikerstreit* (dispute amongst historians) was about responsibility and guilt and coming to terms with the past, and the non-singularity view was very much in keeping with the opinions of young people, who felt that they were given an overwhelming diet of guilt-provoking lessons on history which was made by their grandparents. The fact remains, as Christian Meier shows, that the singularity of the Holocaust lies in three key aspects: a *state* had decided to pursue all members of at least two racial groupings, Jews and gypsies, in all the countries in which it had influence (those which had been annexed or conquered and those which were the Nazis' allies), and to kill them with no exceptions to be made; it had decided to allow such people to be used for appalling medical experimentation; it had reduced them to objects which could be processed on an industrial scale – their clothing, spectacles, prosthetic devices to be recycled, their property to be redistributed, their hair to be used in manufacturing, their gold teeth to be melted down and added to the funds of the Reichsbank, the state's bank (Meier 1990: 39–40). Only the collapse of the Nazi regime saved those not yet murdered. The memory of this criminal behaviour by a *state* remains at the core of *Vergangenheitsbewältigung*.

AKTION SÜHNEZEICHEN AND RECONCILIATION

The attempt to reduce such events to the level simply of philosophical disputation is in marked contrast to the work of Aktion Sühnezeichen (Operation Atonement), an organisation called into being in the mid-1950s to further understanding between Germans and Jews, both in Germany and in Israel. The original members of this group were the children of soldiers or former Nazi party supporters at one extreme, and of resistance fighters at the other. All were motivated by the apparent failure of the FRG at that time to acknowledge the past.

Both sexes are entitled to work voluntarily for the organisation, but male applicants have to be conscientious objectors, who are then allowed to have the work they do recognised as their *Ersatzdienst* (alternative to military service). Volunteers usually spend time in Israel, often working with concentration camp survivors, helping actively to break down the prejudices and hostilities against young Germans, who after all quite clearly have no reason to feel personal guilt. Aktion Sühnezeichen is never short of volunteers, and the organisation is becoming more international as the need to place German history in a broader European context is recognised.

The need felt by members of the post-war generation of Germans to effect reconciliation with the equivalent generation of Israelis whose parents were victims of the Nazis is reflected in the work of Dan Bar-On, of the Department of Behavioural Sciences at the Ben Gurion University of the Negev (1991). His meetings with the children of Nazis and his encounter group Täterkinder – Opferkinder (Children of the Perpetrators – Children of the Victims) successfully demonstrate that one generation's hatreds need not be perpetuated into the next and that the stereotyping of one group by another, whether caused by indoctrination or by history, can be combated when rational human beings are brought together. The fact that close friendships have come about and even marriages taken place between the children of Nazis and of concentration camp survivors provides some grounds for optimism.

RIGHT-WING EXTREMISM AND NEO-NAZISM

Racism and violence

In the 1990s in a newly united Germany, feelings of insecurity and paranoia regarding the past are reinforced – especially amongst young people in the former GDR, where, as in many of the countries of the former communist bloc, the lid which the SED regime tried to keep firmly on any potential fascist inclinations amongst the population has been removed to reveal a brew of xenophobia inflaming the disappointed and disaffected. This mood is nourished by neo-Nazi groupings which try to stir up hatred as they demonstrate the 'pernicious' influence of foreigners, especially Turks, the 'new Jews', and to encourage murderous attacks upon them.

While there had been episodes of aggression towards foreign people living and working in both German states before the fall of the Wall, attacks increased more than fivefold between 1990 and 1991: there were 1,483 racially motivated attacks on foreigners in Germany in 1991 (*die tageszeitung*, 26.08.92: 4). The towns of Hoyerswerda, Hünxe, Solingen, Mölln, and Rostock – hitherto scarcely household names – became for a short time internationally notorious through the cowardly attacks that took place there between 1991 and 1993: in Hoyerswerda in Saxony, thirty tenants in a shelter for asylum seekers were badly injured during attacks on their home in September 1991; in Hünxe in North-Rhine Westphalia two Lebanese children escaped with their lives after being badly injured in an arson attack on their home in October; in August 1993 riots outside a home for Vietnamese guest workers in Rostock-Lichterhagen were captured on film by television cameras, which also recorded the applause of German onlookers and the failure of watching police to intervene until very late in the incident. In June 1993 five Turkish women and children were murdered in an arson attack in Solingen, and in November of the same year in Mölln two Turkish girls and a woman were burnt to death in yet another arson attack. In most of these cases, the right-wing criminal elements involved were caught, some receiving long prison sentences but others being treated with great leniency. This, together with Chancellor Kohl's failure to visit either Mölln or Solingen in the wake of the tragedies there, suggested a lack of concern on the part of the German establishment for the fate of their foreign – and especially Turkish – citizens, which was damaging to Germany's post-war reputation and image. Perhaps as a reaction to the reticence of some politicians, German citizens in their tens of thousands took part in processions and *Lichterketten* (chains of light) throughout the country in solidarity with the Turkish community in the days after the murders. Such a spontaneous attempt to 'come to terms with the present' did much to persuade mounting international Germanophobic reaction that this, rather than the behaviour of neo-Nazi hooligans and the relatively low-key political response to it, was, perhaps, more representative of present-day German attitudes.

Neo-Nazi parties and organisations

Right-wing extremism is not, of course, a new phenomenon in Germany (or anywhere else in Europe). As we have seen, denazification, the process of sifting through the background of the various members of the Nazi party and its organisations, was intended to rid the country of such corrupting political influences, but by the end of the 1940s there were already nationalistic parties such as the DKP-DRP (Deutsche Konservative Partei-Deutsche Rechtspartei) or the SRP (Sozialistische Reichspartei) being founded to represent the extreme right (see Chapter 4, p. 59). The SRP, whose activists were for the most part former Nazis, saw itself ideologically the successor of the Nazi party and was soon prohibited. While such parties did not achieve much success, and although desecrations of synagogues, concentration camp monuments, and Jewish cemeteries were frequently reported – as many as 1,200 separate incidents in 1960 (Benz 1994: 254) – little obvious attempt was made to mobilise any real and general right-wing reaction in the Federal Republic; after all, the *Wirtschaftswunder* (economic miracle) was in full swing (see Chapter 5, p. 70) and the *Gastarbeiter*, the foreigners who had been imported to help run it, were prepared to undertake jobs which the indigenous population were happy to abandon – and in the GDR few would have had the foolhardiness to express fascist sentiments in public. This is not to say that extremist slogans were never heard in the GDR, but until the 1980s and the emergence of the fascist skinhead scene there was some discretion involved in any such indiscretion.

In the FRG it was not until the mid-1960s that old Nazis and youth with the potential for extremist tendencies found a louder voice in the Nationaldemokratische Partei Deutschlands (NPD), which was founded in 1964. For a time the NPD recorded alarming successes, beating the 5 per cent hurdle (see Chapter 4, p. 63) in many of the *Bundesländer*, and peaking in Baden-Württemberg in 1968, where it received 9.8 per cent of votes cast, but then went into decline. For, although it seemed to some political commentators at the time that the NPD, which had drawn to it and united various right-wing factions, would be able to consolidate its position, the 1969 general election resulted in the party's failing to overcome the 5 per cent hurdle, and this defeat marked the end of a period of neo-Nazi resurgence. The fact is that the atmosphere of discontent and deprivation which is a breeding ground for movements such as National Socialism was not apparent in the Federal Republic of the 1970s and certainly the early part of the 1980s. This was after all the period of the Baader–Meinhof terrorists,[4] who for a long time represented left-wing reaction to bourgeois complacency.

By the middle of the 1980s, dissatisfaction was showing itself in the GDR, and unemployment was increasing in the Federal Republic, where a new party, the Republikaner of Handlos, Voigt and Schön-huber, for several years achieved (from the point of view of demo-crats) distressingly positive results (see Chapter 4, p. 59). It was, however, the events leading to the fall of the Wall and the reunifica-tion of Germany resulting from it which brought from obscurity many neo-Nazi splinter groups, whose following, made up largely of hoo-ligan elements, was and is attracted by the militant and militaristic demagogy of their often puerile but at the same time threatening and (for some) convincing leaders. Amongst the most prominent was Michael Kuehnen, the founder of the Gesinnungsgemeinschaft der Neuen Front (GdNF) (this is very difficult to translate; it means something like: 'Community of Like-Minded People [belonging to] the New Front'), who was jailed for his neo-Nazi activities and died of AIDS in 1991.

The man who took Kuehnen's place in the neo-Nazi scene, Ewald Althans, became notorious after a documentary about his life and career, *Beruf Neo-Nazi* (Profession: Neo-Nazi), in which he is seen, for example, at Auschwitz, amused at the idea that people could have been gassed there, since the pipes leading into the gas chambers 'could not have worked' – the gas chambers at Auschwitz had been blown up by the SS before the camp's liberation by the Russians, so that those preserved there are a reconstruction. Althans has now been imprisoned for disseminating Holocaust denial material, an act which is illegal in the FRG, but which has only recently been the object of real pursuit by the legal system. (The illegality of this act is the subject of some dispute, since some would argue that the utterance or distribution of such material is a matter of freedom of speech.) When in 1994 Günter Deckert, a schoolteacher and member of the NPD who had distributed similar revisionist material, was re-tried on appeal by the prosecution after receiving a suspended sentence for this offence, a Mannheim court again gave him a suspended sentence on the grounds that, among other things, he had had a hard time of it as a politician; that he believed the material; that he was pointing out that Germany was still paying for its misdeeds of half a century before, while other peoples had since escaped scot-free after commit-ting similar crimes. The verdict caused a scandal, since it seemed to confirm the suspicion held by many to the effect that German justice is 'blind in its right eye', in the sense that courts have often seemed to be lenient towards neo-Nazis, but not to communists. The judges involved in this case were retired early or transferred to other courts.

There are dozens of neo-Nazi groupings, and they receive much media attention, but their total membership is probably less than 10,000.[5]

NEO-NAZIS AT THE CUTTING EDGE OF TECHNOLOGY

By the mid-1980s the popularity of computers gave neo-Nazis the opportunity to disseminate violently racialist material and games via disks. Simplistic question-and-answer games such as *Anti-Türken-Test* (Anti-Turk Test) and conventional 'shoot 'em' games in which prisoners in camps were shot or hunted by dogs were soon succeeded by more complex simulations. The most notorious of these was *KZ-Manager* (Concentration Camp Manager), a 'Monopoly'-like game whose object was to build a camp with SS barracks, gas chambers, etc. The game was over when a concentration camp was built and 3,000 prisoners had been executed (Benz 1994: 219ff.).

The 1990s have brought the Internet culture, which is available to all and which enables anyone to express any views about anything to a world-wide audience. The neo-Nazis have taken advantage of this development and have sites with which they present their views, insult their opponents, disseminate lies, and pretend to invite dialogue – all in semi-anonymity, since the use of so-called mail-boxes makes it difficult to locate their source. Some employ the bully-boy language of the Brownshirts, but others, striving for respectability and protesting their goodwill, have a dangerously specious quality to their arguments.

The Thule Network[6] has a large site on the World Wide Web.[7] There it publishes: attacks on its critics; pages and pages written in defence of prosecuted (and thus persecuted) Holocaust deniers; attacks on censorship in the Internet; attacks on Freemasons with their 'programme to create a Eurasian Negroid mixed race'; examples of 'falsified history', including lists of supposedly faked atrocity pictures from the Third Reich; reports of Rudolf Hess memorial marches; lists of crimes committed by foreigners in Germany with the intent of pillorying the majority for the – usually imagined – excesses of a tiny minority; calls for the repatriation of foreigners.[8]

Similar literature is distributed from Canada by the Zündel site.[9] Ernst Zündel, an ardent admirer of and apologist for Althans (see

p. 134), publishes bi-lingually on the Net, regaling his readers with attacks on prominent Holocaust survivors such as Elie Wiesel and Simon Wiesenthal, promoting the outpourings of 'gas chamber expert' Fred Leuchter, whose 'scientific investigation' failed to detect any signs of Zyklon-B gas at Auschwitz, and thus nurturing revisionist ideology.

Clearly, there is a danger in such disinformation, as it is written plausibly, without the extremes of language employed by the Nazis during the Third Reich. And, since it is possible to prove anything with false premises, the need to monitor and warn, if not to censor, is felt keenly by the opponents of this modern form of racial aggression. This is a key aspect of *Vergangenheitsbewältigung* since the question is whether verbal and written attacks on foreigners, which are, however disguised, intended to inflame hatred or to incite to xenophobia, can be regarded as merely freedom of opinion and speech or rather as a criminal offence. It is the 'otherness' of the Turk, of the foreigner, which is the object of the neo-Nazis' hatred, and if Mölln or Rostock can be shown to be the result of exposure to such influences, then Net-Nazis – if they can be found – should join Althans, Rudolf, and Deckert in the dock.

THE GOLDHAGEN DEBATE

The central thesis of Daniel Goldhagen's book, *Hitler's Willing Executioners*, which was published in 1996, is that a historical anti-Semitism, endemic through all sectors of the German population, was fertile ground for the Holocaust – which then took place with the full support and connivance of ordinary Germans. This generalisation forms the basis of a controversy which started to rage in Germany even before the translation was published there in the August of that year. Its title is neutralised somewhat in the German, as *Der Spiegel*[10] points out, to *Hitlers willige Vollstrecker* (Hitler's willing executors). It is very much a counterpoint to the *Historikerstreit* of 1986, in that Nolte's starting point was – to paraphrase and simplify it – 'The Holocaust was a terrible thing, but it could have been initiated by any national group and was therefore not a singular crime', while Goldhagen is saying – likewise to paraphrase simplistically – 'It was a terrible thing and it happened because the Germans – not the Nazis, the Germans – were happy to take part in it, and it *was* a singular crime.'

The book documents thoroughly and scientifically the course of anti-Semitism in Germany through its religious beginnings and its political development, and then demonstrates that in some cases it was not the SS but ordinary German police battalions which were involved in mass murder. Equally well researched books have been written before (Martin Gilbert's *Holocaust* and Christopher Browning's *Ordinary Men* to name but two of a myriad), but Goldhagen's argument presents so great an indictment of a people that its thesis has to be debated and some of its conclusions contested. In an interview in 1996[11] Goldhagen allows that the minimum number of Germans directly involved in the Holocaust was 100,000 – an appallingly large number certainly, but even if it were doubled or tripled this is still not to involve all Germans directly. The Germans' burden is to have been apathetic in the face of events at home, to have turned away for fear of involvement or reprisal, and often to have benefited from the disappearance of their neighbours. The eyewitness accounts – including those of the Jewish victims – of the so-called *Reichskristallnacht*, the November pogrom of 1938, for example, suggest embarrassment or consternation amongst broad sectors of the population at the arson attacks on the synagogues and at the looting of Jewish houses and shops by members of the Nazis' para-military organisations, rather than pleasure. None the less, it is, of course, not illogical to interpret the systematic exclusion of Jews from German society and the economy, which was accepted by the population during the 1930s as steps towards exclusion from life itself, and the virtue of this book is that, at a time when Turkish-German citizens are under attack by neo-Nazis, the population has been made to think again about drawing a line beneath the events that occurred during the Third Reich now that fifty years have passed.

CONCLUSION

The Third Reich lasted for just twelve years, yet the policies of its leader left Germany split for forty-five years and a rump of its former self; the war that it brought about led to vastly changed political structures in Europe and beyond. Its history informs all that has happened to and in Germany since 1945. It is their misfortune that coming to terms with the Nazi period is probably more important to the Germans' understanding of themselves than any other part of the nation's heritage.

Exceptional events make history, so that for every xenophobic attack many positive actions go unnoticed. The work of Aktion Sühnezeichen, for example, does not have a high media profile, because, of course, positive action is not as newsworthy as stories about extremist activists. While Unification has revealed a great deal of submerged fascist sentiment, and while clearly there are many incorrigible people who are living in the past (*die Ewiggestrigen*), so that often only a negative picture of modern Germany is transmitted to the world, there are in fact vastly more people committed to peaceful co-existence than the pictures from Rostock or Hoyerswerda might indicate. But that there are still neo-Nazi parties, that there are still revisionists like Deckert, Althans, and Leuchter, that there are still murderous acts perpetrated against people whose 'crime' is to be foreign, that a politician such as Philipp Jenninger could in 1988 unwittingly and out of the best of motives make a statement as President of the Bundestag which was construed widely as being anti-Semitic and which led to his resignation[12] – all this suggests that *Vergangenheitsbewältigung* is still a long way from being accomplished.

NOTES

1 Friedrich names scores of such people, but omits, strangely, the case of Hans Filbinger, Ministerpräsident of Baden-Württemberg until 1978, when he had to resign after it became clear that he had sentenced a young naval deserter to death on the last day of the war – and would have had the sentence carried out if the young man had been available for execution. 'What was legal then, has to be legal today', was his only comment on his judgement and the executions which he had previously had carried out. Filbinger, who had managed to conceal his political interests in the bosom of the CDU party, has since 1979 showed his true position as co-founder and figurehead of an extreme right-wing institute, the Studiumzentrum Weikersheim, which seeks to move German political thought to the (far) right.
2 One of the last trials was that of Joseph Schwammberger, sentenced in 1992 to life for various murders including the burning alive of between 1,000 and 1,500 Jews in a gymnasium and the use of his dog to savage at least ten people to death.
3 Exaggeratedly pro-Jewish sentiment.
4 In 1968, Andreas Baader, together with various like-minded friends, made an arson attack on a department store in Frankfurt. Imprisoned, released, then imprisoned again, he was helped to escape by a left-wing journalist of some repute, Ulrike Meinhof. Together they founded the RAF (Rote Armee Fraktion – 'Red Army Faction'), which proceeded to commit terrorist acts against the German establishment, whose hypocrisy they wished to expose. Eventually caught and incarcerated in Stammheim, a high-security prison, members of the group committed suicide under somewhat suspicious circumstances after an attempt had been made to blackmail the German government into freeing them. The title of a book written by Jillian Becker, *Hitler's Children. The Story of the Baader–*

Meinhof Gang, London, 1977, suggests that left-wing extremists were seeking their own way of coming to terms with the past. The murder of the attorney-general, Siegfried Buback, and of the chairman of the Dresdener Bank, Jürgen Ponto, in 1977 by surviving members of the RAF demonstrated their ruthlessness, as did the kidnapping and murder of Hanns-Martin Schleyer, the president of the German Employers Confederation, but also a former high-ranking officer in the SS, a fact concealed in the subsequent obituaries. While their actions were those of conscienceless terrorists, especially this last target of their murderousness shows how very high culpable members of organisations which had been declared criminal after the war had been able to climb in post-war West German society and how respectable and respected they were allowed to remain.

5 For an overview of the scene, the Bibliothek Rechtsextremismus (Library of Right-wing Extremism) has a large site on the Internet and keeps track of neo-Nazi activities at http://www.nadeshda.org/bib/bib.html, as does the Simon Wiesenthal Institute at http://www.wiesenthal.com/

6 Its name derives from the legendary Nordic kingdom, whence the Thule Gesellschaft (Thule Society), which, founded during the early part of this century, was dedicated to ideas of racial superiority and the founding of a new German Reich. Its symbol was the swastika, and Hitler developed many of his ideas after reading the society's mystical and moronic tracts.

7 http://www.thulenet.com/

8 All references here to be found at the site listed in note 7.

9 http://www.kaiwan.com: 80/~ihrgreg/zundel/english/englisht oc.html

10 Anon 'Riesige Mehrheit: Die deutsche Übersetzung glättet Goldhagens Thesen', *Der Spiegel* 33/1996: 42.

11 With David Gergen, US News & World Report May 1996 (transcript at http://web-cr01.pbs.org/newshour/gergen/goldhagen.html)

12 On the 50th anniversary of the *Reichskristallnacht* (9 November 1988), Jenninger made a speech in the *Bundestag* in which he said: '. . . as far as the Jews were concerned: Had they not in the past presumed to adopt a role – so it was said – which they were not entitled to . . . Had they perhaps not deserved . . .' While clearly he was intending to quote opinions current in the 1930s, he failed to make himself clear and his words were widely misinterpreted.

RECOMMENDED READING

Hockenos, P. (1993) *Free to Hate*, London: Routledge.

BIBLIOGRAPHY

Assheuer, T. and Sarkowicz, H. (1994) *Rechtsradikale in Deutschland*, München: Beck.

Bar-On, D. (1991) *Legacy of Silence*, Cambridge, Mass. and London: Harvard University Press.

Benz, W. (ed.) (1994) *Rechtsextremismus in Deutschland*, Frankfurt am Main: Fischer.

Farin, K. and Seidel-Pielen, E. (1993) *Rechtsruck*, Berlin: Rotbuch.

Friedrich, J. (1984) *Die kalte Amnestie. NS-Täter in der Bundesrepublik*, Frankfurt am Main: Fischer.

Goldhagen, D. (1996) *Hitler's Willing Executioners*, London: Little, Brown & Co.

Meier, C. (1990) *Vierzig Jahre nach Auschwitz – Deutsche Geschichtserinnerung heute*, München: Beck.

Röll, W. (ed.) (1992) *Zur Neuorientierung der Gedenkstätte Buchenwald*, Weimar-Buchenwald: Gedenkstätte Buchenwald.

Smelser, R. and Zitelmann, R. (1989) *Die Braune Elite*, Darmstadt: Wissenschaftliche Buchgesellschaft.

Wistrich, R. (1987) *Wer war wer im Dritten Reich*, Frankfurt am Main: Fischer.

9 The media landscape

Steffi Boothroyd

In 1995, Germans spent on average over three hours per day in front of the television, had the radio switched on for over three and a half hours and took forty-six minutes to read their newspaper (Kiefer 1996: 235). These habits alone justify an examination of the media in this book. In addition, the German media industry is an important economic force – not just on a national level but also on an international scale, with some of Europe's and the world's largest media groups based in Germany. Not least, the mass media deserve attention here also as one of the most influential institutions in Germany, as indeed in any democratic society. After all, they are, for most people, the major source of information about the world, the country and even the region or city they live in. Alongside the provision of information, the media have a variety of other functions to fulfil. They provide entertainment, and they have a significant political role to play. Not only do they make a vital contribution to the opinion-forming process in society, the media also operate in a supervisory capacity, investigating and pointing out defects in the workings of democracy.

The ability of the media to fulfil these functions properly rests, above all, on two key requirements: first, the freedom of the media from state interference and, second, the existence of diversity of opinion in the media landscape. In Germany, the first of these requirements is covered by a number of legal provisions, most importantly Article 5 of the Basic Law (*Grundgesetz*), which stipulates the general right to freedom of information and opinion, guarantees the specific freedom of the media and rules out censorship. The freedom of the media is further underpinned by various concrete regulations: for example, the obligation of public authorities to disclose information to the media. However, the political freedom of the media is not unlimited, and infringements are not uncommon. Some such infringements, for example the close monitoring of children's television, are generally welcomed by public opinion. Other practices, such as the searching of journalists' homes or offices in the interest of state security, are often more controversial. Equally problematic can be measures of self-censorship – for example, the six-week rule in public-service television (Schneider 1996: 73), which is an agreement not to broadcast political satire in the six weeks prior to elections. These few examples illustrate that the implementation of the freedom of the media, as laid down in the German constitution, is not always a straightforward affair.

Diversity, the second main requirement for the media to fulfil their functions, is likewise a difficult issue. As will be shown later in this chapter, much of the diversity of opinion in the German media is contingent upon one of two factors. In the case of public-service broadcasting, it relies on a commitment to ensure such diversity by way of public funding. In the case of commercial print or broadcasting media, the media's ability to fulfil their functions and add to the diversity of opinion not only results from the good will of individual publishers or broadcasting stations, but also depends largely on their economic viability. In other words, even once the political freedom of the media is constitutionally guaranteed, there are economic dependencies to be considered. Of interest, therefore, is the question as to how economic factors – for example the dependence on advertising or the trend towards concentration – may also infringe on media freedom and diversity. The following sections provide a brief overview of the German press and broadcasting media in the context of the parameters that have been sketched out so far. Whilst some topics cannot be discussed in any depth, other issues, such as diversity, freedom from political interference, and economic concentration, will be considered in some detail.

THE PRESS

Private ownership

It may not be surprising that the press of a market economy such as Germany's should be in private hands and subject to the workings of a free market. However, the possibility of other models of media ownership is not an altogether theoretical one, as can be demonstrated by way of example in the case of Germany's own broadcasting system (see pp. 148–50). Moreover, as will be seen, private ownership of the press has brought with it a number of distinct disadvantages,

particularly in view of issues such as press concentration and pluralism or diversity, which will be examined later in this chapter.

The foundations of the current German press structure were laid
by the Allied forces and their policies after the Second World War.
After the defeat of the Third Reich, when the country was split into
four Allied Occupation Zones, it was felt to be of paramount
importance that the previously monolithic media structure, dominated
and controlled as it was by the totalitarian Nazi regime, should be
completely reformed. The media were regarded as important tools in
the re-education of the German people and the introduction of a
democratic system. Consequently, all previously existing publishers
and broadcasters were barred and replaced with operations run by the
Allied forces themselves or by newcomers who were installed within
a strict licensing system.

In the Soviet Occupation Zone, later to become the GDR, the initial
licensing policies effectively created a system in which most of the
available daily and weekly papers were affiliated either to the leading
SED (Socialist Unity Party) or to any of the other political parties in
the government alliance. All publications, including the magazines
which did not necessarily have such party affiliations, were state-
owned and state-controlled. As a result, there was little political
diversity in the GDR's press. Rather, the press served as a kind of
mouthpiece for the slogans and ideas put forward by the country's
leadership. This, however, changed dramatically with unification,
which set in motion the comprehensive restructuring of the GDR
press on the West German model – in particular its transfer into
private ownership. This transfer was achieved largely by way of
West German publishers expanding and taking over former GDR
newspapers and magazines. Since then, many of the old titles have
died, but some peculiarities have remained. There are, for example, a
number of publications which are produced almost exclusively for
readers in the new *Länder*, and some of the old titles to have survived
privatisation have enjoyed healthy sales. The former SED regional
dailies, for example, are now amongst Germany's best-selling regional dailies.

When the Western Allies introduced their licensing system, they
shared with the Russians the concern to ensure that no individual or
company found to have collaborated with the Nazi regime should be
allowed to operate in the newly emerging media landscape. However,
their policies differed in so far as licences were granted to private
companies and entrepreneurs. Bearing in mind the abuse of state
power in the media during fascism, it is not surprising that the media

model envisaged by the Western Allied Forces was based on the principle of keeping the influence of the state down to a minimum (*Staatsferne*). Instead, they regarded private ownership and market forces as the most promising guarantees for a democratic and pluralist press – a view still commonly held today, despite some evidence to the contrary (see pp. 145–8). Indeed, many of today's leading publishers, such as Axel Springer, used the opportunities of those post-war years of licensing to start building their media empires.

The press market today

To any foreign observer, one of the most obvious features of the German press is the large number of titles of both newspapers and magazines. In the newspaper market, a relatively small number of national or supra-regional dailies (*überregionale Zeitungen*) stands in stark contrast to an abundance of local (*Lokalzeitungen* or *Heimatpresse*) and regional papers (*Regionalzeitungen*). In 1993 there were only seven national dailies, in comparison to 370 local and regional publications (Meyn 1994: 48). These local or regional papers have traditionally played a very important role. Quite often people buy them, by way of subscription, not in addition to, but instead of a nation-wide publication, as they provide a wide range of coverage of both national and internal developments (Sandford 1995: 206).

As far as the national dailies are concerned, the main serious publications are *Süddeutsche Zeitung, Frankfurter Allgemeine Zeitung (FAZ), Frankfurter Rundschau* and *Die Welt*. In addition, there are tabloid papers, usually referred to as *Boulevardzeitungen* or *Kaufzeitungen*, which follow a somewhat sensationalist, simplistic and picture-driven approach. Of these, Axel Springer's *Bild Zeitung* has been most successful. Despite the fact that *Bild* has often been criticised and even prosecuted for distortion, unethical behaviour, lies and extreme bias against left-wing, liberal or feminist views (Meyn 1994: 69–70), it is Germany's best-selling daily, with circulation figures of 4.4 million in 1995 (*Media Perspektiven Basisdaten* 1995: 50). Although *Bild* clearly expresses conservative leanings, it is not directly affiliated to any political party. Indeed, very few of the dailies are. One exception, however, is *Neues Deutschland (ND)*, the former paper of the East German SED party, which is now linked with its successor, the PDS, and read almost exclusively in the new *Länder*. As far as the majority of dailies are concerned, there may not be direct party-political affiliations, but the principle of *Tendenzschutz* entitles publishers to express political leanings in their publications, and journalists employed in the publishing houses are obliged to follow their orientation.

Thus, *Die Welt* and the *Frankfurter Allgemeine Zeitung* are generally considered conservative papers, while at the other end of the spectrum the *Süddeutsche Zeitung* and the *Frankfurter Rundschau* are regarded as taking liberal, left-of-centre positions. What appears to be missing or, at least, under-represented in this group of national dailies are papers with a clear left-wing orientation. The notable exception is *die tageszeitung (taz)*, which was founded only in 1979 and is generally regarded as taking a left-wing, alternative approach in both its news selection and its reporting. It is also exceptional in at least two other aspects: its organisation is largely non-hierarchical, and *taz*-ownership is in the hands of a co-operative of contributors (i.e. journalists etc.) and friends of the paper.

There are also some foreign-language newspapers to cater for the interests of some of the ethnic minorities resident in Germany. These tend to be German editions of larger papers otherwise published in Turkey, Italy, Greece, etc.

Of the numerous weekly papers and magazines, most prestigious have been the liberal *Die Zeit* and the news magazine *Der Spiegel*. Founded in 1947 and modelled on the American *Time* magazine, *Spiegel* has been held in high regard for its investigative journalism and critical reporting. It is often referred to as one of the so-called *Leitmedien*, i.e. those media which are considered to be particularly influential in terms of their impact on society as a whole and in terms of the way other media follow and respond to their coverage. The dominance of one publication, such as *Spiegel* in the news magazines market, is not, however, typical of the magazines market in general. There is an abundance of general and special interest magazines, although only a dozen or so achieve sales above the million mark (Röper 1996a: 312ff.).

With close to four hundred local, regional or national newspapers as well as several hundred magazine titles, the German print media market, at first sight, appears to be characterised by a high degree of diversity. However, as the next section reveals, the diversity implied in the great number of titles is somewhat deceptive in the context of an increasing trend towards concentration.

Press concentration

Concerns over press concentration have been on the agenda in West Germany for some decades. In fact, the federal government appointed its first commission to investigate concentration tendencies as early as 1968 and subsequently introduced the 1976 law on the control of mergers (*Pressefusionskontrolle*). Nevertheless, mergers, acquisitions, shareholding arrangements and networks of co-operation have created an increasingly complex ownership structure and advanced the process of concentration quite considerably.

This is particularly evident in the newspaper market, where concentration occurs in four distinct forms (Tonnemacher 1996: 95–96). First, there is editorial concentration (*publizistische Konzentration*), which becomes apparent when one relates the total number of dailies on the market to the number of independent editorial units (*publizistische Einheiten*). Local papers, for example, are often not discrete publishing ventures in their own right. Rather, they tend to be affiliated to larger papers which produce the main, general part of each issue, to which local publishers merely add their own local pages. To take such co-operation and dependencies into account, it has become standard practice to assess concentration on the basis of the number of independent editorial units, rather than the total number of newspapers available. The first indicator of press concentration is, therefore, the fact that the number of editorial units declined from 225 in 1954 to 135 in 1995 (Schütz 1996: 325). This decline in independent editorial units goes hand in hand with what is referred to as *Verlagskonzentration*, i.e. the decline in the number of publishing houses. Third, concentration can be observed in terms of circulation figures (*Auflagenkonzentration*), which have risen from 11.1 million (1950) to 26 million (1993), even though the number of papers and publishers has fallen. In other words, fewer publishers benefit from larger circulation. Finally, and perhaps most worryingly, there is a tendency towards *Lokalkonzentration*, which applies when only one local or regional paper is available in any district or town. This lack of choice in local publications is increasingly prevalent and now affects around half the country's inhabitants (Tonnemacher 1996: 96).

In the magazine market, similar processes of concentration have been taking place, resulting in the current situation where only four publishing groups produce more than 60 per cent of the total circulation (Röper 1996a: 311). From a business point of view, such concentration offers big publishers a number of advantages in a very competitive market. Competition is, of course, largely decided on the basis of sales, but it is also worth remembering that good sales alone cannot guarantee the economic viability of any publisher.

It is only once sales figures attract advertising clients that publishers become viable concerns, as the primary source of income in the German press is advertising, rather than sales. There are some notable exceptions, such as *taz*, which receives only around 10 per cent of its income from advertising. In general, however, this share amounts to between 70 and 80 per cent of the turnover (Meyn 1994: 85). This dependence on advertising adds to concentration tendencies in so far as big publishers with high circulation figures have a built-in competitive advantage when it comes to attracting advertisers. In contrast, the ability of smaller and independent publishing ventures to survive competition from the giants is constantly put to the test. The *taz*, for example, has had to appeal to the loyalty and solidarity of its readers on numerous occasions and has managed to survive only with difficulty.

The effects on the consumer of such concentration and dependence on advertising are ambiguous. On the positive side, they benefit from lower sales prices. Without any advertising revenue, many publications would have to be sold for two or three times their current price (Meyn 1994: 85). Yet concentration ultimately means less choice and, thus, compromises the objectives of pluralism and diversity, particularly in the context of *Tendenzschutz* (see p. 144). It is, therefore, not surprising that the issue of press concentration should have remained on the agenda in Germany. Concerns appear even more justified in view of the media as a whole, as many publishing houses nowadays no longer confine their operations to the publishing arena but have expanded into broadcasting and other related areas. There is some evidence of such cross-media ownership in the following brief survey of the major publishing groups which concludes this section.

The Axel Springer Konzern is Europe's largest newspaper publishing group. In addition to the best-selling *Bild Zeitung*, it publishes various other dailies and Sunday papers as well as numerous magazines. The group is heavily involved in publishing ventures abroad, for example in Eastern Europe, France, Spain and Britain. It also has interests in broadcasting (see p. 152).

Bertelsmann is Europe's largest multi-media conglomerate and the second largest in the world. Its strength in the German print media market rests on its 75 per cent ownership of the publishers Gruner & Jahr. In addition, it has long been developing its international activities all over the world. Bertelsmann is also one of the major players in broadcasting (see p. 152).

The Heinrich Bauer Verlag is the largest publisher of magazines in Europe. Its particular strength in Germany lies in the market of television and radio magazines. In addition, the group is also active in Eastern Europe, the United States and Britain.

Other leading publishers include Burda, Ganske and the Holtzbrinck GmbH, known in particular for its economics publications, such as the daily *Handelsblatt* and the weekly *Wirtschaftswoche*. The WAZ-Konzern, although mainly a regional publisher, has successfully expanded its operations to cover publications and broadcasting interests abroad, mainly in Austria and Hungary. It also has a 10 per cent stake in the RTL television channel.

BROADCASTING: THE DUAL SYSTEM

Since the mid-1980s, dramatic changes have transformed the broadcasting system almost beyond recognition. One of the most radical changes brought about by the media revolution is the emergence of a dual system (*duales System*) in which the traditional public-service provision of television and radio programmes is complemented by private, commercial broadcasting. This commercialisation of broadcasting has gone hand in hand with advances in cable and satellite technology, resulting in the majority of households being equipped with cable or satellite facilities. A total of approximately thirty television channels are currently available to the average household in Germany, which makes the German television market the second largest in the world, surpassed only by the United States. In addition, there are approximately two hundred local, regional and national radio stations.

Public-service broadcasters (*öffentlich-rechtliche Anstalten*)

After the Second World War, broadcasting systems developed in both East and West Germany which were based solely on the principle of non-private ownership. In the GDR, as with the press, this meant that the two national television channels and the numerous national and regional radio stations were state-owned and state-controlled. This was to ensure that the media presented a homogeneous view of the world, in line with the leading party's political and ideological agenda. Unlike in the case of the press, however, these attempts at state control of broadcasting were doomed to failure, because state power did not reach far enough to prevent East Germans from tuning into West German television and radio programmes which most of them could receive. When Unification took place, most East Germans were already quite familiar with West German programmes, although by that time their own national channels, taking advantage of the collapse of state control, had started broadcasting some highly popular, critical and topical programmes, such as had not been possible before. These attempts at self-transformation notwithstanding, and despite fierce campaigns to maintain at least the most popular stations, such as the youth radio station DT64, the East German broadcasting system disappeared almost without trace within just a year or two after Unification. The most instrumental legislation in this context was the 1991 broadcasting treaty (*Rundfunkstaatsvertrag*), on the basis of which the East German broadcasting system was incorporated into the larger financial and organisational structure of broadcasting in the Federal Republic.

The broadcasting media in the Federal Republic, in contrast, were initially neither privately owned nor in the hands of the state. Indeed, because of the terrible consequences of state control of the media during the Third Reich, it was believed by the Allies that broadcasting, like the press, should enjoy the maximum degree of freedom from state influence. A system of public-service provision was developed to ensure that principles such as broadcasting freedom (*Rundfunkfreiheit*) and diversity of opinion (*Meinungsvielfalt*) were not encroached upon by either state or private commercial interests. This public-service provision has been financed largely by licence-fee payments (*Rundfunkgebühren*) from the public, and the broadcasters are accountable to *Länder*-based broadcasting councils (*Rundfunkräte*) or the ZDF television council (*Fernsehrat*). To ensure diversity, these councils are made up of members representing socially significant groups, i.e. representatives of political parties, trade unions, the churches and other organisations in fields such as environmental protection, education or the arts. It is their task to supervise developments in broadcasting and to ensure that principles such as diversity, balance, matter-of-factness and respect are adhered to by broadcasters.

The first television broadcasts were made by ARD (Arbeitsgemeinschaft der öffentlich-rechtlichen Rundfunkanstalten der Bundesrepublik Deutschland), a group of non-commercial broadcasting stations founded in 1950. Under the umbrella of ARD, these regional stations have produced national as well as regional programmes. On a national level, ARD broadcasts as the so-called first programme or channel (*Erstes Deutsches Fernsehen* or *Erstes Programm*). The regional broadcasts are produced in any of, currently, eleven regional stations and shown mainly on the third channel (*Drittes Programm*). The location of these regional stations is based largely on the federal structure of Germany, with *Länder* either having their own stations or co-operating in joint operations. After Unification, two regional stations were added to cover the new *Länder*.

In addition to ARD, a second public-service provider, ZDF (Zweites Deutsches Fernsehen or *Zweites Programm*), has been operating since 1963. Whilst the structure of ARD with its regional stations closely follows the federal administrative system, ZDF is a centralised provision based in Mainz. It is financed, like ARD, mainly from licence fees, although for some years now both have been able to complement their income by revenue from advertising which they are allowed to broadcast at certain limited times of the day. More recently, both ARD and ZDF have also set up joint television channels with other European broadcasters – for example, 3SAT (with Austrian and Swiss participation) or ARTE (with French channel LA SEPT).

ARD, as a public-service broadcasting organisation, is also responsible for radio transmission – both nation-wide and regionally. Overall, there are around fifty different regional transmissions which are broadcast by the same stations responsible for regional television. In addition, there are two channels provided by *Deutschlandradio* and *Deutschlandfunk* for national transmission and a third, *Deutsche Welle*, which targets listeners abroad. Apart from *Deutsche Welle*, all public-service radio programmes are financed in the same way as public-service television, i.e. through licence fees and advertising revenue (Tonnemacher 1996: 165).

Commercial broadcasters

Up until the mid-1980s, the three television channels and the radio programmes available in Germany were provided almost exclusively by public-service broadcasters. Yet this monopoly was not to survive for much longer. Advances in cable and satellite technology provided private broadcasters with the long-awaited opportunity to enter the arena and challenge the public-service monopoly – with some success. Today, the majority of German television channels and radio stations are privately owned.

Unlike their public-service counterparts, private television channels, such as SAT.1, RTL, VOX, PRO 7 and others do not benefit from any licence-fee income. They are highly dependent on advertising revenue and, therefore, under great pressure to gain and maintain large audience figures. They too, however, are accountable to public institutions, the *Länder*-based media regulators (*Landesmedienanstalten*), which are responsible for granting their operating licences and supervising their output. Nevertheless, private channels enjoy more freedom as regards programme output, since they are not bound, like the public-service providers, by the obligation to supply a balanced and diverse basic provision (*Grundversorgung*) of television programmes, which will cater for all, including minority, interests (see pp. 155–6). As their funding rests solely on advertising revenue, they also benefit from less restrictive advertising regulations than their public-service counterparts, allowing up to 20 per cent of their output to be broadcast as advertising, including on Sundays and after 8 p.m., and the interruption of feature films for commercial breaks.

Much of the above applies not only to commercial television channels but also to private radio stations. And, even though most commercial radio stations transmit on a local or regional level only, the radio market is just as competitive as the television market. In fact, the *Länder*-based regulatory institutions have noted many instances where the original stipulations on programme format and content, on whose grounds radio licences are granted, are flouted by stations when deviant practices promise higher audience ratings. This drive for audience ratings has entered a new dimension with the emergence of the dual system. Indeed, audience ratings appear to have become the single main concern, certainly, of commercial broadcasters, but also, to some degree, of public-service providers, all of whom are now competing with one another. This new competitive climate in broadcasting is, however, not without its problems.

Problems of the dual system

When, in the 1980s, commercialisation of broadcasting started and the dual system of public-service and private television and radio emerged, it was hoped that these developments would lead to greater choice and diversity for media users. On the face of it, this is, indeed, what has happened. With the dramatic increase in television channels and radio stations, viewers are bound to have a greater choice than that offered by the handful of stations in the mid-1980s. It has since become clear, however, that the link between an increased number of channels and more diversity is not as straightforward as had been assumed, since the concentration tendencies already existing in the German media have been progressing at the same time.

Concentration

Concentration tendencies, already referred to in the context of the press (see pp. 145–8), become even more pronounced once broadcasting is taken into account as well. The emergence of local commercial radio stations, for example, was originally welcomed in the hope that they would be able to add to the diversity of local reporting and thus to counteract some of the concentration tendencies in the local press (see pp. 145–8). This, however, has not happened, as most local publishers are involved in and even dominate local radio and because reporting, as opposed to music, plays a very minor part in many local stations anyway (Tonnemacher 1996: 170). These problems notwithstanding, commercial radio has received rather less critical attention than other commercial media. It is, primarily, the extent of their involvement in television and the press that has alerted observers to the emergence of multi-media monopolies around the three major players: Bertelsmann, Kirch and Springer.

The Bertelsmann Group, in addition to its publishing and other activities (see p. 147), has developed a lively broadcasting division, UFA, through which it has interests in a number of television channels, such as RTL, RTL2, SUPER RTL, VOX and PREMIERE. UFA's recent merger with the Luxemburg-based CLT has resulted in CLT-UFA becoming Europe's largest media company, operating nineteen television and twenty-three radio stations in ten European countries. Part-owned by the group is also Britain's new Channel 5.

A similarly complex web of interests can be observed in the case of the Springer Group which, in addition to being Europe's largest publisher of newspapers (see p. 147), holds interests in television channels, such as SAT.1 and DSF, numerous regional radio stations and production companies. Whilst Springer's influence in the media at large is remarkable, as far as broadcasting is concerned it does not match that of Bertelsmann or the Kirch group.

The Kirch group's main interests are in film rights, distribution and production. In addition, Kirch is a major shareholder in channels such as SAT.1 and PRO 7, and holds a 35 per cent stake in the Springer press empire. Kirch's major strength results from the fact that the group owns the rights to a staggering number of films and television programmes which it has been buying since the 1950s. These are a very valuable commodity, as the amount of broadcasting time to be filled by channels has gone up dramatically with the increase in channels since the advent of commercial broadcasting. In addition to almost inexhaustible archives of old movies, the group has also acquired unique access to the latest Hollywood productions. It has made deals with several major Hollywood studios, including Rupert Murdoch's 20th Century-Fox (*Der Spiegel* 29/1996: 23). This gives the Kirch group a distinct advantage over its competitors in broadcasting, particularly as the shortage of programmes is going to be fuelled by the advent of digital television, also first introduced in Germany by Kirch. Digital television offers the opportunity to make available an even larger number of channels. And in future, as Kirch has demonstrated with his launch of pay-TV DF1, the emphasis will be on channels which viewers subscribe to or pay for on a pay-per-view basis. Yet again, the success of such operations will depend largely on the availability of attractive programmes that viewers are willing to pay extra money for, and the Kirch group appears singularly well prepared to satisfy this requirement.

If the television market as a whole looks set to expand further, then this, naturally, offers companies potential for growth. For some time now, debates have, therefore, focused on the question of how much influence any one broadcasting company should be allowed to have, and what restrictions should be imposed in order to prevent it from dominating the television market. These questions have been addressed in the latest broadcasting treaty (*Rundfunkstaatsvertrag*), in force since January 1997, which puts the maximum threshold for any television company's market share at 30 per cent, calculated on the basis of audience ratings. At first sight, this figure may appear low enough to safeguard diversity and prevent dominance. However, concerns have already been expressed about the ability to control concentration on the basis of these new regulations (Röper 1996b: 610–614, 618). Apart from the difficulties of obtaining reliable audience figures, concern focuses on the fact that the regulations target only those companies which hold a minimum of 25 per cent shares in any broadcasting station. In practice, this means that the Springer group, for example, is considered irrelevant in the television market because its shares in both the DSF channel (24.9 per cent) and the SAT.1 channel (20 per cent) are below this threshold. This appears problematic, as the group, although a relatively small player in the television market, has substantial influence in the press. Yet such networks of cross-media ownership are only taken into account in the case of companies which are close to reaching the 30 per cent threshold in their television market share. In other words, investigations of cross-media ownership affect only the big players in the television market, rather than big media companies in general. Many regard this as a shortcoming and fear that it restricts, at the outset, the work of the newly founded commission for the investigation of concentration, the KEK (Konzentrationsermittlungskommission). Even the increased degree of transparency about shares and interests that the new treaty requires from media companies could be compromised, if calculations fail to take into account the complex web of cross-media ownership – not just of broadcasting companies but also of those primarily active in publishing, production, distribution, rights and licences and many other related fields.

Without doubt, the issue of media concentration could have been addressed with much more stringency had it not been for economic considerations. The individual *Länder*, within whose cultural sovereignty broadcasting falls, have long been aware of the economic benefits of media companies being based in their respective regions. On a national level, too, such considerations have played an important role. Having observed the increasing power of international media giants, politicians of all major parties now seem to agree that German media companies must be allowed to grow in order to compete successfully on an international level – even if this means more concentration.

It remains to be seen what impact the recent deregulatory policies will have on the German media in the longer term, and to what degree concentration tendencies will jeopardise diversity in broadcasting. One thing, however, is certain: whilst there is still some commitment to public-service broadcasting in Germany, commercial stations have not only established themselves successfully in the dual system but are also likely to push for further deregulation in the future.

Competition between public-service and private broadcasters

The arrival of commercial broadcasters on the scene has had dramatic consequences for the public-service providers. Both ARD and ZDF have lost audience figures and substantial advertising revenue to private stations, resulting in serious financial difficulties and prompting extensive cost-cutting operations. Yet the funding shortage has been much too substantial to be addressed by internal reforms alone. In recognition of these difficulties, the new licence fee agreement, in force since 1997, stipulates an increase in licence fees from DM 23.40 to 28.25 per month. This has, undoubtedly, relieved some of the financial pressures on public-service channels and radio stations. Yet the debates surrounding the new licence fee agreement are set to continue. Various reform proposals are still on the agenda. The commercial channels, unhappy with ARD's and ZDF's double income from fees and advertising, have questioned whether such preferential treatment of the public-service broadcasters is justified. At the core of the debate has been the question of whether there is still a need for publicly funded channels.

The evidence suggests that there is and that the commercial leg of the dual system rests heavily on the continued existence of the public-service channels. One of the key arguments in this context concerns the notion of *Grundversorgung* (basic provision). The Federal Constitutional Court ruled in 1986 that public-service channels were to be relied upon for a basic provision of programmes. This basic provision is defined, above all, in terms of the overall diversity and balance of programmes, which must provide wide-ranging information and programmes to satisfy varying educational, cultural and entertainment interests. Commercial channels, in contrast, were not expected to fulfil these requirements to the same degree and were allowed to design programmes largely on the basis of commercial considerations, i.e. with ratings and advertisers in mind. Whilst this key ruling provides a justification and guarantee for the future existence of publicly funded channels, it also indicates their basic dilemma: a programme format which upholds the principles of diversity and balance cannot, by definition, attract high ratings at all times. For diversity is the result of a programme mix whose different parts appeal to different, including smaller, audiences. As far as commercial broadcasters are concerned, the ruling clarifies that their existence and ratings success depends on public-service channels delivering this basic provision of programmes, providing diversity and creating a counter-balance to the 'ratings fetishism' prevalent in commercial broadcasting. In practice, this means that specialised commercial sports, music or news channels (*Spartenkanäle*), such as DSF, VIVA or N-TV, can be appreciated as additions to a basic, varied provision of programmes guaranteed elsewhere. Similarly, this basic provision provides the necessary counter-balance also to those commercial channels which claim to provide a comprehensive programme (*Vollprogramm*) but whose programme formats may revolve around films, chat shows, game shows and soaps, which are known to pull in big audiences and which are, therefore, attractive to advertisers, too.

In short, there seems to be a division of labour of sorts between public and private channels, and this division is borne out by evidence on media usage. Bearing in mind that information and entertainment are the two primary motivations for television viewers, it appears that German viewers seek out different parts of the dual system to satisfy either of these interests. They rate public-service channels more highly in terms of their provision of information, whereas commercial channels are appreciated primarily for their entertainment value. These attitudes are reflected in viewing habits: in 1995 viewers received over 70 per cent of their daily television information from public-service channels. In contrast, they turned to commercial channels for almost two-thirds of their television entertainment (Darschin and Frank 1996: 180–2). These viewing habits, as well as indicating viewers' preferences, are also a reflection of the overall balance in programming. In 1994 the category of entertainment accounted for over 70 per cent of the commercial channels' output, but only for 40 per cent in the public channels (Kiefer 1996: 247). It should, however, not be assumed that the public-service channels are only appreciated for being informative. They are also the producers of some of the most popular entertainment programmes, crime series, children's programmes and music shows. In fact, half the German viewers list ARD and ZDF amongst their three favourite television stations (Darschin and Frank 1996: 184).

If these figures indicate that the basic provision by public-service channels is indispensable for many Germans, further evidence suggests that they may also be rather more reliable in terms of quality. Many of the private channels have been criticised for bowing to the lowest common denominator in their drive for high ratings. In contrast, all but one of the sixteen *Grimme Preis* awards for quality television in 1995 went to public-service programmes. The significance of such awards should, of course, not be overestimated. Nor are all criticisms regarding the quality of commercial broadcasting necessarily valid. Yet it appears that at least some of the concerns are not unfounded. There is clearly a danger that the pressure to achieve high ratings may tempt commercial stations to take a sensationalist approach and compromise where ethical considerations and journalistic integrity are concerned. This danger was highlighted by the case of television journalist Michael Born, who in December 1996 was sentenced to four years' imprisonment after having invented and staged sensationalist news stories. In his trial, judges also expressed severe criticisms of the commercial television companies which had broadcast Born's programmes without having shown the necessary care and attention in examining their authenticity and truthfulness. As exceptional as this case may have been, it has highlighted the dangers resulting from the obsession with ratings of commercial channels and will, no doubt, have implications for the future. In the words of Hermann Meyn, head of the German association of journalists:

'Audiences will, in future, be much more sceptical, when certain programmes, particularly by commercial stations, broadcast sensationalist items' ('Vier Jahre Haft . . .' 1996: 1).

RECOMMENDED READING

Humphreys (1994) and Sandford (1976) in English. Somewhat shorter, but focusing on developments after Unification is Sandford (1995).

In German, Meyn (1994) and Tonnemacher (1996), both excellent introductions. For the most up-to-date information and research on all media, see the monthly journal *Media Perspektiven*. In its 12/96 issue, Röper and Dörr provide commentaries on the latest deregulatory reforms in broadcasting. For a discussion of commercialisation, the impact of new technology and other recent developments in television, see Monkenbusch (1994).

BIBLIOGRAPHY

Anon. (1996) 'D. e. F.' *Der Spiegel* 29: 22–34.
Darschin, W. and Frank, B. (1996) 'Tendenzen im Zuschauerverhalten', *Media Perspektiven* 4/96: 174–185.
'Das entfesselte Fernsehen', in *Der Spiegel* 29/1996: 22–34.
Dörr, D. (1996) 'Maßnahmen zur Vielfaltssicherung gelungen?', *Media Perspektiven* 12/96: 621–628.
Drösser, C. (1995) *special: Fernsehen*, Reinbek bei Hamburg: Rowohlt.
Heinrich, H. (1991) *Deutsche Medienpolitik*, Nauheim: Verlag R. Koch.
Humphreys, P. J. (1994, revised edn) *Media and Media Policy in Germany: The Press and Broadcasting since 1945*, Oxford and Providence, USA: Berg.
Kiefer, M.-L. (1996) 'Massenkommunikation 1995', *Media Perspektiven* 5/96: 234–248.
Media Perspektiven Basisdaten 1995.
Meyn, H. (1994, revised edn) *Massenmedien in der Bundesrepublik Deutschland*, Berlin: Edition Colloquium.
Monkenbusch, H. (ed.) (1994) *Fernsehen: Medien, Macht und Märkte*, Reinbek bei Hamburg: Rowohlt.
Röper, H. (1996a) 'Konzentration im Zeitschriftenmarkt gestiegen', *Media Perspektiven* 6/96: 309–323.
—— (1996b) 'Mehr Spielraum für Konzentration und Cross ownership im Mediensektor', *Media Perspektiven* 12/96: 610–620.
Sandford, J. (1976) *The Mass Media of the German-Speaking Countries*, London: Oswald Wolff.
—— (1995) 'The German Media', in Lewis, D. and McKenzie, J. (eds) *The New Germany: Social, Political and Cultural Challenges of Unification*, Exeter: Exeter University Press.
Schneider, N. (1996) 'Ein Uber-Winter-Märchen: Satire im Fernsehen', in Abarbanell, S., Cippitelli, C. and Schwanebeck, A. (eds) *Fernsehzeit: 21 Einblicke ins Programm*, Munich: Verlag Reinhard Fischer.

158 *Steffi Boothroyd*

Schütz, W. J. (1996) 'Deutsche Tagespresse 1995', *Media Perspektiven* 6/96: 324–336.

Sternburg, W. von (ed.) (1995) *Tagesthema ARD: Der Streit um das Erste Programm*, Frankfurt am Main: Fischer.

Tonnemacher, J. (1996) *Kommunikationspolitik in Deutschland: Eine Einführung*, Constance: UVK Medien.

'Vier Jahre Haft für TV-Fälscher Born', in *Berliner Zeitung*, 24 December 1996: 1.

10 Culture

Steffi Boothroyd

Considering the wealth of cultural activity in contemporary Germany, the following accounts of literature, film, the theatre, the visual arts and popular music are bound to present an incomplete picture – incomplete not only because much has had to be excluded, but also because this chapter takes a somewhat narrow and traditional approach to culture. It provides a brief survey of some of the recent developments in the cultural sphere and introduces some of the recent debates. Its focus is largely on those works and figures that are widely regarded as influential – either as part of Germany's commitment to creating a cultural identity for itself, or as part of an established mainstream. More avant-garde activities on the fringes, however, are not considered in any detail, nor is the process by which these impact on and feed into the established mainstream culture. These limitations should be borne in mind by readers of this chapter.

KULTURSTAAT GERMANY

What distinguishes the Federal Republic's cultural landscape from that of many other Western countries is, above all, the visibility of cultural activity all over the country. If New York is often regarded as the cultural capital of the United States, or London as that of Great Britain, there is no one single city to claim this title in Germany. Alongside Berlin, Frankfurt, Munich, Hamburg, Cologne and other major cities, smaller towns and even rural areas often boast their own distinctive cultural scene and offer cultural attractions to locals and visitors alike. This cultural infrastructure has partly evolved from the historically strong identity of regions in Germany, but it would not have been possible to maintain and develop without the prosperity that the Federal Republic has enjoyed in recent decades and its overall commitment to a notion of Germany as a *Kulturstaat* (cultural state).

Within this general commitment to culture, the federal state is, primarily, in charge of Germany's cultural representation abroad – a role performed, for example, by the Goethe Institute with its one hundred and fifty or so branches in seventy-seven countries. Far more important, however, for those living in Germany, are the local provisions by individual *Länder* which, following the federalist principle of cultural sovereignty (see Chapter 3, p. 33), carry the main responsibility for fostering culture. It is primarily at this *Länder*-level, and within local city and community authorities, that the general commitment to culture is translated into practical arrangements of funding and patronage which have created much of the country's cultural landscape. In recent years, however, Germany's precarious economic situation has forced authorities to impose cuts and freezes in the cultural sector, and some observers even speak of a policy of deliberate underfunding (Grasskamp 1996: 51). For various projects, lack of funding has already resulted in closure. Others have, increasingly, resorted to private sponsorship, but a large proportion of cultural ventures continue to depend on injections of public finance.

The FRG's system of state funding and patronage has often been praised as beneficial for artistic development and for making culture more accessible to the public. Doubtlessly, it has contributed to the existence of a lively and prolific cultural scene – one which is both open to international, particularly Anglo-American, influences and committed to fostering its own distinctive expressions of traditional and contemporary culture. However, state involvement in the cultural sphere is not unproblematic. At its most extreme, such involvement may be part and parcel of a political agenda which disrespects the freedom and autonomy of the arts and reduces culture to a vehicle for expressing a dominant ideology. This was the case in the Third Reich, where patronage of culture and the arts by the fascist state was generous, but where the role of the state as a sponsor of culture was inseparable from its role as censor. Its commitment to culture extended only to those projects which were regarded as affirmative of or, at least, compatible with the fascist ideology, while everything else was banned and often, quite literally, destroyed. This cultural policy forced countless writers, artists and film-makers into exile and almost succeeded in annihilating major parts of the country's entire cultural tradition. In the infamous book-burning (*Bücherverbrennung*) ceremonies, the works of countless writers – Jewish, left-wing or simply experimental – were thrown into the fire. Paintings and other works of art considered degenerate (*entartet*) were destroyed or removed from public display. Film production came under the control of one central authority (Reichsfilmkammer) which was responsible for commissioning, subsidising and approving all film projects. Thus, culture in the Third Reich was allowed to exist only as state culture, as an extension of the fascist state's ideological and political agenda.

In the GDR, too, there was a close relationship between cultural production and the state. Here, the responsibility of the state towards culture was clearly defined in the constitution as the promotion and protection of a socialist national culture. On the one hand, this guaranteed many artists a material basis for developing their projects. It also translated into generous subsidies, for example to keep prices of books and theatre tickets low, so that culture was accessible to people from all income groups. On the other hand, this cultural practice excluded all those artists whose ideas did not fit in with the definition of a socialist national culture. In this respect, the GDR's state apparatus, too, performed the double role of sponsor and censor of culture. Projects which officials regarded as detrimental to a socialist culture were banned or simply denied access to the state-owned production facilities. Many artists, whose works were thus excluded from the public sphere, saw no alternative but to leave the country. However, in the field of culture, the boundaries between what was and what wasn't regarded as acceptable at any one time were rather more fluid than, for example, in the media. Certainly, many artists engaged in the often tiresome and frustrating attempt at extending these boundaries – and with some success. Whilst outright criticism of the political and social set-up was rarely tolerated by the authorities, there was, nevertheless, some leeway to address controversial issues, often implicitly, by way of allegory or by challenging the audience to read between the lines. There was also some experimentation in genres and styles, and even the preferred style of socialist realism itself underwent transformations and became more critical over the years. Many activities also took place on the fringes, where banned books and manuscripts or experimental films were introduced to small audiences. And even big state-sponsored events, such as the annual international Political Song Festival in Berlin, often provided a space of encounter and communication between GDR audiences and artists and foreign guests which was, to a degree, beyond state control. In other words, the state did not succeed, if that was its aim, in creating a homogeneous affirmative state culture. Rather, the relationship between culture and the state was constantly renegotiated.

This process of negotiation of differences is relevant also in the context of the Federal Republic, and some conflictual aspects of the relationship between culture and the state may be seen to apply here, too. As the freedom of the arts is enshrined in the Federal Republic's Basic Law, there is, unlike in the GDR, no legal basis which allows the state to discriminate between different forms of cultural expression and to foster only those projects which fit into an exclusive concept of state culture. Yet the commitment to fostering culture and the arts requires, in practice, decisions to be made, for example, about which projects should receive public funding. As there are also varying ideas about what makes for adequate cultural policy and a desirable culture landscape, it comes as no surprise that the practicalities of the German *Kulturstaat* have often been regarded as problematic. Traditionalism, for example, is a charge frequently levelled with regard to the preoccupations of prestigious cultural institutions, such as the 300-year-old Berlin academy of arts, but also in the context of the aesthetic value judgements underlying individual state-sponsored projects. More importantly, considering Germany's difficulties following two world wars and four decades of division, in defining a positive identity for itself, the commitment to a *Kulturstaat* does not merely express a recognition of culture as an important part of the fabric of society, but must also be seen as having a political dimension. As such, the notion of *Kulturstaat* is closely linked with the political commitment to creating a national cultural identity. This process of identity-formation has been particularly topical since Unification, as the ensuing cultural effort has offered the opportunity to re-assess past traditions and developments in both Germanys as well as to shape a new identity for the new Germany. In this context, culture within the German *Kulturstaat* cannot be regarded merely as an expression of a more or less traditionalist aesthetic interest, but must be understood also as a topical political concern, as will be evident in the next section on literature.

LITERATURE

Approaching Germany via the contemporary book market with its lists of new publications and bestsellers reveals, first of all, a remarkable presence of foreign literature. In contrast, neither the country's rich literary tradition nor the wealth of its contemporary activity is immediately apparent in the same way. A rather different picture emerges from the literary review pages and the, at times, prolonged debates following articles and essays on or by German writers. These reveal that the impact of Germany's own writers on the cultural and political climate, which was considerable in both East and West, continues to be so in the unified Germany too.

In the GDR, literature was held in high regard by both the state and the general public. The state, unsurprisingly, encouraged the production of literature that unquestioningly identified with the political system. In contrast, many readers appreciated literature for its ability to provide a forum which, although it did not question the validity of the socialist world-view as such, offered reflection on those contemporary issues which were ignored and left out of public discourse elsewhere in society, especially in the media. Its authors, by extension, were often perceived as being at the forefront of the battle for a more democratic and open socialist society. The literary efforts and other public expressions of such authors were, of course, closely monitored by the state, and those who overstepped the mark would find themselves without a publisher or, worse, face recriminations. It is, however, to those writers who were successful at performing the balancing act of being published, while maintaining a degree of autonomy, that GDR literature owes much of its diversity and appeal. Amongst them are Christa Wolf, Volker Braun, Christoph Hein, Jurek Becker, Irmtraud Morgner and others.

In the FRG, too, there has been a tradition of socio-critical and emancipatory literature which has responded to contemporary social and political concerns in subject matter, genre and style, and explored the imbalances and injustices prevalent in society. Within this tradition, the literary author has come to be regarded as a figure of some authority, ideally suited to comment on contemporary issues, not only through literary works but also in essays, interviews, speeches and such like. This tradition, which includes writers such as Heinrich Böll, Günter Grass, Hans Magnus Enzensberger, Günter Wallraff, Martin Walser, Max von der Grün and many others, has strongly influenced the entire cultural scene and produced some of the most highly regarded literary works. Since Unification, however, this tradition, alongside that of critical writing in the GDR, has come under review. In the so-called *Literaturstreit* (debate on literature), conducted by critics, observers and writers during the years following Unification, the political and ethical commitments of leading protagonists of the literary scene were challenged and re-assessed in an attempt to redefine the role of literature in the new Germany. Whilst literature was called upon to move away from political towards more aesthetic concerns, the peculiarities of the review undertaken in the *Literaturstreit* themselves testify to the continuing political dimension assigned to literature and writers in Germany.

Contrary to what the term *Literaturstreit* suggests, the debates focused less on actual works of literature, their quality, relevance and interpretation, than on the perceived flaws in the personal integrity and political convictions of individual, particularly East German, authors. There were some specific charges of collaboration with the East German secret police, as in the much-publicised case of Christa Wolf, who had briefly, informally and rather inconsequentially collaborated with the secret police twenty years previously. But on a more general level East German authors were criticised for writing and publishing in East Germany and thus 'lending credibility to the GDR in one way or another' (Mellis 1995: 233). It seems paradoxical at first sight that the focus of attention was precisely on writers who had previously been regarded as serious and critical enough not to be categorised as 'state writers'. Yet the argument holds in so far as most of them, while considering the status quo in the GDR as unsatisfactory and in need of reform, felt in some way committed to socialism, its ideals and objectives. It was this commitment, above all, that appears to have been challenged in the *Literaturstreit*.

If East German literature was thus scrutinised in view of its potential position in the new Germany's canon, the *Literaturstreit* did not stop there, but also targeted some West German writers of the sociocritical tradition. Grass, Böll and others were now attacked for their left-of-centre ethical and political concerns which, it was argued, had not only been overemphasised in their literary works but had also dominated the country's cultural scene as a whole. There are significant parallels between the 'essentially political nature of the attack on GDR culture' (Parkes 1997: 190) and the attacks on West German writers and intellectuals which also expressed 'not so much objection to political stances as such, but rather to certain specific stances' (Parkes 1997: 195). As such, the *Literaturstreit* gave expression to the wider political tensions and shifting balances of power in the new Germany. Certainly, its 'projection . . . flew in the face of much of German cultural tradition' (Carr and Paul 1995: 341). For to demand that German literature should return to aesthetic concerns and liberate itself from an overtly political function means in effect to call for an end to a valued humanist tradition of socio-critical literature, which has offered unique responses to many issues of topical relevance – not least that of the division of Germany, now in principle overcome.

Indeed, the divided Germany is amongst the many themes to have preoccupied writers in East and West Germany alike. It is the subject of Christa Wolf's early work *Der geteilte Himmel* (1963), Peter Schneider's *Der Mauerspringer* (1982), Thorsten Becker's *Die Bürgschaft* (1985) and Martin Walser's *Dorle und Wolf* (1987), to mention but a few.

Similarly, the common fascist past, problematic in the historical and political discourses of both the GDR and the FRG, has been a theme to which literature has responded in unique ways. Probably the most successful attempt at literary *Vergangenheitsbewältigung* has been undertaken by Günter Grass in his *Die Blechtrommel* (The Tin Drum) (1959), which explores Nazi Germany and the period of restoration in the FRG through the eyes of maverick Oskar Matzerath who deliberately turns himself into an outsider by refusing to grow after the Nazis take power. In Christa Wolf's *Kindheitsmuster* (A Model Childhood) (1976) an examination of the fascist past is initiated when an adult woman revisits her childhood home, and Jurek Becker's *Jakob der Lügner* (Jacob the Liar) (1968) tells a story of hope and despair amongst the victims of fascism in a Jewish ghetto.

Another theme taken up in both East and West German literature is that of the patriarchal society and the limitations it imposes on women. Amongst the key works to come out of the GDR was Irmtraud Morgner's *Leben und Abenteuer der Trobadora Beatriz nach Zeugnissen ihrer Spielfrau Laura* (1974). In the West, Elfriede Jelinek's controversial *Lust* (1989) explores with shocking directness the impact of male desire, power and violence.

Alongside these and other themes which literature in both Germanys has given voice to, there are many works which explore specific social and political tensions in each of the two German states. Ulrich Plenzdorf's *Die neuen Leiden des jungen W.* (1972), for example, had cult status in the GDR, and Volker Braun's *Die unvollendete Geschichte* (Unfinished Story) (1975), although to a lesser extent owing to censorship, offers an even more poignant condemnation of a state distrusting its citizens. In the FRG, during a period of paranoia about left-wing extremist terrorism, Heinrich Böll's *Die verlorene Ehre der Katharina Blum* (The Lost Honour of Katharina Blum) (1974) provides a unique insight into the relationship between the individual and the state, by placing an ordinary unpolitical heroine in the context of terrorism, state surveillance and a media witch-hunt. And Günter Wallraff's *Ganz unten* (1985) alerted the West German public to the prevalence of racism in its society.

In view of the strength of this and other socio-critical writing, it remains to be seen how post-Unification literature is to proceed in the long term. It has, however, already responded to the recent political and cultural upheavals, and various examples of *Wenderoman* (novels about the changes of Unification) have been published. Volker Braun's *Wendehals* (1995), Thomas Brussig's *Helden wie wir* (1995) and Günter Grass's *Ein weites Feld* (1995) are all interesting in this respect.

FILM

Since its emergence a century ago, the German film has largely been a national concern. With the exception of the silent era and the New German Cinema in the 1970s and 1980s, the German film industry's prolific output has rarely met with much international recognition or commercial success. Even in Germany itself, commercially viable German productions have been the exception rather than the rule, and around 80 per cent of cinema turnover has, traditionally, been accounted for by American productions. On the other hand, there has often been international recognition of the artistic quality of German films and the work of directors such as Fassbinder, Herzog, Schlöndorff and Wenders. Moreover, recent developments suggest that German films may be enjoying a revival in popularity and thus offer not only artistic but also commercial potential.

The early German film industry of the 1920s and early 1930s was one of the most successful and influential in the world. Despite economic depression and inflation, the film industry flourished in Weimar Germany and held an enormous appeal with audiences. Nowadays, it is largely the art films of this early period which are acclaimed for their experimentation in Expressionist and other styles, their startlingly stylised settings, their general visual quality and, not least, their exploration of new camera techniques. Many of these early works are now regarded as cinema classics, for example Robert Wiene's *Das Cabinett des Dr Caligari* (1919), F. W. Murnau's *Nosferatu* (1922) and Fritz Lang's *Metropolis* (1926).

After the Second World War, the very studios at Babelsberg which had produced many of the classic movies of the 1920s became the centre of film production in the GDR. They were now state-owned, and their productions under the imprint of DEFA suffered from constraints similar to those in other areas of cultural life in the GDR. Nevertheless, some high-quality films were made which often attracted large audience figures in the GDR itself as well as finding some international acclaim. To mention but a few: Konrad Wolf's 1964 production of Christa Wolf's *Der geteilte Himmel* and his last work *Solo Sunny* (1979), Heiner Carow's *Die Legende von Paul und Paula* (1973) and *Coming out* (1988/89) or Lothar Warneke's *Einer trage des anderen Last* (1988). When the Babelsberg studio complex was privatised after Unification, the West German film director Volker Schlöndorff, now also one of its managing directors, expressed a vision to return Babelsberg to its former glory as the birthplace of German cinema and turn it into a 'European Hollywood'. Some years on, however, the realisation of this vision appears a long way off. An extensive programme of modernisation has gone hand in hand with diversification, and film productions for cinema release are now outnumbered by productions for television, advertising and video.

In the Federal Republic, the film scene began its most interesting phase with the emergence, in the 1960s, of the New German Cinema (*der Neue Deutsche Film*), which was to be critically acclaimed throughout the following two decades. This new style of film-making was not clearly defined in terms of genre, style or theme. Rather, it covers a very diverse range of intelligent, experimental and political films. There were adaptations of literary works, such as Volker Schlöndorff's *Die verlorene Ehre der Katharina Blum* (The Lost Honour of Katharina Blum) or *Die Blechtrommel* (The Tin Drum), which won the Palme d'or at Cannes in 1979 and the Oscar for Best Foreign Film in 1980. There were Werner Herzog's exotic existentialist films, such as *Fitzcarraldo*, which was awarded the Cannes prize for best direction in 1982. Other important directors include Alexander Kluge, Wim Wenders, Margarethe von Trotta, Peter Lilienthal, Helma Sanders-Brahms and the immensely prolific Rainer Werner Fassbinder who, until his death in 1982, directed over forty films and series for cinema and television. Many of Fassbinder's works, which were highly controversial at the time, are now regarded as classics. His largest success came in 1979 with *Die Ehe der Maria Braun*. However, popularity with audiences and commercial success were not, on the whole, typical of the New German Cinema. It was, with the notable exception of Schlöndorff, largely a cinema of auteurs (*Autorenkino*) who sought to express their aesthetic, political and intellectual concerns without seeking wide box office appeal. And whilst the New German Cinema includes remarkable cinematic contributions to the social and political conflicts of the time, as well as artistically commendable explorations of the medium film, there was a degree of aloofness *vis-à-vis* popular culture and mass audiences. Consequently, commercial viability became the exception.

The liveliness, despite this lack of commercial success, of the New

German Cinema in the 1970s and 1980s must be attributed, at least in part, to the system of funding, subsidy and promotion of film from the *Länder* budgets and the public-service television channels. On the other hand, it has been suggested, even by some film-makers themselves, that this very system has actively invited commercial failure by encouraging the production of 'art house'-style movies for small audiences, rather than insisting on achieving a balance between artistic quality and commercial appeal. Recently, however, there have been indications that German productions are beginning to compete more successfully with American imports. It is, probably, no coincidence that a number of comedies, in particular, have recently attracted large audience figures, for example Rainer Kaufmann's *Stadtgespräch* (1995), Doris Dörrie's *Keiner liebt mich* (1995), Detlev Buck's *Männerpension* (1996) and Sönke Wortmann's *Der bewegte Mann* (1995). With audience figures of 2–6 million, these films and others indicate that the German film is breaking out of its niche existence. The audience share of German productions, previously only around 10 per cent, reached 22 per cent in the first seven months of 1996 (*Der Spiegel*, 38/1996: 215) – a reward, it seems, to a younger generation of film-makers committed to providing intelligent entertainment. If, as a result, the market has become bigger and film-making is no longer considered a loss-making venture, then this must be good news for the German film as a whole. Yet it remains to be seen whether the current enthusiasm for a new heyday of the German film is justified. The export value of German comedies is traditionally rather low, and even in the German film scene there has been little evidence that the new popularity extends beyond the genre of comedy. Romuald Karmakar's serious, non-mainstream feature *Der Totmacher* (The Deathmaker), for example, was awarded three of the 1996 German film prizes for best director, best film and best actor. At the box office, however, it attracted less than half a million viewers, a fate shared by many other recent non-comedy productions, such as Joseph Vilsmaier's *Schlafes Bruder* and Michael Verhoeven's *Mutter Courage*.

It is to be hoped that recent successes have instilled new interest and confidence in the German film amongst audiences and that, in time, this interest will extend to high-quality, non-mainstream features, too. There is much talent in the German film scene, and the cinema market appears big enough to accommodate both large-scale international productions and a distinctive cinema made in Germany.

THEATRE

The German theatre is a boring and marginal affair, according to Carl Hegemann, chief dramaturge of the Berliner Ensemble, one of the country's most prestigious theatres (Detje and Koberg 1996: 50). Such a sweeping statement, even coming from an insider, cannot do justice to the diversity within contemporary theatre work in Germany. It does, however, highlight a problem that the theatre scene has had to face with particular urgency in the wake of recent cuts and freezes in public funding. With around half of Germans never visiting the theatre and fewer than 10 per cent describing themselves as frequent theatre-goers (*Datenreport 1994*: 533), it seems that the theatre has, with some exceptions, not been able to overcome a somewhat elitist and traditionalist appeal. Although current funding policies, even after recent cuts and freezes, suggest that the theatre is still regarded as one of the most important national cultural institutions, it seems that theatres are now called upon to tighten their belts and to re-think their role in Germany's cultural landscape. One vision as to what this role might be was expressed by Federal President Roman Herzog when he addressed the German stage association on the occasion of its 150th anniversary in 1996. He spoke of finding ways for the theatre to become a place with which the people in any given city could identify, as they would with their local football club (Herzog 1996: 5).

This is an enormous challenge which, so far, not many theatres have seriously taken up. Arguably, it is not easy, in the current climate of cuts and freezes, for theatres to face the challenge of carving out a new role for themselves and increase their appeal. Apart from suffering a reduction in public funding, they have also had to operate in a climate where television is seen as the main medium for leisure time. And whilst the public-service television channels used to show some commitment to fostering theatre work, they now appear less willing and able to fulfil this role. ZDF, for example, recently axed its *Aktuelle Inszenierung*, a slot devoted to broadcasting contemporary theatre productions, and justified its decision by pointing out the minority appeal of such programmes.

Patronage, funding and its distribution are issues at the core of much discussion about the contemporary theatre scene. Most observers and theatre workers themselves agree that reforms are necessary, and various models are under discussion. Although there has been no consensus as to how the system should be changed, much criticism focuses on the current funding policies, often described as being based on the *Gießkannen-Prinzip* (watering-can principle). Whilst this principle has ensured funding for a large number of theatres across the country, it has also been argued that this emphasis on quantity rather than quality is to blame for much of the complacency and provincialism observed in the scene. It has encouraged lavish spending habits in some of the established public theatres (*feste Häuser*), whereas independent companies (*Privat- und Off-Theater*) receive only short-term funding on a project basis or have to fend for themselves entirely.

Interestingly, the financial crisis has not affected all theatres. Many commercial theatres, which operate rather more independently of public funding, have always been aware of the need to attract large audiences in order to play to full capacity. It is they who have benefited most from the recent boom in the popularity of musicals which has resulted in commercial musical ventures mushrooming all over the country (Büning and Rückert 1996: 9–10). Even if traditional theatres do not see themselves in direct competition with these ventures, such commercial success illustrates that the prospect of 'a night out' at the theatre can have great pulling power with audiences – a potential which many of Germany's public theatres have yet to realise. One that has is the small-town Meiningen theatre which appears to have built a remarkable presence in the south-eastern region of Thuringia. With a diverse repertoire of classical and new plays, operas and musicals it plays to over 90 per cent capacity – a record percentage amongst public theatres in Germany. If Meiningen's theatre can attract 190,000 visitors per season, i.e. more than six times the number of inhabitants in the area (*Der Spiegel*, 3/1996: 142–3), then, amid funding and identity problems, there must also be reason to be optimistic about the future of Germany's theatres.

And there are other reasons, too. Above all, the scene is very lively and there is much evidence of productivity and talent. Furthermore, the German theatre has arguably been at its most interesting when it has responded to contemporary social and political issues. Certainly in East Germany the theatre often fulfilled 'the function of a political forum' (Patterson 1995: 262), by reflecting aspects of contemporary life which the official political discourse did not address. This was true of contemporary plays, for example by Volker Braun, Christoph Hein, Ulrich Plenzdorf and, in particular, of the highly complex and political works of Heiner Müller, and it was an aspect of many productions of classical plays which were imbued with topical political references. It was also in the East, at the Berliner Ensemble, that

Bertolt Brecht, upon his return from exile after the Second World War, developed his theatre style which was to have an enormous impact on playwrights, directors and actors all over the world. Brecht's theatre, by abandoning traditional modes of empathy-inducing, psychologised theatre in favour of a rational, didactic style, revolutionised and politicised theatre work.

In West Germany, too, playwrights such as Rolf Hochhuth, Peter Weiss and others have been part of a tradition of political theatre, and topical political themes will, no doubt, continue to play an important role in the newly unified theatre scene. Unification and its effects have themselves become a subject for exploration in the theatre, for example in Hochhuth's recent *Wessis in Weimar: Szenen aus einem besetzten Land* and in Klaus Pohl's *Wartesaal Deutschland*. The concern about right-wing extremist activities has also found expression in new plays, for example Franz Xaver Kroetz's *Ich bin das Volk* and Tankred Dorst's *Schattenlinie*. Overall, the contemporary scene is very diverse. Alongside established directors of international acclaim, such as Peter Zadek and Peter Stein, a younger generation of artists have been making their mark, amongst them directors Frank Castorf, Leander Haußmann and Einar Schleef. They and many other theatre workers, not least the great number of committed and talented actors, are the main reason why the German theatre looks set to survive its current funding crisis.

THE VISUAL ARTS

The German art world, which had exhibited great diversity and gained much international recognition in the early decades of this century, visibly suffered from the rupture induced by fascism. Whilst artists such as Max Beckmann, Max Ernst, Oskar Kokoschka, George Grosz and many others continued their careers abroad, in Germany itself the arrival of fascism in 1933 spelt the beginning of a long period of decline into uniformity which could be said to have continued until well into the 1950s and 1960s. The Nazi campaigns to rid the country of 'un-German art', as it was described, culminated in 1937 in the infamous Munich exhibition of '*Entartete Kunst*' (degenerate art), where many works, particularly of abstract modernist art, were presented to the public for ridicule before, finally, being destroyed or sold off to buyers abroad.

In the Federal Republic, the almost unanimous turn to abstract art after the end of the Second World War was symbolic of the liberation from the Nazis' obsession with heroic and dull figurative art and their extreme dislike of non-representational art. In addition, this turn to the abstract expressed the divisions created by the Cold War, with realism being viewed, in the West, as somewhat backward and anti-quated (Gohr 1986: 462). Consequently, realist and representational art became almost entirely the domain of artists in the GDR, where, in turn, experimentation with other styles was generally not welcomed. Thus, in the east, artists like Fritz Cremer, Werner Tübke, Wolfgang Mattheuer and Willi Sitte explored the style of socialist realism. Others, such as Georg Baselitz and a. r. penck, settled in the Federal Republic where they developed their distinctive individual styles, Baselitz becoming particularly well known for turning his motifs 'upside down', and penck for his characteristic figures reminiscent of primitive cave paintings.

West German artists, in turn, sought their inspiration and themes almost exclusively in the Western international arts scene and refrained from references to specifically German historical and con-temporary themes. This international orientation and the resulting break with national tradition was not, however, rewarded with inter-national recognition. Rather, it has been blamed for contributing to the provincialism that the West German arts scene exhibited for many decades (Damus 1995: 19). The most notable exception to this trend was Joseph Beuys whose works, crossing the boundaries of genres and styles, offered a radically new approach to sculpture and art in general. In his installations, Beuys made use of materials previously unheard of in sculpture, and his happenings were attempts at over-coming the boundaries between art and life. He was exceptional also for the consistency with which his work confronted questions of German identity in the aftermath of fascism and war. On the whole, however, it was only in the 1970s that a somewhat less radical, but distinctively German dimension established itself in the West German arts scene, with Anselm Kiefer, Markus Lüpertz, Jörg Immendorff and others exploring themes and motifs from German history, mythology and landscape, and gaining national as well as international recognition in the process.

POPULAR MUSIC

It is usually composers like Beethoven or Wagner that come to mind when one thinks of music made in Germany. Yet there has been a distinctive and lively contemporary music scene, particularly in the prominent sphere of popular music, where home-grown music has developed both alongside and in collaboration with the strong Anglo-American influence.

One of the most recent imports, referred to under the umbrella term 'Techno', has been building up an ever larger following in Germany, and with it has developed the dance or rave culture with its distinctive dance fashions and lifestyles. Strictly speaking, Techno and HipHop have not simply been imported to the German scene. Apart from the fact that they exist in many distinctive styles and permutations across the country, Techno has, in a way, returned to Germany, where electronically produced music and the so-called industrial sound were experimented with long before the actual beginnings of House and Techno in the American cities of Chicago and Detroit. Klaus Schulze, Tangerine Dream, Einstürzende Neubauten and, above all, Kraftwerk are regarded as influential precursors of Techno (Henkel and Wolff 1996: 41). The current German Techno-scene has many distinct identities. It has its own record labels, such as Low Spirit, and its very own star DJs, such as the Love Parade's Dr Motte, WestBam and Marusha, as well as Techno-magazines and communication networks. With Mayday and the Berlin Love Parade, Germany also hosts two of the world's biggest Techno events.

It is remarkable how quickly Techno has progressed from being a youth sub-culture to becoming a vital part of German mainstream culture. Even though the music itself is still very much produced within the scene, rather than by big record companies, the rave culture as a whole has fast become an attractive target and source of inspiration in youth marketing, with agencies employing trend-scouts and fashion and lifestyle companies keen to sponsor Techno events. Even state authorities and the media have realised the growing appeal of this youth culture. Whilst still opposing the drugs culture associated with the scene, they are waking up to its commercial and tourist potential, as can be illustrated by the fact that the city of Frankfurt has offered DM 1 million for the transfer of Berlin's Love Parade to Frankfurt (Henkel and Wolff 1996: 7).

Many insiders are wary of this mainstreamisation of Techno which, in their view, has watered down its intrinsic message, such as the Love Parade's 'Love, Peace and Unity'. However, the diversity of the scene has made it difficult to identify one single unifying message in the Techno culture. The music, no doubt, creates a unifying experience amongst many ravers and thus offers scope for developing a free and open relationship with other ravers, as expressed by Hakim Bey's idea of 'loving contact' in pursuit of individual happiness (quoted in Böpple and Knüfer 1996: 152). There is also no doubt that Techno has taken the relationship between human beings and technology to unprecedented heights. However, whether this is generally experienced as a 'reconciliatory merger of machine and primeval instinct, of future and past' (Böpple and Knüfer 1996: 168) appears rather more doubtful. After all, there are many for whom weekend raving is mainly a leisure-time excess, sought as an antidote to everyday routines and stresses, and those who have embraced Techno as an apolitical hedonist lifestyle in which dress codes, consumption patterns and choice of venues are the primary concerns. Such diversity of views and motivations is, perhaps, to be expected, considering the enormous popular appeal of Techno. It is estimated that around 3 million 16-to-25-year-olds consider themselves part of the Techno culture in Germany, which is credited with having created the most important youth scene of the 1990s, as well as the first all-German youth culture, since it has attracted young people in East and West alike (Deese *et al.* 1995: 212). Moreover, there have been some crossovers of Techno into other mainstream music styles in Germany.

The German *Schlager*, for example, a melodious, easy-listening music with mostly banal German lyrics, has been around for decades and has quietly outlived all other imported or home-grown music styles. Recently, it has seen a distinct boost in popularity, not just with the older generations but also with young people. Alongside much-loved *Schlager*-veterans, like Marianne Rosenberg, there is no shortage of new singers, for example Dieter Thomas Kuhn or the Swabian group Pur. *Schlager* has even become a reference point for Techno music which, by adding its beat to classic hits, has created the hybrid of *Houseschlager*. Ironic and humorous silly references to the *Schlager* tradition, such as by Helge Schneider or Die Doofen (The Stupids), have also proved a successful recipe and are part of the general revival of interest in a certain kind of nonsensical comedy.

Another style of music made in Germany has successfully withstood the test of time and seems to be experiencing a similar boom. German *Volksmusik* (folk music) has been around for decades and is much loved for its up-beat, clean image. Television stations regularly devote prime-time slots to *Volksmusik*, and sold-out concert halls all over the country testify further to its popularity.

Whilst both *Schlager* and *Volksmusik* have been popular for many decades, the current boom in the German music business appears to be also a product of the continuing impact of the so-called New German Wave (*Neue deutsche Welle*) in the late 1970s and early 1980s. Whilst its subversive punk element was relatively short-lived, the New German Wave gave a distinct boost to the popularity of rock and pop music made in Germany and illustrated that there is a lot more to German music than banal rhymes strung together in the tradition of the *Schlager* or *Volksmusik*. Rock veterans, such as Udo Lindenberg, Herbert Grönemeyer, Ulla Meinecke or BAP, former indie bands like Die Toten Hosen, and newcomers, such as Snap or Die Fantastischen Vier, are testimony to the fact that contemporary mainstream music, although influenced and dominated by Anglo-American imports, nowadays includes the German element as a matter of course – even if it is still under-represented on the radio, a fact which has prompted the German association of rock musicians to campaign for a quota to be introduced. The demand is that the proportion of German music played by radio stations, currently between 10 and 20 per cent, be raised to 40 per cent. Somewhat ironically, such a quota to promote home-grown music is reminiscent of the 60:40 quota that the GDR authorities imposed in order to limit the exposure of East German radio audiences to foreign influences. In view of this, and the liveliness of the contemporary pop music scene, it must remain doubtful whether such a quota is desirable and necessary.

RECOMMENDED READING

In English, Burns (1995) offers a detailed interdisciplinary discussion of German culture from 1871 to the present. For a survey of German literature of the same period, see Humble and Furness (1994). An account of East German literature in the transition period around the time of Unification is provided by Mellis (1995), and literary developments after Unification are discussed by Rohlfs (1995), with the *Literaturstreit* figuring in both. The *Literaturstreit* and other aspects of the contemporary intellectual climate also feature in Chapter 9 of Parkes (1997). For recent developments in the theatre, see Patterson (1995). The post-Unification film scene is discussed in Hughes and Brady (1995). *German Quarterly* is a useful journal.

For a detailed overview of culture in the FRG in German, see Benz (1983) and Glaser (1991). The most up-to-date information and discussions can be found in journals such as *Theater heute*, *epd Film* and *film-dienst*, *Sinn und Form* and *neue deutsche literatur*.

BIBLIOGRAPHY

Anon. 'Das Lachen macht's', *Der Spiegel*, 38/1996.
Anon. 'Jedermanns gute Stube', *Der Spiegel*, 15 January 1996.
Baumgart, R. (1995) *Deutsche Literatur der Gegenwart: Kritiken, Essays, Kommentare*, Munich: Deutscher Taschenbuch Verlag.
Benz, W. (ed.) (1983) *Die Bundesrepublik Deutschland: Geschichte in drei Bänden. Band 3: Kultur*. Frankfurt am Main: Fischer.

Bohn, V. (1995) *Deutsche Literatur seit 1945*, Frankfurt am Main: Suhrkamp Taschenbuch Verlag.

Böpple, F. and Knüfer, R. (1996) *Generation XTC: Techno und Ekstase*, Berlin: Volk und Welt.

Büning, E. and Rückert, S. (1996) 'Schale Gefühle und sterbliche Melodien', *Die Zeit*, 9 February.

Burns, R. (ed.) (1995) *German Cultural Studies: An Introduction*, Oxford and New York: Oxford University Press.

Carr, G. and Paul, G. (1995) 'Unification and its aftermath: the challenge of history', in Burns, R. (ed.) *German Cultural Studies: An Introduction*, Oxford and New York: Oxford University Press.

Damus, M. (1995) *Kunst in der BRD: 1945–1990*, Reinbeck bei Hamburg: Rowohlt.

Datenreport 1994: Zahlen und Fakten über die BRD, Munich: Verlag Bonn Aktuell.

Deese, U., Hillenbach, P. E., Michatsch, C. and Kaiser, D. (eds) (1995) *Jugendmarketing: Das wahre Leben in den Szenen*, Düsseldorf and Munich: Metropolitan.

Detje, R. and Koberg, R. (1996) ' Das ist die Liebe der Gespenster', *Die Zeit*, 2 February.

Durrani, O., Good, C. and Hilliard, K. (eds) (1995) *The New Germany: Literature and Society after Unification*, Sheffield: Sheffield Academic Press.

Glaser, H. (1991, revised edn) *Kleine Kulturgeschichte der Bundesrepublik Deutschland: 1945–1989*, Bonn: Bundeszentrale für politische Bildung.

Gohr, S. (1986) 'Die Kunst der Nachkriegszeit', in Joachimidis, C., Rosenthal, N. and Schmied, W. (eds) *Deutsche Kunst im 20. Jahrhundert: Malerei und Plastik 1905–1985*, Munich: Prestel.

Grasskamp, W. (1996) 'Die Zeit des Klinkenputzens', *Die Zeit*, 8 March.

Henkel, O. and Wolff, K. (1996) *Berlin Underground: Techno und HipHop zwischen Mythos und Ausverkauf*, Berlin: Fab Verlag.

Herzog, R. (1996) 'Kultur: Das Pfund mit dem wir wuchern', in *Theater heute* 7.

Holert, T. and Terkessidis, M. (eds) (1996) *Mainstream der Minderheiten: Pop in der Kontrollgesellschaft*, Berlin and Amsterdam: Edition ID-Archiv.

Horx, M. (1996) *Der erste große deutsche Trendreport*, Düsseldorf, Vienna, New York and Moscow: Econ Verlag.

Hughes, H. and Brady, M. (1995) 'German film after the Wende', in Lewis, D. and McKenzie, J. (eds) *The New Germany: Social, Political and Cultural Challenges of Unification*, Exeter: University of Exeter Press.

Humble, M. and Furness, R. (1994) *Introduction to German Literature 1871–1990*, Basingstoke and London: Macmillan.

Mellis, J. (1995) 'Writers in transition: the end of East German literature', in Lewis, D. and McKenzie, J. (eds) *The New Germany: Social, Political and Cultural Challenges of Unification*, Exeter: University of Exeter Press.

Parkes, S. (1997) *Understanding Contemporary Germany*, London and New York: Routledge.

Patterson, M. (1995) 'The German theatre', in Lewis, D. and McKenzie, J.

(eds) *The New Germany: Social, Political and Cultural Challenges of Unification*, Exeter: University of Exeter Press.

Rohlfs, J. (1995) 'German literature after Unification', in Lewis, D. and McKenzie, J. (eds) *The New Germany: Social, Political and Cultural Challenges of Unification*, Exeter: University of Exeter Press.

11 German language

David Kaufman

INTRODUCTION

The German spoken and written in the FRG is largely standardised; none the less, anyone travelling there will surely become aware of differences in sounds and dialects – as would be the case in any country. A linguistician would be able to identify very many dialects and sub-dialects, but for our purposes it suffices to know that apart from the *Hochsprache*, the standard language of educated speakers, the roots of which are in the north and which is the norm taught in schools throughout the country, three major dialect areas can be distinguished: *Niederdeutsch* (Low German [in the north]), *Mitteldeutsch* (Central German), and *Oberdeutsch* (Upper German [in the south]). There are great differences in pronunciation, so that *ich*, for example, varies from *ik* (*Niederdeutsch*) at one extreme to *i* (*Oberdeutsch*) at the other (König 1983: 162).

Some regional accents and dialects such as Saxon (East *Mitteldeutsch*) or Swabian (*Oberdeutsch*) are regarded with snobbism by some 'standard' speakers; none the less there is much pride taken in dialect and there is some dialect publishing. While we are dealing here with the German spoken in the FRG, it should be pointed out that standardisation of the language is such that on the whole Austrian and Swiss speakers of German can communicate with natives of the FRG without problems (just as the British can communicate with Americans or Australians and vice versa). On the other hand, there is sufficient variation in vocabulary for there to be separate national dictionaries, and indeed there is enough variation within the dialect areas of Germany for there to be a dictionary entitled *Wie sagt man anderswo?* (How do they say it elsewhere?) for German native speakers (Seibicke 1972). Anyone monitoring German television will also be aware that it is often necessary for programmes in which there are dialect speakers of southern German, Austrian and Swiss, and of *Plattdeutsch* (Low German dialect spoken in North Germany) to be presented with sub-titles for native speakers of standard German, for whom these dialects are almost incomprehensible. It should, however, be remembered that most Germans who are brought up speaking a dialect at home, Swabian, for example, must also learn *Hochdeutsch* at school, and are usually able to switch from dialect to standard when speaking to Germans from different areas or indeed to poor foreign nationals who think they have achieved a good standard of comprehension and are suddenly confronted with a version of German which makes them think they need to start again.

There are not only regional variations in the German-speaking countries – there are, of course, also those characteristics which distinguish German from the other languages with which it is related: the Dutch and Flemish of Holland and Belgium, for example, and the Scandinavian languages, and English. In this chapter we will be looking at German's close relationship with English and examining some of the ways in which it has been influenced during the twentieth century, which is ending for the German language with a scarcely revolutionary but certainly controversial spelling reform.

GERMAN IN A HISTORICAL CONTEXT

Whenever we open our mouths to speak, what pours forth is what we might call a 'linguistic archaeology', since every word we use is the descendant of other words and has a history, which can often be traced back. If, for example, in English we look at the words 'lord' and 'lady' it is not immediately obvious to us that they originally meant 'guardian of the bread' and 'kneader of the bread'. In the same way, it does not necessarily occur to us, as modern linguists, that the European languages we are studying are related to one another and to those of India and Iran. Yet they *are* all related. The languages of Europe and India, which developed out of an Indo-European mother tongue, can be categorised into family groups. We would probably all know, or at least be able to guess, that French and Spanish, and Italian and Portuguese, are descended from Latin, and that the languages of Germany, the Netherlands, Flemish-speaking Belgium, and Scandinavia are also closely related. What is not always evident to English native speakers (or even to students of German) is that English too is a Germanic language. Indeed, if we were living a thousand or so years ago, we would, as English native speakers, be using Old English (Anglo-Saxon), with which we would be able to make ourselves understood certainly in the north of Germany. Unfortunately, languages tend to change over time, so that now it is impossible for monolingual native speakers of German or English to understand one another. While it is not the intention of this chapter to look at the history of the German language, it is worth while to examine the way in which German and English have gone off in different directions, since it is possible, if we know one or two things about the way they have developed, to perform some simple tricks to predict the meanings of some German words and to see the changes of meaning which have taken place between English and German in words which have a common history.

THE RELATIONSHIP BETWEEN GERMAN AND ENGLISH

Germanic in Britain

From the fifth century, Angles, Jutes, and Saxons came to England speaking similar German dialects; their language became dominant, displacing the local Celtic dialects, and is the ancestor of modern English.

The conquest of England by the Normans brought a great admixture of French to what is called Old English, the language inherited from the Saxons and others. They failed to obliterate this language, but the vocabulary became enriched as the languages intertwined, while grammatical structures were modified. Meanwhile continental German continued to develop, and the changes were dramatic because many of the sounds 'shifted' so that their pronunciation altered. This 'shift' did not take place in Old English.

Take the German words *Ding, Knecht, Zaun*. They look or sound similar to some English ones: *Ding* sounds a bit like 'thing', which is what it means; *Knecht* looks very much like 'knight', but it means 'farm labourer', and both words derive from a word meaning 'young man'; *Zaun* sounds like a rather sibilant 'town', but it means 'fence', and indeed a town was originally a place which was fenced in. These pairs of words, which are closely related and which in each case derive from one word, demonstrate several linguistic phenomena: namely that the pronunciation, spelling, and meaning of words often change over time, and that where part of a linguistic community leaves its homeland to live elsewhere, taking its language with it, this language will develop separately and differently from that of the community which has been left behind. This was particularly the case historically when little contact was possible because of the difficulties of long-distance communication. The emigrating language, isolated in its new home, tended to retain words or meanings of words which had died out in the mother country, while modifying its vocabulary and grammar through influences emanating from the host country.

Some tricks

There is a correlation between the following sounds of English and German:

English	German	Example
/v/	/b/	(give:geben)
/ð/ (spelt 'th')	/d/	(this:dies)
/f/ (spelt 'gh')	/χ/ (spelt 'ch')	laugh:lachen
		night: Nacht
		(the English *gh*
		having become silent)
/t/	/ts/ (spelt 'z')	town:Zaun
/p/	/pf/	plough:Pflug
/tʃ/ (spelt 'ch')	/k/	church:Kirche

Additionally there are the *sch* + consonant combinations *schl-*, *schm-*, *schn-*, *schw-* corresponding with *sl-*, *sm-*, *sn-*, *sw-* in English, e.g. *schlau/sly*, *Schmied/smith*, *Schnee/snow*, *Schweden/Sweden*. We are able to see relationships like this within English pronunciations too. Think of American Brooklyn 'dese' and 'dose' for 'these' and 'those', or Cockney 'wiv' for 'with'. Given the relationship between certain sounds, it is possible to predict the English versions of many German words (some will have exactly the same meanings, others will have similar ones, while others will demonstrate unexpected semantic changes). Look at the following list, and make your predictions:

Dach, denken, Distel, Dorf;
Kalk, Kammer, Kanzler, Käse;
Pfanne, Pfeffer, Pflug;
tief, Haufen, reif;
zählen, zahm, Zange, Zeitung, Zimmer;

Rabe, Knabe;
Nacht, Recht, Licht, dachte;
Schleim, schlachten, schmerzen.

The following list shows the above words with their cognates, the words they are related to, and the present-day meanings where these differ.

German word	*English cognate*	*Meaning (where different)*
Dach	thatch	roof
denken	think	
Distel	thistle	
Dorf	thorpe	village
Kalk	chalk	calcium, lime
Kammer	chamber	chamber, store-room
Kanzler	chancellor	
Käse	cheese	
Pfanne	pan	
Pfeffer	pepper	
Pflug	plough	
tief	deep	
Haufen	heap	
reif	ripe	
zählen	tell	count
zahm	tame	
Zange	tongs	pliers
Zeitung	tidings	newspaper
Zimmer	timber	room
Rabe	raven	
Knabe	knave	boy
Nacht	night	
Recht	right	
Licht	light	
dachte	thought	
Schleim	slime	mucus
schlachten	slaughter	
schmerzen	smart	hurt

The above are just a few of the many such words which have cognates in English. The link between such words as *Zimmer* and *timber*, and *Zimmermann* (carpenter), in which the connection with wood is preserved, or *Dach*, and *thatch*, and *roof*, are examples of the way in which meaning can change, usually quite logically. Similarly, words like *schlachten* and *slaughter* are quite clearly related and have the same meaning, so that application of the sound-shift rules can help you to guess meanings as well.

LEXICAL CHANGES IN THE TWENTIETH CENTURY

Political movements and social developments during this century have brought about great changes in the area of vocabulary. Nazis and communists, sociologists, scientists, young people, feminists – all have had an influence on the language, the effects of which have sometimes been short-lived, sometimes far-reaching.

Language in the Third Reich

It is a characteristic of totalitarian governments that they seek to influence *every* facet of national life. So in the Nazi period the attempt was made to impose changes of meaning on to the language. The *Sprachbrockhaus*, a pictorial dictionary first published in 1935 and thus the product, largely, of the Weimar period, went through four editions between 1935 and 1940. It is not uncommon for a new dictionary to be revised after three or four years, at a time, for example, of great technological progress when many new terms may be coined; four editions in five years is extraordinary. A comparison of entries between, for example, the 1935 and 1940 editions of the *Sprachbrockhaus* can give us some idea of the way in which the Nazis sought to modify the nation's mind-set. Take the definitions of the words *Schule* (school), *Gewerkschaft* (trade union), and *Führer* (leader):

- *Schule* (1935): 'Die Schule dient der Erziehung und dem Unterricht' (School serves the purpose of educating and teaching). By 1940 the entry is headed 'Die deutsche Schule' (the German school) and the definition is: 'Die deutsche Schule ist ein Teil der nationalsozialistischen Erziehungsordnung' (The German school is a part of the National Socialist educational order).

- *Gewerkschaft* (1935): 1) 'bergbauliche Genossenschaft' (mining co-operative); 2) 'Arbeitnehmerverband' (employees' association).

Clearly, the Nazis' language monitors failed to point out to the dictionary's compilers in 1935 that since 1933 the trade unions had ceased to exist. By 1940 the second meaning has been modified to correspond with Nazi reality: 'Verband von Arbeitnehmern, im Deutschen Reich durch die Deutsche Arbeitsfront überwunden' (Employees' association, superseded/taken over by the German Labour Front).

- *Führer* (1935): 'leitende Persönlichkeit, im besonderen der, Führer des deutschen Volkes' (personality in leading position, especially the leader of the German people). By 1940, the primary definition of the word is given thus: 'Adolf Hitler in seiner Stellung an der Spitze der NSDAP und als Oberhaupt des Deutschen Reiches' (Adolf Hitler in his position at the head of the NSDAP and as leader of the German Reich). A secondary definition, 'eine überlegene Persönlichkeit, in der andere die Verkörperung ihres Willens wiederfinden' (a superior personality, in whom other people discover the embodiment of their will), helps any reader with learning difficulties to grasp the implications of the first. (*Sprachbrockhaus* 1935, pp. 580, 224, 196; *Sprachbrockhaus* 1940, pp. 581, 224, 196)

Such tamperings are but examples of the way in which language was used as a weapon in the Nazi ideologue's 'philosophical' armoury: they helped to taint knowledge and learning, and are mirrored in the political system of Orwell's *Nineteen Eighty-four*. The attempt to control language was not limited to dictionary definitions: the Nazis used language to hide their criminal behaviour, so that euphemisms such as *Sonderbehandlung* (special treatment, i.e. murder) and *Endlösung der Judenfrage* (final solution of the Jewish problem, i.e. the extermination of the Jews) were used by the Nazi establishment to mask the murderousness of the acts behind them. Likewise events were given names which had little to do with truth. Thus the history surrounding Hitler's accession to power in 1933 was called the *Machtergreifung* (seizure of power) as if a revolution had taken place and not a political deal.

Altogether the Nazis brought with them a proliferation of abbreviations, acronyms, and word coinages, which were necessary to deal with the large number of party and political organisations: NSDAP (Nationsozialistische Deutsche Arbeiterpartei – 'National Socialist German Workers Party), SA (Sturmabteilungen – storm detachments), NSKK (Nationalsozialistisches Kraftfahrkorps – NS Motor Corps), HJ (Hitlerjugend – Hitler Youth), BDM (Bund Deutscher

Mädel – League of German Girls), KdF (Kraft durch Freude – Strength through Joy), DAF (Deutsche Arbeitsfront – German Labour Front), Gestapo (Geheime Staatspolizei – Secret State Police), stand here for very many more.

Language specialists who were sympathetic to the Nazis were wont to bemoan this tendency, albeit because the abbreviations concealed the elegance of the words for which they stood. Thus one Germanist well in tune with his times wrote in 1935: 'Unfortunately the National Observer is having its name ruined by being called the VB'; and: 'Sad and incomprehensible that people would like to force the merry Hitler Youth into the strait-jacket of an acronym' (translated from Wustmann 1935: 381, 383–384).

Such was the demand for terms to cover newly introduced concepts that words needed to be coined or resuscitated from a moribund state. *Blockwart* (block warden, a political caretaker in charge of a group of households), *Braunhemd* (Brownshirt), *arisieren* (Aryanise, i.e. to take property from Jews and put it into the hands of non-Jews), *Gleichschaltung* (bringing into line politically), *Deutscher Gruß* (German greeting, i.e. 'Heil Hitler'), *Jungmädel* (girl member of the Hitler Youth), *Bann* (Hitler Youth regiment) – these are examples of the myriad words introduced, or reintroduced, from a medieval context during the Nazi period, and while they no longer belong to the active vocabulary of Germans they still belong to the political-historical stock of the language.

GDR and FRG

The division of Germany into two countries for the (historically) relatively short period of forty-five years still caused some divergence in the language because of the influences to which it was exposed and because of the tendency anyway for the language of split linguistic communities to develop along different lines, however artificial the split might be. On the one hand there were the lexical peculiarities of the East German political system and the exposure to Russian, on the other the influence of American and British English and the need for the vocabulary of 'affluence' in a West German society which had at its disposal all the fruits of its economic success and the technological innovations which were widely available as soon as they were developed. On an intellectual level, one problem was that certain terms which had one meaning in the West had undergone a politically charged change of meaning in the East. So, for example, a word like *Abgrenzung* (walling off, dissociation) had in the GDR the further specific meaning of 'demarcation from the FRG' (Kinne and Strube-Edelmann 1981: 19).

While there were idiosyncrasies in the language of the former GDR, the fact that many East Germans could see and hear what was going on in the West, because they were able to watch Western television and to preserve some contact with friends and relatives, meant that they could keep abreast of linguistic developments, so that with the fall of the Wall there was on the whole no communication problem for them.[1] As far as the West Germans were concerned, there was anyway no question of their resorting to East German usage: linguistic absorption was clearly going to be one way, given the enthusiasm with which the majority of the inhabitants of the former GDR approached unification and Western German values and their desire to throw off ideological shackles, and given the poor-relation status which they soon acquired in the eyes of the citizens of the old federal states.

The linguistic usages of the former GDR – expressions and acronyms such as *anti-faschistischer Schutzwall* (anti-fascist protective wall, i.e. Berlin Wall), *Kombinat* (concern, in the industrial/business sense), *HO* (Handelsorganisation – [state-owned] trading concern), *NVA* (Nationale Volksarmee – National People's Army), *Subbotnik* (from the Russian meaning '[unpaid, voluntary] Saturday work') (Kinne and Strube-Edelmann 1981: 29, 105, 82, 128, 197) – have thus already become part of political and social history, much in the way that most of the jargon of Nazi Germany, while still necessary for the discussion of the period, swiftly disappeared from use in the active vocabulary of German native speakers after the Second World War.

FOREIGN WORDS IN GERMAN

Languages have a tendency to borrow words from one another, since whenever an area of knowledge or technology is taken or developed from another culture and requires words for which there is no indigenous provision, native speakers look to the source of these ideas for the words with which to express them. German is no exception and has thus been historically a borrower, especially from Latin, Greek, French, and English, and since the end of the Second World War very extensively from British and American English.

From the seventeenth century there was a movement to cleanse the language of 'unnecessary' borrowings, embodied in the work of the

Sprachgesellschaften (Language Societies). Thus words such as *Rechtschreibung* (orthography) and *Briefwechsel* (correspondence) were coined to replace *Orthographie* and *Korrespondenz*. In 1801 the lexicographer J. H. Campe had produced *Wörterbuch zur Erklärung und Verdeutschung der unserer Sprache aufgedrungenen fremden Ausdrücke* (Dictionary for explaining and translating into German those foreign expressions which have forced their way into our language) in which words such as *Feingefühl* replaced *Takt*, and *Lehrgang* replaced *Kursus*. While these Germanisations have remained in common use, the words they were meant to suppress have not necessarily died out and have often continued to exist side by side with their newly coined German counterparts. Words introduced by the end of the nineteenth century to replace French expressions such as *Retourbillet* (*Rückfahrkarte* – return ticket) or *Perron* (*Bahnsteig* – platform) were more successful in supplanting the Gallic intruders, although they do still remain in Swiss usage.

This attitude towards *Fremdwörter* (foreign words), which at first was based on a rational desire to make words easier to understand for German native speakers, became less rational and more xenophobic with the rise of nationalistic feeling, so that in a dictionary of foreign words in German, published during the First World War, its author could write in his introduction:

> With justified pride in the high level of intellectual wealth which German science and German literature have given to humanity, popular feeling resists the unjustified/needless dressing up of our vocabulary . . . Let everyone see to it that this emphasis on things foreign disappears and is eradicated. We owe that to our brave men in field grey.
>
> (Translated from Partenschmitt n.d.: 1)

This xenophobia was further promoted by the Nazis, and where words could not be 'translated into German' there was an attempt by Bernhard Rust, Hitler's incompetent education minister, to modify words like *Philosoph* and *Theater* to *Filosof* and *Teater*. Although his attempts were considered even by the Nazis to be the ideas of a buffoon, it has to be admitted that there has been great inconsistency in the rendering of words with Greek roots, since alongside *Philosoph*, for example, *Fotograf*, *Telefon*, and *Grafiker* are today the norm, so that there has been a – perhaps unconscious – academic snobbery which has allowed *ph* to become *f* in some words but not in others.

British and American influence

The influence of British and American English on German is all-pervasive. Since the Second World War the strong economic and political links with America and Britain on the one hand, and the enthusiasm of young Germans for the popular music culture of those countries on the other, have made a great impact on the language. A trawl of German television programmes or the perusal of any newspaper or magazine reveals a plethora of English words for which there are often perfectly suitable German equivalents and which seem to be used purely to demonstrate familiarity with all things fashionable and *cool*.

In a random monitoring of two hours of German television on 27 July 1996 the following titles of programmes/programme segments could be noted: *news & business* (n-tv), *Ticker* (n-tv), *Yesterday* (3SAT), *hot clip* (VOX/Bayrisches Fernsehen), *NORDtour Tips* (N3). A glance at the linguistic content of the programmes reveals much use of *Fixing*, *Put*, *Call*, and *Timing* in stock market reports, while the weather service for businesspeople on n-tv is called *Businesswetter*. In *NORDtour Tips* a decisive woman is *eine resolute Lady*; the promotion slogan for SAM (PRO7) is 'Don't be late for SAM!', while the same programme has its *VIP-Clips* – 'video clips of very important people' – and Bayrisches Fernsehen *hot clips* – 'the only way to rock the day'. Most of these words appear in *Das Große Fremdwörterbuch* (1994) and can presumably be understood by their target audience;[2] yet it remains difficult for the objective observer to accept, for example, that there is any argument for a news presenter to substitute one *Fremdwort* for another when she says: 'die Wirtschaft [von Simbabwe] stagniert auf dem *Level* [= *Niveau*] der 60er Jahre'([Zimbabwe's] economy is stagnating at its level in the Sixties).[3]

The language of marketing, business and advertising is likewise permeated with English. Products thus have names demonstrating their provenance or simply the fact that they are used in the English-speaking world, e.g. *Rexona-sensitive* and *AUTAN-sensitive*,[4] both with an extra (English) *e*. Many advertisements catch the eye by making the major slogan English, or even by avoiding German altogether, e.g. *after shave adidas – feel the energy;*[5] *falke – FOR TOMORROW'S PEOPLE.*[6] Mitsubishi even makes use of an English pun – *King-Off-Road. King-On-Road*[7] – for one of its cars. In its newspaper advertisement Garant Schuh AG shouts: *Sorry, Herr Waigel, wir bieten 6,6%!* (Sorry, Mr Waigel, we're offering 6.6%!) –

while Holiday Inn seeks our attention with: *Endlich. DON'T DIS-TURB! Ein Weekend lang* (At last . . . For a whole weekend).[8]

Similarly the language of whole areas of professional life, whether science and technology, psychology, sociology, or linguistics, etc., is derived from disciplines which have often been developed by American expertise, and even if much is borrowed from Latin and Greek the direct influence of such words on German (or indeed any other language) is English. So, for example, the world of computers and the Internet has given German *Computer* (the word *Rechner* does occur, but the loan word is much more popular), *Laptop, PC, CD-Roms, Mailing* and *mailen, Daten-Superhighway, Cyberspace, on-line, Chip*, and hundreds more. Recently there has been something of a reverse trend so that terms such as *downloaden*, which are felt even by the most computer-literate to be linguistically uncomfortable and which had not yet been recorded by *Das große Fremdwörterbuch* in 1994, are being back-translated, e.g. *downloaden* to *herunterladen*.

Borrowings and apparent borrowings from the English

There has been a post-war tendency for German to take words directly from the English and to use them with different meanings, or to invent words as apparent borrowings which do not exist in English at all, e.g. *Slip* (briefs/knickers), *Oldtimer* (veteran car), *Twen* (person in his/her twenties), *Showmaster* (compère), *last not least* (with missing 'but'), *Pullunder* (tanktop), *Straps* (suspender belt), *Dressman* (male model), *Handy* (mobile telephone). The explanation for this seems to lie in the vogue for things American and English which are perceived, as we have seen, to be up-to-date and *cool*.

JUGENDSPRACHE

That young people should speak differently from their elders is nothing new: slangs develop with each generation, and the technological developments of the last decades have led to comprehension gaps between the generations which we have all witnessed. In the German-speaking areas, jargons, especially amongst young people, have been a frequent linguistic feature, the language of students being particularly influential (Ehmann 1992: 9). Yet there has been nothing quite like the phenomenon of late-twentieth-century *Jugendsprache* (young people's language). Older speakers of *Hochdeutsch* confronted with young people speaking in a standard German accent are often unable to follow what is being said since the usage which has developed over the last thirty years bears little resemblance to anything recorded in dictionaries of slang. A whole new publishing activity has come about in order to provide non-*Jugendsprache* speakers (e.g. *Gruftis* – people so old and 'uncool' that they belong in a tomb) with the wherewithal to interpret the language of their children or grandchildren. The influence of English is unmistakable: *checken* (to check/cotton on to), *Feeling, Fashion-Freak, heavy, down, anturnen/abturnen* (to turn on/off) are just a few of the many expressions which have been borrowed. But *Jugendsprache* has plundered German vocabulary too: *ätzend/echt ätzend* (both 'really good' and 'really bad', depending on context), *brutal* (really good), *Lungentorpedo* (cigarette) are examples of the way in which many words have been given new meanings. Some of these expressions have entered the language of the *Gruftis*, so that idioms such as 'ich kann ihn nicht ab' (I can't stand him) can be heard in older circles too.

FEMINIST INFLUENCES

While the results of Nazi attempts to effect change in the meaning of words for cynical political ends lasted, largely, only for the period of the Third Reich, the efforts made in the name of feminism in the late twentieth century seem more likely to endure. For example, the fact that in German the names for so many professions have a basic masculine form from which the feminine equivalent has to be derived was justifiably a great thorn in the side of feminist thinking. The most obvious victory in the struggle against linguistic sexism has been the introduction of the capitalised suffix *-Innen* into the plurals of words denoting professions. While until very recently the plural form *Lehrer*, for example, was understood to mean teachers of either sex, first *Lehrer/innen* and now *LehrerInnen* are commonly used to express the idea that both genders are covered by the word. It is felt to be a creation of great ugliness by some, but it is seen in respectable journals everywhere, and certainly in many job advertisements. In the latter it is in fact now illegal for the female version of the noun not to appear in the job specification, e.g. *Versicherungskaufmann/kauffrau* (insurance salesperson).

An attempt to introduce a feminine version of *man* ('one', 'you'), namely *frau*, has had less success, although recently it is to be heard more and more, though somewhat self-consciously, in television programmes with a women's rather than a feminist slant, and in newspaper and magazine articles directed at women. *Frau* has also established itself together with *mensch* (person) – which has, however, much less currency – amongst students on many university Internet homepages.

SPELLING REFORM

As late as the nineteenth century there was little standardisation in written German, so that Goethe was quite happy to write the same word in different ways. Words like *Rat* (advice) and *Tal* (valley) were spelt *Rath* and *Thal*, with a silent *h*, which was no aid to pronunciation. Words derived from the French like *Kritiker* had an initial *c*, *zitieren* (to quote) was spelt *citieren* – linguistic conventions which were illogical in the German orthographical system. The capitalisation of nouns was an invention of the sixteenth and seventeenth centuries, unknown before that period, and from the 1870s there was a movement to introduce *Kleinschreibung*, i.e. the writing of nouns with small initial letters. After the Second World War, German language specialists in the British zone of occupation voted for its introduction; in the 1970s the German PEN Centre and the Association of German Authors took part in a symposium in Vienna at which writers as distinguished as Heinrich Böll, Ingeborg Drewitz, Rudolf-Walter Leonhardt and Gerhard Zwerenz as well as members of the Duden publishing company, which is considered to represent the norms of German orthography, spoke in favour of reform of the language and produced a book, *vernünftiger schreiben* (a more sensible approach to writing) based on their findings. There remains much resistance to abolishing the capitalisation of nouns, and no reforms have come about in that respect. In 1901, Konrad Duden, the great lexicographer, with his supporters, set forth his ideas on spelling reform, which he regarded as but the first stage of a more radical re-working of German orthography. He argued successfully for the modification of the spelling of foreign words and for the removal of unnecessary letters such as the illogical *h*, and the *d* in *todt* (*tot* – dead). While there were other, relatively minor, changes (e.g. the *f* sound in *Efeu* (ivy), *Rudolf*, *Westfalen*, *Elefant*, *Elfenbein* (ivory), *Fasan* (pheasant), and *Sofa* having previously been spelt *ph*), little else has changed until today or, to be more precise, until the end of 1994 when far-reaching decisions were taken by the Internationaler Arbeitskreis für Orthographie (International Orthographical Study Group). Most of these were ratified by the education ministers and minister presidents of the German federal states in November and

December 1995, after consultation with representatives from Austria, Switzerland, and other interested countries. A final joint declaration on the new rules for German orthography was signed in Vienna in July 1996. The spelling reform is to come into force on 1 August 1998, with a transition period lasting until 31 July 2005, during which time the previous spellings will not be regarded as wrong, but as obsolescent. Any newly published books, and particularly school-books, will be able to make use of the new orthographical rules before August 1998, and in eight federal German states the reforms were introduced for first-year primary-school pupils at the beginning of the autumn term 1996.

Although the reform is intended to remove anomalies and to make German orthography (and punctuation) simpler to learn, some of the new rules for spelling have proved controversial (an opinion poll conducted by the Infas-Institut in 1995 suggested that 70 per cent of the German population considered a spelling reform to be unnecessary!). They are likely to seem nightmarish to those who have spent their working lives trying to persuade their pupils and students, whether native speakers or foreign learners, that the subordinating conjunction *daß* (that), for example, has to be spelt thus and not with *ss* (see below for new rules). An appeal by Professor Gröschner of the University of Jena, who approached the Federal Constitutional Court on the grounds that the reform was unconstitutional, failed, so that now, it seems, nothing stands in its way.

The reform seeks to rationalise spelling and the use of small and capital letters, and to simplify the rules for *ß* and punctuation. So, for example, the new rulings on noun/verb and verb/verb combinations will eliminate many anomalies such as *Auto fahren* (to drive a car), but *radfahren* (to ride a bike), or *gefangennehmen* (to take prisoner), but *getrennt schreiben* (to write as two words). The new rule is: always separate such combinations, e.g. *radfahren > Rad fahren*, *gefangennehmen > gefangen nehmen*. The anomalous compounding of *so* and *wie + viel/e* is likewise abandoned, so that *soviel/e > so viel/e* (so much/many), *wieviel > wie viel* (how much). On the other hand, in analogy with *irgendein* (any), combinations with *irgend* will be written as one word, e.g. *irgend etwas > irgendetwas* (anything), *irgend jemand > irgendjemand* (anyone). Nouns which can at present be written capital or small according to context – with no rational explanation – are all to be capitalised so that, for example, the illogical *in bezug auf* (but *mit Bezug auf*, both meaning 'with regard to') becomes *in Bezug auf*. Likewise adjectives used as ordinal numbers, indefinite numerals used after indefinite pronouns, and adjectives used in set prepositional phrases are all to be capitalised. The following versions will thus become the standard: *der/die/ das Erste* (the first one), *der/die/das Letzte* (the last one), *der/die/das Nächste* (the next one), *jeder/jede Zweite* (every second person), *im Allgemeinen* (in general), *Folgendes* (the following), etc. The names of languages as objects of prepositions will now also be capitalised, e.g. *auf deutsch* > *auf Deutsch* (in German).

These changes are probably sensible, since even the most literate of German natives are often confused by the illogicalities of capital/not capital. On the other hand, allowing alternatives to co-exist might have been a simpler and cheaper solution, given the long-term expense involved in the transition.

More difficult to understand are modifications which affect a small number of words and which suggest tinkering with rules rather than any large-scale reform. So, for example, where formerly a spelling failed to make clear the root of the word from which it was derived, such an anomaly will be removed, e.g. *überschwenglich* (root: *Überschwang*) thus becomes *überschwänglich* (effusive); the small number of words involved suggests limited benefits. The doubling of consonants after short vowels in words with foreign roots is introduced, e.g. *numerieren* > *nummerieren* (to number); yet if there was some concern about hidden roots, then there are grounds for suggesting that in this example the alteration should perhaps have been in the opposite direction, given that the Latin root of *Nummer* has one *m*.

The tinkering continues with the re-introduction of a third identical consonant hitherto dropped from compound words, e.g. *Schiffahrt* > *Schifffahrt* (shipping), *stillegen* > *stilllegen* (to close down) – which look like misprints and will take some getting used to! A missing *h* is restored in *Roheit* (> *Rohheit* [rawness]) and *Zäheit* (> *Zähheit* [toughness]), and a superfluous one is removed from *rauh* (> *rau* [rough]), and *Känguruh* (> *Känguru* [kangaroo]). The new rulings make hyphenation an option in compound nouns, so that, for example, *Balletttänzer* can exist side by side with *Ballett-Tänzer* (which would eliminate the ugly triple consonant). There are some changes to the hyphenation of words at the end of lines, the most striking of which is that the rule for splitting of *ck* into *k-k* lapses, e.g. *Zuk-ker* > *Zu-cker* (sugar), while the rule to the effect that a word may not be separated after an initial vowel representing a whole syllable lapses, e.g. *aber* (but) can now be separated as *a-ber*. These changes will do little to facilitate the reading of a text and seem to provide solutions to problems that were not widely perceived as such.

Words which are historically nouns but in adverbial combinations

have lost their capitals will, somewhat unappealingly for those familiar with the old system, have them restored, e.g. *heute morgen > heute
Morgen* (this morning), *gestern nachmittag > gestern Nachmittag*
(yesterday afternoon). The second person familiar forms, *du* and
ihr, and their inflected forms, *dich, dir, euch*, which were written
capital in correspondence, will henceforth be written small; this
alteration of informal usage will be seen – by those who were aware
of it in the first place – as an impoverishment rather than an
enrichment.

Perhaps the most controversial of the reforms is to be the modification of the rules relating to the use of *ß/ss*, since there is a strong
argument to the effect that if a change was to be made, then might this
not have been the time to eliminate *ß*, as has already been done in
Switzerland? The new rules do, however, represent a great simplification: henceforth the spelling will be *ß* when preceded by a long or
double vowel, and *ss* everywhere else, e.g. *Haß > Hass* (hatred),
Kuß > Kuss (kiss), *läßt > lässt* (leaves/lets), *muß > muss* (has to). On
the other hand, *Gruß* (greeting) and *schließen* (to close) retain their *ß*
because of the preceding long vowel sounds. To judge by popular
reaction, it seems that those who have been brought up to write *muß,
daß*, etc., are likely to find this new spelling – at least optically –
offensive.

In the latter months of 1996 and the beginning of 1997 there was a
popular movement to rescind or reform the reforms: various eminent
authors, who seem to have been unaware of the approaching uphea-
val, signed petitions, and there was much protest in the press, particularly after it was discovered that some new editions of dictionaries
which were meant to take account of the reform had failed to be
consistent in the way they showed some of the changes. Looked at
objectively, the whole exercise has a somewhat half-baked flavour,
but the fact remains that any spelling system is a matter of convention, so that what is perceived as strange today will inevitably be
accepted as the norm by tomorrow's adults, who in thirty years' time
will probably consider the pre-reform spelling of the 1990s to be as
quaint as our perception of the pre-1901 *todt* and *Rath*.

CONCLUSION

This is the state of the German language at the close of the twentieth
century. It seems likely that the influences of English and American
'coolness' will continue, while some controversial reforms, which in
the eyes of many are unnecessary, seem set to take place as a

Germany which is both physically and linguistically reunited enters the next millennium.

NOTES

1 There were, however, occasional misunderstandings. For example, requests from former-GDR citizens for a *Broiler* (West German *(Brat)hähnchen* – roast or grilled chicken) were greeted with some incomprehension in West German shops.
2 However, older German citizens who had less opportunity to learn English may well find themselves nonplussed when confronted with some of these expressions.
3 n-tv, 27July 1996.
4 PRO7 and SAT1, 27 July 1996.
5 PRO7, 27 July 1996.
6 *Der Spiegel* 19, 1996.
7 *Der Spiegel* 23, 1996.
8 FAZ, 23 May 1996.

RECOMMENDED READING

Clyne, M. (1984) *Language and Society in the German-Speaking Countries*, Cambridge: Cambridge University Press.
Heller, K. (1996) *Rechtschreibung 2000*, Stuttgart: Klett.
Priebsch, R. and Collinson, W. E. (1966) *The German Language* (6th edn), London: Faber.

BIBLIOGRAPHY

Das große Fremdwörterbuch (1994) Mannheim: Dudenverlag.
Der Sprachbrockhaus (1935) Leipzig: F. A. Brockhaus.
—— (1940) Leipzig: F. A. Brockhaus.
Ehmann, H. (1992) *affengeil: Ein Lexikon der Jugendsprache*, München: Beck.
Kinne, M. and Strube-Edelmann, B. (1981) *Kleines Wörterbuch des DDR Wortschatzes*, Düsseldorf: Schwann.
König, W. (1983) *dtv-Atlas zur deutschen Sprache*, München: dtv.
Partenschmitt, K. F. (n.d.) *Dem Deutschen sei seine Sprache heilig! Ein Fremdwortverdeutschungsbuch*, Leipzig: Helios.
Seibicke, W. (1972) *Wie sagt man anderswo?*, Mannheim: Duden.
Wustmann, G. (1935) *Sprachdummheiten* 10. Auflage vollständig erneuert von Werner Schulze, Berlin: de Gruyter.

12 Germany and Europe

Nigel Thomas

Germany occupies a central position in Europe, and has common frontiers with nine European states – Denmark, Poland, the Czech Republic, Austria, Switzerland, France, Luxembourg, Belgium and the Netherlands – more than any other country except Russia. Whenever Germany has been united it has wielded enormous power owing to its large population, economic might and military strength, factors which combine to give Germany's political leaders great influence, and which have in the past seemed to threaten its smaller neighbours and to challenge other leading European powers.

This chapter will concentrate on the developing German relationship with the rest of Europe as expressed by German foreign policy since 1949 and relate it to the 'German Question' which has preoccupied European states since at least 1871 and which, in the closing years of the twentieth century, may have reached a mutually satisfactory solution.

THE ORIGINS OF MODERN GERMANY

During the Middle Ages, Germany had been a powerful, united empire dominating Central Europe, but from the end of the thirteenth century had split into hundreds of states. Some, like Prussia and Bavaria, were significant powers in their own right, but many were city-states with only local importance. The disunity of this diverse and fragmented territory led to its defeat in 1806 by the forces of Napoleonic France, a disaster which was to strengthen German determination to seek unification and to develop strong armed forces.

In July 1870, France, then the most powerful state in continental Europe, declared war on Prussia, which, since its defeat of Denmark in 1864 and Habsburg Austria in 1866, had become the most powerful German-speaking state. After six weeks the Prussian army had crushed the French and occupied Paris, and in January 1871 the Prussian King Wilhelm was crowned Kaiser of a new German Empire, the Second Reich, in the Hall of Mirrors in Versailles. France's humiliation was total and Germany's victory indisputable. Europe woke up to a new great power in Central Europe with Count Otto von Bismarck, formerly the Prussian Chancellor and the architect of German unification, as Reichskanzler – Imperial Chancellor.

THE GERMAN QUESTION

The emergence of Germany in 1871, as a new nation-state unifying the majority of ethnic Germans, was a respectable political achievement in the age of nationalism, when many European peoples were expelling foreign influences and asserting their own right to independent statehood. However, since Germany had just fought three wars, German unification – unlike, for instance, the Italian unification of 1861 – was perceived throughout much of Europe as an aggressive act, and the new German nation as a country to be feared.

The economic, military and political characteristics of a newly established Germany seemed to confirm this fear. Unification and a large, well-educated workforce had produced a robust economy based on a manufacturing sector which, invigorated by a large internal market, had the strength to penetrate European export markets. Similarly the large German army, well trained, with recent battle experience, and well equipped by a modern and innovative industrial base, was soon regarded as the greatest military power in Europe.

'What should be Germany's role in Europe?' was the German Question. If Germany became as powerful as she then felt she was entitled to be, then the rest of Europe would feel threatened. If she were weak, as Great Britain, France and Russia (the established European great powers) seemed to prefer, and had been accustomed to before 1871, then Germany would herself feel undervalued and constricted. There was a European consensus that Germany was entitled to join the ranks of the European great powers and to play her part in maintaining the post-Napoleonic balance of power. However, the suspicion grew that Germany might not be content with this, and aspired to becoming the leading European power, an act that would upset this balance. At the root of the German Question was, therefore, 'the compatibility of a unified German state with its external environment' (Smith *et al.* 1996: 135).

This question would remain open as long as there was a mismatch between European perceptions and German perceptions of Germany's role, and would only be resolved when Europe and Germany could agree on the role Germany should play in European affairs.

THE FIRST UNIFIED GERMANY

Germany's first experience as a unified nation, spanning seventy-four years from 1871 to 1945 and two pan-European conflicts, showed the disastrous consequences that this persistent mismatch of perceptions was to cause.

At first, however, the omens were good. By 1877, Bismarck had established himself as the *ehrlicher Makler* (honest broker) in European negotiations, but the accession of Wilhelm II as Emperor in 1888, his abrupt dismissal of Bismarck and his adoption of an aggressive foreign policy created an atmosphere of tension and suspicion which contributed to the outbreak of the First World War in August 1914.

This war left Europe in ruins with a legacy of bitterness towards Germany, blamed as the perpetrator of such mass destruction, a view she disputed. The war concluded in November 1918 with an armistice, leading to the Treaty of Versailles in June 1919. This treaty could have served as a basis for a lasting reconciliation between Germany and Europe, but its authors' intentions were to humiliate Germany and keep her economically and militarily weak for the foreseeable future. Friedrich Ebert, first president of the new Weimar Republic, earned widespread unpopularity in Germany by his courageous acceptance of the treaty in the interests of pan-European reconciliation, but he unintentionally helped to discredit Weimar as a political system amongst many Germans. This erosion of legitimacy, coupled with the deteriorating economic situation and the rise of the NSDAP (Nazi party), fatally compromised the Republic. In January 1933 Adolf Hitler came to power (democratically) and proclaimed the Third Reich. He promptly defied the rest of Europe by formally rejecting the Treaty of Versailles, introduced a violently racialist and anti-democratic regime, and expanded the armed forces, the Wehrmacht. His deliberate rejection of European reconciliation in favour of an aggressive programme of territorial expansion and European domination plunged Europe into the Second World War, the second European war within less than twenty-five years and the most ruinous war Europe had ever experienced.

The defeat of Hitler in May 1945 dragged Germany to the lowest point in her history, a time of despair vividly described as *Jahr Null* (Year Zero). Any semblance of a positive relationship between

Germany and the rest of Europe had vanished, apparently for ever. Convinced that Germany could never be trusted again, the Allies (the United States, the Soviet Union, Great Britain and France) confiscated all her territory east of the Oder and Neisse rivers (East Prussia, East Pomerania and Silesia, the 'Eastern Territories') and occupied the rest of Germany. The German armed forces were disbanded and the German government replaced by four Occupation Zones, each under an 'Allied Military Government', controlling economic and political life. The savagery of the Nazi regime seemed to confirm the fears of some that Germany was not fit to be an independent European state. For some observers it looked as if Germany had returned to the 'geographical concept' it had been before 1871.

THE CHANGED ARCHITECTURE OF POST-WAR EUROPE

If in 1945 the rest of Europe could have returned unscathed to the political and economic life it had lost in 1939, then Germany's humiliation might have been permanent, but such a restoration proved impossible. Germany was ruined by war; Great Britain and France were economically weakened, their status diminishing as their huge empires began to fall away, and they could not resume the European great power status they had formerly enjoyed. Only two countries – the United States and the Soviet Union – could be fairly called 'superpowers', and after February 1948 Europe had been partitioned between them: a liberal democratic capitalist West, under United States protection, and a communist East, under the Soviet Union. This European fault-line, defined as the 'Iron Curtain', bisected Germany, leaving the British, American and French Zones in the West, and the Soviet Zone in the East, a division symbolising a global trial of military and political strength between the two superpowers that became known as the 'Cold War'.

In this atmosphere of East–West confrontation the three Western occupation powers were anxious to conclude a peace treaty with Germany before restoring a unified German state as a bulwark against further Soviet expansion westwards. The Soviet Union, however, insisted that a united Germany be neutral, a condition which the West rejected, on the assumption that a neutral Germany would inevitably fall under Soviet political control. Thus on 23 May 1949 the three Western zones combined as the Federal Republic of Germany (FRG) under Bundeskanzler Konrad Adenauer. The Soviet

Union reacted on 7 October 1949 by converting the Soviet Zone into the German Democratic Republic (GDR). German political life had been re-established after a fashion, but there were two Germanys, not one.

ADENAUER AND *WESTPOLITIK*

The first Federal Republic of Germany, usually referred to outside Germany as 'West Germany', lasted almost exactly forty-one years, a time which can be considered as an extended probationary period, as a profoundly sceptical Western Europe accustomed itself to the re-establishment of a distinctively German political entity, watching its progress carefully, too slow to give credit for richly deserved democratic successes, and too eager to label the occasional lapses as confirmation of their worst fears. West Germany was governed by only six federal chancellors (see Chapter 4, pp. 47–48) – this fact alone brought political stability – but was dominated by four: Konrad Adenauer (CDU), Willy Brandt and Helmut Schmidt (both SPD), and Helmut Kohl (CDU), all distinctive political figures with different political agendas (see Chapter 4, p. 55), all united in their determination to rehabilitate Germany in the eyes of Europe and the rest of the world.

The Federal Republic of 1949 was a semi-sovereign state, since the Western Allies were not ready to grant it complete freedom of action lest it abuse its freedom as it had done during the Third Reich. Occupation forces remained, German armed forces were still banned (until 1955), initially there was no Defence Ministry, and even West German foreign policy required Allied approval.

Adenauer's first priority was to work for full sovereignty. Sovereignty would restore German political life and would advance the process of the German rehabilitation, but it could only be granted by the three Western Allies, whose confidence Adenauer had to gain by pursuing foreign and security policies compatible with the West. It should be stressed here that Adenauer was principally concerned with only two Western countries – the United States, the superpower-patron, and France, the hereditary enemy in Europe. Great Britain, the remaining Western ally, constituted a third, but very much less important consideration.

Adenauer had three very clear foreign policy objectives: 'a sense of community with the Western powers, extreme aversion to the prospect of Communist rule and commitment to the "European idea" in place of a discredited nationalism' (Richardson 1966: 11).

These three can be summed up as *Westpolitik*. The first, 'Atlanticism', was based on the clear observation that Western Europe and North America (the United States and Canada) formed a coherent political community sharing the same liberal democratic values which Adenauer wanted for the Federal Republic. In April 1949 twelve countries, amongst them the United States, Great Britain and France, had formed the North Atlantic Treaty Organisation (NATO) as a military alliance to defend 'Western Europe' (a term that included Norway and from 1952 Greece and Turkey) from Soviet military and political incursions. Adenauer was reluctant to re-establish armed forces which had been Germany's ruination in two world wars and which might once again unsettle her neighbours. He did, however, accept that membership of the 'Atlantic Club', which guaranteed German security *vis-à-vis* the Soviet Union, would eventually require German entry into NATO.

The second objective, which defined Adenauer's internal policy of 'democratic values', also underlined his concern at the precarious position in which the infant Republic found itself. The Soviet Union had confiscated the Eastern Territories and held the GDR within its grip. The Federal Republic, and especially West Berlin, seemed vulnerable – not to a direct military threat (Atlanticism was likely to guard against that) then more probably to a steady contamination of West German political values, as had happened in Czechoslovakia in February 1948. Truly democratic political institutions, enshrined in the West German constitution, the *Grundgesetz*, or Basic Law, would allow the will of the majority to prevail. That was to be Adenauer's best protection against such a threat.

If Atlanticism was the first pillar of Adenauer's foreign policy, the third objective, European Integration, was the second. Adenauer wished for a permanent reconciliation with all his Western European neighbours, but especially with France, which since the Napoleonic era had been the hereditary enemy of Germany. France had endured three defeats and three brutal occupations within eighty years at the hands of Germany and retained a profound scepticism of the Federal Republic's good intentions. Adenauer reasoned that such a reconciliation would be all the more credible if the Federal Republic agreed to subordinate its growing economic strength to promote European economic regeneration and eventually European political integration. It was from these motives that the Federal Republic joined France, Italy and the Benelux countries in the European Coal and Steel Community in April 1951.

Adenauer's *Westpolitik* necessitates two further comments. First, there is an inherent tension between Atlanticism, which emphasises European subordination to the United States, and European Integration, which aims at a self-sufficient Europe – a tension exacerbated by French mistrust of the United States. Torn between two intrinsically incompatible policies Adenauer, the consummate politician, was thus forced to appease both France and the United States in order to maintain both policies.

There is also the matter of German reunification. For the West German public, many of whom had relatives in East Germany and the eastern territories, or who had once lived there, reunification was a fourth policy issue at least as important as Adenauer's *Westpolitik*. Adenauer, however, correctly understood that reunification would require the consent of both superpowers, and Soviet consent would only be gained through a 'policy of strength' (*Politik der Stärke*). If the Federal Republic at that time had attempted to negotiate from a position of political and military weakness, then it would have risked losing its independence. It was perhaps not until the 1980s that she became strong, as the Soviet Union became weak. From 1952 to 1955 the Soviet Union repeatedly offered reunification on condition that a reunited Germany abandoned the Western Alliance and embraced a strict neutrality, a proposal that Adenauer rejected as a stratagem to subjugate the Federal Republic to Soviet political domination.

By 1952 it had become obvious to the United States that a coherent Western European defensive strategy against Soviet aggression required West German armed forces, and Adenauer agreed to rearm on condition that the Federal Republic be granted more sovereignty. This was a bargain that led to the abolition in May 1955 of the occupation regime – the troops remained as allies – and the Federal Republic's membership of NATO.

When Adenauer resigned in October 1963 after more than fourteen years as Chancellor the Federal Republic's position as a loyal member of NATO and the Western democracies was undisputed. Furthermore, in January he had signed the Franco-German Treaty of Co-operation with General de Gaulle, achieving a historic reconciliation with a former bitter enemy, and initiating a Franco-German axis of co-operation that was to power the motor of European integration.

Atlanticism was well established, and the West German armed forces, the Bundeswehr, effectively under NATO, not German control, were perceived as an asset, not a threat, to Western security. Lord Ismay, the first NATO Secretary-General, had quipped that NATO's function was 'to keep the United States in, the Soviet Union out, and Germany down', but this point of view was now fast becoming obsolete and excessively cynical. The newly established army, Bundeswehr, proved to be a perfect reflection of the Federal Republic: the philosophy of *innere Führung* (leadership from within) stressed that a German soldier's first duty was to his conscience, not blind obedience to a superior; whilst the Bundeswehr, as the largest NATO armed force in Central Europe, decisively rejected the bellicose traditions of the former Wehrmacht, and remained totally subservient to civilian, even pacifist civilian control. It seemed to relish NATO international command, and was content to remain militarily inactive, saving its energy for the Soviet attack which never came.

European Integration had continued apace with the development of the European Economic Community, or EEC, as the ESCC was rechristened in 1957. Soviet pressure on the Federal Republic had proved counter-productive, and had, as a bonus, even convinced the SPD, the main West German opposition party, that a neutral unified Germany was not a real possibility in the circumstances of that time and that German membership of NATO was a positive policy. By the end of his long premiership Adenauer had, from inauspicious beginnings, largely achieved the rehabilitation of his country.

BRANDT AND *OSTPOLITIK*

Before the Second World War, Germany had dominated an ill-defined region called Central Europe, but the Iron Curtain and the partition of Germany had effectively abolished this concept, and the Federal Republic had joined Western Europe, principally for the protection that such membership offered.

Although Adenauer made a controversial trip to Moscow in September 1955, securing diplomatic recognition and the release of the last Wehrmacht prisoners held by the Soviet Union, he had tended to neglect relations with Eastern Europe as risky in the prevailing circumstances, and indeed had endorsed the 'Hallstein doctrine' which regarded any recognition of the GDR by any other country as an unfriendly act towards the Federal Republic.

The Grand Coalition government (1966 to 1969) signalled a final break with the Adenauer era, and Federal German foreign policy, under the SPD Foreign Minister, Willy Brandt, felt securely enough anchored to the West to begin to explore links with Eastern Europe. This emergent policy matured during the period of SPD–FDP coalition governments (1969–82), when German foreign policy, and to some extent security policy, took on a new direction. Willy Brandt, Federal Chancellor from 1969 until 1974, believed that although the risk of a Soviet-bloc attack had been successfully deterred by NATO membership, tension remained. Central Europe remained a potentially dangerous region, vulnerable to superpower rivalries. He concluded that a policy of negotiations with the Soviet bloc, *Ostpolitik* (a policy of *rapprochement* with the East), combined with a continuing *Westpolitik*, would reduce tension, and further enhance West German security.

In August 1970, Brandt concluded a non-aggression treaty with the Soviet Union. The Warsaw Treaty in December 1970 confirmed the Oder–Neisse Line as Poland's western border, and the Prague Treaty of December 1973 endorsed Czechoslovakia's western borders. Finally, in December 1972, Brandt concluded the 'Treaty for the basis of relationships between the German Federal Republic and the German Democratic Republic', whereby each state recognised the other's right to exist, whilst retaining the prospect of reunification. This developing German–German *rapprochement* duly received NATO's blessing as a contribution to the relaxation of regional tension, and in September 1973 both states joined the United Nations.

SCHMIDT: THE STEADY HAND

Brandt's achievements earned him the Nobel Peace Prize in December 1972, but in May 1974 he was forced to resign following the revelation that Günter Guillaume, his personal aide, had been a GDR spy. Helmut Schmidt (SPD), who succeeded him as Federal Chancellor, and governed until 1982, was widely perceived in the West as more reliable than Brandt, whose judgement had been called into question by the Guillaume affair. Schmidt determined to continue Brandt's *Ostpolitik*, and to make it compatible with Adenauer's *Westpolitik*.

The focus of Schmidt's contribution to *Ostpolitik* was the German Democratic Republic. Under Party Secretary Erich Honecker the GDR stressed its independence as a German state, but its economy, impressive by Eastern European standards, lagged far behind the Federal Republic and its performance deteriorated throughout Schmidt's period in office. Informal meetings between Honecker and Schmidt in August 1975 and May 1980 led to Schmidt visiting the GDR, the first Federal Chancellor to do so. Federal German aid to the GDR increased steadily, and Honecker reciprocated by easing travel restrictions between the two states; but the states remained part of opposing European alliances, and NATO forces remained vigilant and at full strength on the Inner German Border.

The Federal Republic's influence within NATO increased, commensurate with its military contribution to the Alliance, and in 1978 General Gerhard Schmückle became Deputy Commander of NATO Forces in Europe, the first German officer to achieve this very influential position, succeeding a British general. Schmidt's premiership was also dominated by the efforts of NATO and the Warsaw Pact, NATO's Eastern equivalent, to reduce the amount of nuclear weapons in Europe, a process that had begun under Brandt. The immediate issue which the Federal Republic faced was the stationing of nuclear weapons on its territory, and the unthinkable prospect of Germany becoming a nuclear battlefield in the event of a third world war, a situation which explains West Germany's continuing equivocation on the nuclear issue. Strategic Arms Limitation Talks (SALT) began in November 1969, followed in May 1972 by talks in Vienna to achieve balanced NATO–Warsaw Pact force reductions. The Conference on Security and Co-operation in Europe (CSCE), intended to act as a forum to reduce East–West tension, opened in Helsinki in November 1972, culminating in the 'Final Act' in August 1975, which the Federal Republic signed. In June 1982, Strategic Arms Reduction Talks (START) opened in Geneva.

KOHL: A NEW EUROPEANISM

In October 1982, Helmut Kohl (CDU) became the last Chancellor of the first Federal Republic, and embarked on a foreign policy course which re-emphasised *Westpolitik* at the expense of *Ostpolitik*.

The key goal of *Ostpolitik*, the normalisation of relations with Eastern Europe, had been largely achieved by Brandt ten years before, and since then the policy had been dominated by relations with the GDR, a policy which mainly consisted of Federal financial aid to the GDR in return for a gradual liberalisation of a basically illiberal regime.

Kohl turned to Adenauer's *Westpolitik* with more enthusiasm. Building on the principles of Atlanticism, he fostered particularly close relations with the United States – to the chagrin of the British, who felt, with some justification, that the Federal Republic was steadily usurping their traditional role as the United States' closest European ally. German commitment to NATO returned to the forefront, and in July 1988 Manfred Wörner, the Foreign Minister, became the first German to become NATO Secretary-General, a post he filled with distinction during the vital period of German reunification before his untimely death in 1994.

Kohl believed that continued German membership of NATO and the UN would inevitably require Bundeswehr units to deploy outside the 'NATO area', defined as the territory of existing NATO members, but that this would require a change in the constitution, the basis of West German democracy. Nevertheless in October 1987 three German naval frigates assigned to NATO were sent to the Mediterranean to replace Allied ships transferred to the Persian Gulf during the Iran–Iraq War. In the ensuing years Kohl consistently infringed the Basic Law by sending nominal Bundeswehr contingents on UN, WEU and NATO missions, earning the approval of his allies at the expense of controversy within the Federal Republic.

But if Kohl's NATO policy was only marginally distinguishable from that of his predecessors, he showed an unprecedented commitment to European Integration, a view most clearly demonstrated by his enthusiasm for greater EEC economic and political integration, a goal he shared with French President François Mitterrand, with whom he had formed a close personal relationship. Kohl, like Mitterrand, wanted the EEC to develop a common foreign policy, backed by military forces which, unlike European forces in NATO, could operate independent of United States command and with the full participation of France. It was therefore no coincidence that in June 1984 the seven European states belonging to NATO and the European Community (formerly the EEC) decided to reactivate the dormant 'Western European Union' as a European military force. In June 1987, Kohl announced the formation of the WEU's first dedicated unit, the Franco-German Brigade, consisting of West German and French companies and battalions fully integrated into a mechanised brigade with a joint WEU and NATO combat role. This was followed up in January 1988 by the formation of a Franco-German Security Council to explore further co-operation. Thus Kohl expressed his determination to force the pace on European Integration in order to achieve a European State with a common defence policy and armed forces. This policy, fully endorsed by France but only half-heartedly by Great Britain, demonstrated Kohl's newfound proactivity and self-confidence in foreign policy.

UNIFICATION: A VINDICATION OF WEST GERMAN POST-WAR POLICY

In May 1989 the reformist communist Hungarian government unilaterally, and for purely humane reasons, dismantled the barbed-wire frontier fence with Austria (see Chapter 1, p. 6) and refused to use force to prevent refugees crossing the border. This apparently local decision was to have two incalculable consequences for the whole of Europe. It enabled Eastern Europeans, particularly East Germans, physically to cross into Western Europe, and it heralded the impending collapse of East–West confrontation and the end of the Cold War in Europe.

The Cold War had partitioned Germany, and so the Germans became the principal beneficiaries of its demise. Thousands of ordinary East Germans fled to the Federal Republic, in September there were demonstrations in East German cities for more democracy and in November the Berlin Wall was breached. This unpredictable manifestation of East German 'people power', its only apparent aim being greater internal democracy, seemed to encourage dangerous political instability in Eastern Europe and the Soviet Union. Although Kohl had not predicted these shattering events, any more than anyone else had done, he showed astute political judgment by calculating that the best resolution of this European power vacuum would be a reunited Germany. On 28 November 1989 he proposed a ten-stage programme for achieving reunification, a goal which even six months before had seemed as unattainable as it had been in 1949.

Kohl recognised that reunification could never remain an internal German matter. The very existence of two German states, with limited sovereignty, had been presided over by the four Allied powers (the United States, the Soviet Union, Great Britain and France) as a consequence of German aggression in the Second World War. Reunification would require the approval of these states, as well as that of Germany's allies in NATO and the EC, and Germany would have to offer tangible reassurances that these states would have nothing to fear, and everything to gain, from a reunited Germany.

It was at this point that the positive post-war policies of successive federal chancellors paid off handsomely. The United States, soon to be the last remaining superpower as the Soviet Union commenced its own internal collapse, happily endorsed Kohl's plan, recognising that reunification would extend Western influence further east at the expense of the ideological communist rival. The Federal Republic's Western European allies, including France, were, however, less

enthusiastic. Although they had accepted West German rehabilitation, the prospect of a new pan-German state awoke old fears of
German militarism which forty years of good behaviour by Bonn
had not entirely eradicated. Nevertheless, the Federal Republic's
positive membership of the EC and NATO, coupled with American
and German reassurances, eventually appeased them.

Soviet reaction to German reunification was predictably hostile,
since Gorbachev had not calculated the demise of the GDR. Nevertheless, believing that reunification was inevitable, and in any case
already preoccupied with ethnic conflicts within the Soviet Union
itself, Gorbachev was prepared to countenance German reunification
as long as it was accompanied by heavy economic and security
conditions and an understanding with the United States as to the
shape of post-Cold War Europe.

The ensuing negotiations, inelegantly entitled the 'Two plus Four
Talks', which took place in Paris from May to July 1990, defined the
relationship between the two German states and the United States, the
Soviet Union, Great Britain and France, the four principal Allied
powers in the Second World War. It led to the Moscow Treaty, signed
in September 1990, the peace treaty formally closing the Second
World War, which had in reality ended forty-five years earlier. Unlike
the Treaty of Versailles, intended to punish and weaken Weimar
Germany, it offered reunification and reconciliation, a proof that
post-1945 Germany was finally rehabilitated politically.

On 3 October 1990, Germany was formally reunified, enjoying full
sovereignty, Adenauer's historic goal. It was hardly coincidental that
during these negotiations NATO, in July 1990, acknowledged that the
Soviet Union was no longer an enemy, and that the 45-year-old Cold
War, the longest and least bloody war in recent European history, was
over.

UNITED GERMANY: THE NEW STATUS QUO

Germany's Unification was an unprecedented act, perhaps even more
radical than the unification of 1871, since it involved an economically
strong West absorbing an economically and politically bankrupt East.
This took place beside a rapidly evolving Eastern Europe which was
quickly rejecting communist hegemony and rediscovering its nationalistic roots. Kohl determined, therefore, that German foreign and
security policy must show a stability and consistency that would
reassure her allies and neighbours. He promptly reaffirmed
Germany's continued and deepening commitment to 'multilateralism'

through membership of the five international organisations – namely, OSCE (Organisation for Security and Co-operation in Europe), UN, NATO, EC and WEU – which, with their interlocking memberships and divergent overlapping aims, seemed to be Germany's best guarantee of peace and prosperity in post-Cold War Europe. He also recognised that the end of the Cold War had impacted across Europe, and that these organisations themselves would have to adapt to new realities, and that Germany must adapt with them.

Germany's Atlanticist policy, evidenced by close US–German relations and the NATO alliance, deepened. The Bundeswehr absorbed the Nationale Volksarmee, but fears of a new Wehrmacht proved unfounded. Only 338,000 strong, the new united Bundeswehr was integrated into five international NATO corps – the Franco-German–Belgian–Spanish 'Eurocorps', two US–German corps, a Danish–German corps, the Dutch–German Multinational Corps, and the international Rapid Reaction Corps. The new German armed forces began to participate fully in international peacekeeping, a new role permitted in July 1994 when the Federal Constitutional Court sanctioned deployment 'out of area' as constitutional, and German contingents have been sent to United Nations operations in Cambodia, Iraq, Somalia and Zaïre, WEU patrols in the Adriatic and NATO guard duties in Bosnia-Herzegovina. Germany has also endorsed 'NATO Enlargement' eastwards by encouraging the applications of Poland, Hungary and the Czech Republic to join NATO, not least in order to allow Germany to relinquish its forty-year-old role of front-line NATO state.

Kohl's greatest impact on German foreign policy has been in the field of European integration. At the Maastricht conference in December 1991 the European Community (EC) became the European Union (EU), with a clear agenda to progress towards a unified European state with a single currency and a common fiscal, foreign and defence policy. Kohl has persistently promoted this course as guaranteeing a peaceful and prosperous Germany within a peaceful and prosperous Europe. Nevertheless he has awoken widespread fears, especially in Great Britain, that political and economic unity would not tame German economic power, despite the financial strains of East German reconstruction.

With the demise of East–West confrontation 'Central Europe' has re-emerged as a European region, with Germany as its most important state. Kohl has moved quickly to establish a positive dialogue with states which, as former victims of Nazi aggression, had reason to fear a reunited Germany. He recognised that German security would be enhanced by a historic reconciliation with Russia comparable to that secured by Adenauer with France in 1963. He has accordingly made Russo-German relations a priority. In November 1990 he negotiated no fewer than three German–Soviet treaties – the 'General Treaty', regulating future bilateral relations and including a non-aggression clause; the 'Economic Treaty', guaranteeing East Germany's financial debts to the Soviet Union; and the 'Transition Treaty', regulating the withdrawal of the Soviet occupation forces from East Germany and their resettlement in the Soviet Union. German aid to the Russian Federation has been massive, and Kohl now enjoys such confidence with President Yeltsin that he was asked by NATO to mediate in the NATO–Russian dispute over NATO enlargement. Has Kohl become the new *ehrlicher Makler*?

He has also successfully developed good Polish–German relations. In November 1989 he affirmed that Poland's western borders were inviolate and Germany would not claim Eastern Pomerania and Silesia as German territory. In June 1991 he signed a Friendship Treaty in Warsaw, and even secured Poland's consent to allow joint Polish–German military manoeuvres on Polish soil.

Relations with Czechoslovakia have proved more difficult, owing to a vociferous community of former Sudeten Germans in Bavaria who demand compensation and apologies from the Czech government for their brutal expulsion from Sudetenland in May 1945. Czech President Havel duly apologised for Czech brutalities, and in October 1991 a Czech–German Friendship Treaty was signed; relations remain cool, but correct.

Unification has also encouraged Germany to play a larger role on the world stage. Chancellor Kohl is now able to send German troops on observer, humanitarian and peacekeeping missions. Similarly Kohl has supported the Organisation for Security and Co-operation in Europe (OSCE) – until January 1995 the CSCE – as a comprehensive pan-European forum promoting peace and democracy, and in 1993 Bundeswehr observers visited Georgia on a CSCE mission. Finally, Germany plays a full role as a member of the G7 group of advanced industrial states.

A SOLUTION TO THE GERMAN QUESTION?

The first and second Federal Republics have been well served by their senior politicians, who have provided political stability and continuity of foreign policy. This has been rare in Western Europe. All eighteen Federal Cabinets except one (Adenauer's third Cabinet,

1957–61) have been coalitions of either the CDU or the SPD plus the FDP, a fact which in Germany has promoted consensus and political stability. This means that the tiny FDP has spent more years in government than either of the two large parties (see Chapter 4, pp. 57–8). Furthermore, and most significantly, the key post of Foreign Minister has since 1969 been held by the FDP – Walter Scheel (1969–74), Hans-Dietrich Genscher (1974–92) and Klaus Kinkel (since 1992) – creating a tradition of consistency and political moderation in foreign affairs.

In 1945, Adenauer understood that Germany could no longer afford a foreign policy which treated its European neighbours with contempt, and from 1949 he and his successors ensured that the Federal Republic followed policies which locked it into a network of overlapping alliances. This had the effect of building confidence amongst the Federal Republic's allies, and potential enemies, that it would not, in fact could not, act independently and, by implication, resume its aggressive pre-1945 policies.

By the same token, this action forced the Federal Republic to forgo its own national interest in favour of international compromises, a restriction which initially many Germans welcomed as absolving them from the costs of armed forces or a separate foreign policy. Whilst Germany has remained compliant, indeed timid, regarding NATO and Atlanticism, it has sought a more independent role within the EU, a new attitude illustrated by Genscher's controversial unilateral recognition of Slovene and Croatian independence in December 1991, and Kohl's determination that a European single currency should be introduced in 1999. Nevertheless, such actions have taken place within the context of an international organisation, the rules and restrictions of which Germany continues to accept, and in no way signal a return to pre-1945 policies.

It therefore looks as if perhaps an answer has finally been found to the German Question – that is, Germany's role in Europe. Germany wishes to remain an equal partner in NATO and the EU, which are tried and tested European politico-economic and security alliances, but has, within the definition of equality, moved from the submissiveness of 1949–87 to active and vigorous participation. Kohl is prepared to court unpopularity in a way his predecessors were not, but remains bound by the rules of these alliances. Germany's neighbours continue to hold widely varying opinions of Germany, as Verheyen and Søe clearly and entertainingly demonstrate (Verheyen and Søe 1993: 72), but since 1949 Germany has consistently defined its conduct as peaceful and neighbourly, and it is likely that it will continue to do so for the foreseeable future.

RECOMMENDED READING

Smith *et al.* (1996), especially Chapters 8–10.

BIBLIOGRAPHY

Richardson, J. L. (1966) *Germany and the Atlantic Alliance*, Cambridge, Mass.: Harvard University Press.

Smith, G., Paterson, W. and Padgett, S. (eds) (1996) *Developments in German Politics 2*, Basingstoke and London: Macmillan.

Verheyen, D. and Søe, C. (eds) (1993) *The Germans and their Neighbours*, Oxford: Westview.

Index